Media Research Methodology

Media Research Methodology

S.K.Sikka

CYBER TECH PUBLICATIONS
4264/3, Ansari Road, Daryaganj New Delhi - 110002
Phone : 011-43559448, Fax : 011-23280028
Email : cybertechpublications@gmail.com

Media Research Methodology

CYBER TECH PUBLICATIONS
4264/3, Ansari Road, Daryaganj
New Delhi - 110002 (India)
Phone : 011-23244078, 011-43559448,
Fax : 011-23280028
E-mail : cybertechpublications@gmail.com
Website : www.cybertechpublications.com

First Published : 2009

ISBN 978-81-7884-465-7

Price, 1200.00

Printed at :

New Green Print Solutions, New Delhi 110078

Preface

Regarding the present state of the relations between politics, the media and the public, the relevant discourses in communication studies, political communication, and discourse analysis are very sceptical. There is criticism that it falls short of the democratic ideal according to which free, objective and scrupulous media inform the public on political decisions and issues, at the same time controlling the actors in the political sphere by insisting on the transparency of the political process and on the justifcation of its decisions to the public.

Instead, the media are accused that, due to time constraints and other production pressures, they have fallen into rigid routine, which in turn leads to the simplifcation of complex states of afairs. Also, due to the commercial pressure excerted through audience ratings or number of copies sold, the media are said to be giving in to a tendency to make political discourse more entertaining by trivializing, personalizing, dramatizing, conversationalizing, in short by "boulevardizing" a social domain which depends on an informed public, respectively electorate for democracy to work (Swanson 1992; Blunder & Gurevitch 1995; Curran 1991; Curran & Gurevitch 1991; Negrine 1996).

The politicians for their part are criticised for using the mass media to infuence public opinion instead of providing factual information, by employing professional public relations strategies and "spinning" what information they do provide.

The relations between politics, the media and the public have been captured in the model of a system of political communication created by Blumler and Gurevitch (1995).

The model comprises four interrelated subsystems: the system of political institutions with respect to their communication aspects, the system of the media with respect to their political aspects, the system of the publics expectations and orientations regarding political communication, and communication-relevant aspects of political culture. Depending on the aims of inquiry, one can focus on one subsystem at a time, while keeping in mind its relations to the others.

—Author

CONTENTS

1

Introduction

The analysis of political discourse on television should, ideally, be an interdisciplinary enterprise: political communication, media studies, and cultural studies are only some of the disciplines that could provide valuable contextualization for the discourse analytic study of verbal data taken from the mass media. Although the contributors to this volume all work within a framework of discourse analysis, in some papers a response to the pressure to cross disciplinary boundaries into the domain of the visual code of television can be observed (e.g. Lauerbach, Sauer, Scheithauer, Schiefi). Also, all authors are aware of the importance of the social, cultural and situational context of their data by providing background for their analyses. But since the scope of an empirical paper rarely leaves room for the discussion of the wider issues of the exercise one is involved in, there are two interrelated points that shall be briefly addressed in this section. The first is what the theory and method of a constructivist approach to the analysis of political discourse involves, and the second is the relation between politics, the media, and the public sphere.

As to the first point, constructivism is the dominant view in media studies, cultural studies and discourse studies alike: the phenomena under scrutiny are not conceived of (merely) as static domains whose structural characteristics are the object of inquiry, but as being achieved or produced through the dynamic interaction of the members of the social domain under review. This is the classical view of ethnomethodology, and it marks the turn from the analysis of social structures to the analysis of social processes, that is, to the *methods* the members of a social group themselves use in collaboratively producing those structures. This view also involved a turn away from the analysis of the macro-level of social institutions to the analysis of the micro-level of conversational interaction, and earned ethnomethodology the label of "micro-sociology" (see e.g. Heritage 1984; Levinson 1983). The problem ever since has been how to account for the relations between the micro and macro-levels, a problem that also besets the analysis of political discourse in the media. A *moderate* constructivist approach involves the assumption that the micro-structural interactions of social members *only partly* construct, maintain and change the macro-structures of a society, i.e. its institutions, just as they are in turn partly constructed, maintained and changed by them-complex systems of further factors and processes on various levels are involved in the relations of the micro and macro levels of social organization (cf. for instance Faircloughs 1995, 1998 models for how this may work for the micro-level of text and the orders of discourse that construct what elsewhere would be called the macro-level institutions of say, education, law, religion, economics or politics).

Turning to the second point, politics, the media and the public sphere have traditionally been conceived of as macro-structural phenomena and much theorizing on the part of sociology, media studies and political communication has gone into elucidating the relations between them. The political discourse disseminated in the mass media, for instance, has been conceptualized as "symbolic politics". The term is based on a distinction by Edelman (1976) between an instrumental and an expressive dimension of politics, which Sarcinelli (1987) calls the production and the presentation of politics. The production of politics for the greatest part takes place behind the scenes, and the public very rarely has access to it (if it does-as is the case e.g. in the case of parliamentary commissions publicly probing into political scandal-this happens only in retrospect and within strict limits). The presentation of politics by contrast takes place on the public stage that the media provide (televised parliamentary debates would seem to be a complex boundary case). The term "symbolic politics" may create confusion however, since any type of politics is done through language and, thus, symbolically constituted (Fairclough 1998; Chilton & Schaffner 2002). Yet due to the access problem mentioned, most of the data that discourse analysis deals with belong to mediatized politics, that is to say not to the production but to the presentation variety. And this latter variety, due to the staging constraints and commercial interests of the mass media, has become ritualized, formatted and schematized to such an extent that it is justifed to speak of a "semblance" of political reality (Sarcinelli 1994; Bentele 1992, translation G.L.). It is this negative interpretation that has become the dominant meaning of "symbolic politics" in political communication studies (Tenscher 1998). This reading should also not be confused with the "symbolic politics" of celebrating national holidays, for instance (cf. Sauer, this volume).

The relations between politics and the media have also been described as an "existential exchange system" (Sarcinelli 1987:218; translation G.L.) or a "happy symbiosis" (Boorstin 1987), in which information (on the part of the politicians) is exchanged for publicitiy (on the part of the media)-a bond that keeps growing tighter as the media become more and more subject to the commercial imperative (Tenscher 1998). Such a "happy symbiosis" between politics and the media runs counter to the media's role as a neutral mediator and critical monitor of politics, and it is not democratically legitimated. It is therefore unlikely to show itself on the surface of "symbolic politics". Rather, it is to be expected to manifest itself in other phenomena, such as e.g. the staged antagonism observable in political interviews. Such covert practices are hard to capture with the methods of media studies, but they fall squarely into the field of discourse analysis with its focus on the micro-level phenomena of not just explicit, but also implicit communication.

Regarding the present state of the relations between politics, the media and the public, the relevant discourses in communication studies, political communication, and discourse analysis are very sceptical. There is criticism that it falls short of the democratic ideal according to which free, objective and scrupulous media inform the public on political decisions and issues, at the same time controlling the actors in the political sphere by insisting on the transparency of the political process and on the justifcation of its decisions to the public. Instead, the media are accused that, due to time constraints and other production pressures, they have fallen into rigid routine, which in turn leads to the simplifcation of complex states of afairs. Also, due to the commercial pressure excerted through audience ratings or number of copies sold, the media are said to be giving in to a tendency to make political discourse more entertaining by trivializing, personalizing, dramatizing, conversationalizing, in short by "boulevardizing" a social domain which depends on an informed public, respectively electorate for democracy to work (Swanson 1992; Blunder & Gurevitch 1995; Curran 1991; Curran & Gurevitch 1991; Negrine 1996). The politicians for their part are criticised for using the mass media to infuence public opinion instead of providing factual information, by employing professional public relations strategies and "spinning" what information they do provide (Cook 1998).

The relations between politics, the media and the public have been captured in the model of a system of political communication created by Blumler and Gurevitch (1995). The model comprises four interrelated subsystems: the system of political institutions with respect to their communication aspects, the system of the media with respect to their political aspects, the system of the publics expectations and orientations regarding political communication, and communication-relevant aspects of political culture. Depending on the aims of inquiry, one can focus on one subsystem at a time, while keeping in mind its relations to the others. Possible complementary participant roles for the agents in the subsystems are hypothetically proposed as follows (1995:15):

Audience	*Media personnel*	*Politicians*
Partisan	Editorial Guide	Gladiator
Liberal citizen	Moderator	Rational persuader
Monitor	Watchdog	Information provider
Spectator	Entertainer	Actor/performer

Diferent confgurations of participant roles across the subsystems will yield different types of political communication in a society, a culture, or a media corporation. The table shows how difcult a comprehensive analyis of all three components would be. Blunder and Gurevitch's model has informed their own cross-culturally comparative research on the agenda-setting role of British (BBC) and US-American (NBC) television in reporting on election campaigns (1995). It also provides a useful frame of reference for empirical research beyond communication studies. In discourse analysis, for instance, the focus of inquiry in media discourse has so far mainly been on the study of journalistic practices in certain genres, or on the discourse practices of politicians, less frequently on how they interact, and discourse analytic audience reception research is so far still a fairly neglected field (but see Holly 1996; Holly, Püschel & Bergmann 2001).

The goal of discourse analysis is to describe the coding and interpretation conventions of a culture in certain discursive domains, as well as the cultures underlying common ground assumptions. In cross-cultural analysis, it then goes on to confront its results with comparable phenomena of another culture. Such comparative research, according to Gurevitch and Blumer (1990:308f), possesses signifcant advantages over a mono-cultural approach: Due to its wide and varied data base, and the constant comparison between culturally specifc ways of doing things, comparative research counteracts any culture-centric bias that may remain unrefected in mono-cultural analysis. Further, the process of comparison renders visible the unchallenged assumptions in the analysts own culture. And lastly, the confrontation with diferent ways of doing the "same" thing, which is advocated by critical discourse analysis in order to de-naturalize the dominant readings of a culture, is built into the very heart of the comparative method.

CULTURE AND CROSS-CULTURAL DISCOURSE ANALYSIS

Culture is a concept whose defnition is ofen presupposed in the domains of linguistics, pragmatics and discourse analysis. In other disciplines, it has been defned for instance as the world view refected in the classifcation systems of languages, as systems of beliefs, values and attitudes shared by the members of a community, as shared ways of doing things or as the sum of the artefacts produced by the members of a culture over time. Some views involve a static perspective on culture, focusing on a culture's products and ideas, some a dynamic one, focusing on the interactive processes employed by members in collaboratively creating them. Some views favour a cognitive perspective, focusing on the knowledge shared by a culture's members about the physical, the social and the subjective world. Most traditional views conceive of culture as an autonomous, homogeneous, territorially confined unity that is "contained" within the boundaries of a nation state and that contains, in turn, all the properties that define it and make it different from other cultures.

What is of relevance for this volume on political media discourse across cultures is the premise that members of a speech community know about their community's appropriate ways of producing and interpreting explicit and implicit meaning, about its discourse practices and genres and about the socio-cultural contexts of their use, and that they are not necessarily familiar with the ways of other communities (Hanks 1996; Ochs 1996). We shall therefore approach the problem of defining culture by asking what constitutive conditions need to be satisfied for members of a culture to successfully interact with each other (cf. Lauerbach 2002). Very briefly, the position taken here is that three dimensions are necessarily involved when we talk about what is necessary for members of a culture to be able to communicate: they have to share knowledge regarding symbolic sign systems, above all language; they have to share knowledge about systems of pragmatic principles and social practices, above all those of verbal interaction; and they have to share systems of knowledge about the physical, the social and the subjective world (which worlds also include the artefacts of a culture). They also have to share knowledge about how these systems interact. In addition, there are stores of knowledge involving normative conditions on appropriate interaction in all three dimensions. These relate e.g. to standards of social tact and politeness, and of rational argumentation, and to how these are expressed in speech acts and genres in culturally situated discourses. There are many open questions here regarding the dimensions of this interactionally relevant knowledge, for instance of how explicit these types of knowledge have to be, and how consistent and free of contradictions within and between the systems, about meta-levels of knowledge, about how the systems interact, how they are accessed and continuously monitored in interaction, about how this complex of knowledge is socially distributed, etc. All of these questions are well beyond the scope of this introduction, except the last.

The store of interactionally relevant knowledge is a potential, a resource from which members of a culture can choose for the realisation and interpretation of contributions to discursive events. If there are, between members, grave asymmetries between the stores of interactionally relevant knowledge, miscommunication will occur. This is aggravated if members of different cultures are involved (see Günthner & Luckmann 2001). In the context of intercultural communication, marked deviations from expected interactional norms become a rich source of cultural stereotyping. However, interpersonal communication between different cultures *is* possible, and this points to the fact that there has to be a core of interactionally relevant knowledge that is universally shared.

Cross-cultural discourse analysis is about both: about a core which can be presupposed as shared, and about the rest, where languages and other semiotic systems, social and discursive practices, and conceptualisations of reality are culturally specific to a degree that may be communicatively disruptive (or interesting for e.g. social, political or philosophical reasons). For the dimension of language, the project of cross-cultural analysis includes all levels of the linguistic system, from prosody to textual organisation. For the dimension of interaction it addresses the ways in which the social and discursive practices of a culture work But the focus is also on what happens if interactants are unaware of this and are led to to misguided evaluations regarding e.g. the group membership of their interlocutors, their social status, personality features, or even their intelligence (see Gumperz 1982). In the domain of world knowledge, cross-cultural analysis is about how the dominant discourses of different cultures shape their members' perspective on the world.

Depending on the dimension of knowledge and the type of product looked at (sentence or discourse), scholars attempt to reconstruct the grammar of a language and speakers' knowledge of linguistic principles, categories and relations, or they try to reconstruct the "grammar" of interaction and speakers' knowledge about pragmatic principles, categories and relations. Earlier Chomskian grammars, with their reconstruction of linguistic competence, are examples of the first approach. The ethnography of communication (Hymes 1974; Saville-Troike 1989), with its reconstruction of communicative competence in contexts of culture, is a case of the second. Interactional meaning, according to Hymes (1974), can be captured through a number of contextual factors which constrain appropriate linguistic behaviour. He has assembled them in his well-known s-p-e-a-k-i-n-g acronym, anchoring a speech community's knowledge about linguistic code and social practice to the components of situation, that is the physical setting and the psychological scene, participants, viz. speaker, hearer and audience and their statuses, ends, namely the goal and the purpose of the speech event from a socio-cultural viewpoint, act sequence, that is *how* something is said as regards message form and sequence, and *what* is said as regards message content, key, e.g. mock or serious, instrumentalities, e.g. channels (spoken, written, visual, etc.) and forms (vernacular, dialect or standard) of speech, norms of interaction and interpretation, and genres.

Yet a focus on interaction does not necessarily imply one on cultural context as well, as the enthnomethodological paradigm shows. According to the ethno-methodological enterprise of reconstructing participants' orientation to principles of conversational organisation, cultural context does not pre-exist the interaction. Rather, it is interactionally constituted and collaboratively constructed by its members in and through the process of communication (Prevignano & Thibault 2003). Consequently, the research paradigm of ethnomethodological conversation analysis focusses on the methods of interaction with which participants produce the structural components of discourse, while ignoring the cultural and social contexts in which the interaction takes place. The extreme position that social context is constructed solely through the interaction of the participants, rather than facilitating and constraining it, has not gone without criticism. The argument of the critics is that the approach precludes the possibility of contextual factors informing a critical analysis (see the debate between Billig and Schegloff in *Discourse and Society:* Billig 1999; Schegloff 1997, 1999). A cross-cultural discourse analysis will need to complement such approaches by theories that allow for the fact that in communication, interactants collaboratively construct their relevant context(s) for producing and interpretating utterances, without the implication that context arises wholly and solely as a product of interactive construction. Such theories have to account for the fact that, to use John Gumperz' felicitous phrase, context is both brought along and brought about.

In the tradition of Foucault and Bourdieu, Fairclough (1995) has formulated such a theory, with a focus on media discourse. The goal of the theory is to account, in a multilevel model, for the relations between the linguistic/semiotic micro-structure of the text and the context of the sociocultural macro-structure. Fairclough understands the macro-structural *Order of Discourse* as a configuration of *Types of Discourse* of social domains or institutions (e.g. the family, education, politics, the mass media). Types of Discourse, in their turn, are constituted by *Genres* and *Discourses.* The latter are a society's representations of a social domain under a particular perspective (e.g. politics from a liberal, socialist, or marxist perspective). *Texts* are produced and consumed according to *discursive practices,* and these, in turn, are embedded in *sociocultural practices.* Text analysis has a double focus-on the structure of the text and on the discursive practices with which it was produced within the wider context of the type of discourse it is a part of. The key categories for the mediation between the Order of Discourse and the Text are those of *Genre* and of *Discourse,* and the key processes are those of the *discursive practices of production and consumption* (which, in Faircloughs framework, are more than just coding and interpretation but include the conditions of the production and reception situation of, e.g. media products). Let us focus here on the category of genre.

The category of *Genre* is central to discourse analysis and can be taken to be its basic unit of analysis. Communicative genres (rather than literary ones) or *activity types* (Levinson 1979) are conventionalised patterns for the communicative solution of social "problems". These problems give rise to a genres external (social, institutional) structure, while the communicative practices of working through those problems yield its characteristic internal (discursive, textual) structure (Luckmann 1986, 1988; Kress 1993). Genres can vary across cultures, historical eras, social classes and sub-cultures (Luckmann 1986, 1988; Günthner & Luckmann 2001), and they are indicators of social change (Bakhtin 1987; Fairclough 1995; 2003). The internal-external-structure constitution of communicative genres points to their function as points of articulation between the socio-cultural and the textual, or between culture and language. Levinson (1979:368), drawing attention to the category's indeterminate boundaries, defnes *activity type* (which corresponds to genre) as a fuzzy category whose focal members are goal-defned, socially constituted, bounded events with *constraints* on participants, setting and so on, but above all on the allowable contributions.

Genres provide a context for understanding "over and beyond whatever meaning the words or sentences may have *in vacuo*" (Levinson 1979:367), and a cognitive frame of reference, which is strongly infuenced by sociocultural constraints, for the interpretation of implicit meaning:...there is another important and related fact, in many ways the mirror image of the constraints on contributions, namely the fact that for each and every clearly demarcated activity there is a set of *inferential schemata*. These schemata are tied to (derived from, if one likes) the structural properties of the activity in question. (Levinson 1979:370)

To sum up, communicative genres are socio-culturally conventionalised, sometimes even ritualised patterns for dealing with recurring social problems, they provide standardised frames of interpretation and genre-specific ways of inferring implicit meaning. Actual texts, on the other hand, always offer a range of potential reading positions but suggest preferred interpretations by privileging one of those positions over the others. The privileged reading positions reaffirm shared cultural coding conventions, interpretation rules, norms and values.

They may therefore appear to be the only ones, to be "natural". From the point of view of cultural studies and of critical discourse analysis, these preferred interpretations are nothing but the naturalization of the hegemonial view, achieved due to the relations of power in a society and by the privileged access of the powerful to the public sphere (cf. Bell & Garrett 1998; Fowler 1987, 1991; Fowler & Kress 1979; Fairclough 1989, 1992, 1995; Hall 1973, 1980). Genres, due to their conventionality, must be considered a powerful factor in promoting such preferred interpretations. This can be taken to hold in particular for the standardised genres of the mass media.

The view that cultures are well-bounded, homogeneous unities based on systems of naturalised meanings, as well as the role of the mass media in the processes of naturalisation, has provoked critical inquiry from various quarters. In critical discourse analysis, for instance, with its goal of addressing relations of discursive power within a society, the method is to lay open a society's underlying naturalized assumptions, coding conventions and preferred reading positions by close linguistic analysis. These are then confronted with alternative ones that are also possible, but not commonly realized in a culture (cf. Wodak & Meyer 2001). In cultural studies, Hall (1980) introduced the idea that recipients actually do use more ways of reading a text than the ones priviledged by the culture. Over and above the dominant reading, by which recipients accept the interpretation preferred by the text, he distinguishes two further types: negotiated and oppositional readings. In both, recipients do not follow the preferred interpretation offered by the text. In the negotiated reading, recipients modify the offered interpretation to some extent without totally rejecting it, in the oppositional reading, they reject this interpretation altogether and substitute it with their own. Deviant readings point to sub-cultural differences of dealing with discursive meaning and thus challenge the presumption of the homogeneity of cultures. But if cultures are internally differentiated according to sub-cultural milieus, lifestyles and communication practices, then this presents a complication for cross-cultural discourse analysis.

Another complication comes from outside the individual culture. The acceleration of the globalisation process has led to world-wide economical, political, social and cultural connections which render it problematic to continue speaking of separate, autonomous, territorially defined cultures (Welsch 1999). Traditional cultures have been modifed by forms of life and cultural styles which are not contained within their boundaries. Rather, they traverse them. These lifestyles cannot be captured within the old concept of culture, which is why Welsch proposes the term of *transculture* (cf. also Hepp 2006:63). In a similar vein, Hall (1997), in a paper on "The centrality of culture", argues that, due to advanced communication technologies and world-wide media networks, a cultural revolution has taken place which has made cultural products a major factor in the global economy. The media, above all the internet but also television, have become a major force in the globalisation process, and the motor of world-wide social and cultural change. We may add that world-wide media networks, globally operating media corporations and international television channels, like CNN International, BBC World, Al Dschazira or the newcomer Al Dschazira English, create new cultural spaces whose extension coincides with the reaches of their airwaves. These new territories are inhabited by a global audience which, due to the international distribution of information and advertising in a few world languages, is in the process of becoming a global information elite. For these audiences, global media events, especially in times of crisis, are not only "sites of maximum visibility and turbulence" in the flow of global discourses (Fiske 1996:7), but also arenas for the construction of transcultural identities.

What is the influence of global cultural products on local contexts? Is it a unidirectional process, from Western-dominated media to the rest of world? Naturally, there is a way in which global culture leaves traces in local contexts, but global products are also selected and imported according to local preferences, and these preferences, in turn, have an effect on production. The production and global marketing of television soap operas or the advertising campaigns of globally operating corporations are examples of such strategies of "glocalisation". Due to the fact that cultural products and signifying practices have become available transculturally, there is indeed an effect on local cultures, in that cultural differences are beginning to show structural similarities (Hannerz 1992:53). We can hypothesise that such changes will show up in the communicative genres of a culture, presumably as a tendency towards hybridisation.

To sum up, there are two factors that cast into doubt a homogenous, autonomous, territorially bounded concept of culture: the sub-cultural diferentiations from within a culture, and the transculturalisation processes that afect it from outside. What are the consequences of this for the methods of culturally comparative research? Cross-cultural analysis is, after all, based on the premise of independent systems with definite boundaries as objects of its analyses (cf. Pfetsch & Esser 2003:28). Does not the existence of internal differentiation and of trans-cultural processes undermine the comparative enterprise by depriving it of its objects of inquiry?

The answer to this is twofold, concerning the underlying concept of culture on the one hand, and the units and methods of inquiry on the other. As to the first, the concept of culture as formulated above is based on the constitutive and normative conditions of verbal and nonverbal interaction of the members of a speech community. As such, it is not bound to territory, nor does it presuppose the homogeneity of the speech community. But what kinds of cultural manifestations, in terms of texts and genres, can be the objects of transcultural discourse analysis? Is there a way in which cross-cultural diferences as well as transcultural communalities can be captured? For the study of transcultural communication, Hepp (2006:78f.) proposes what he terms an *international comparative semantics*. This includes a comparative analysis of the media system of culture one and culture two, *complemented* by an analysis of areas of intensified cultural contact, involvement, exchange on the level of global media capitalism. Such areas could be from sub-cultural domains such as popular culture, religious and social movements, diaspora groups, or politics. In this manner, transcultural phenomena could be put into relation to mono-and cross-cultural ones. The approach seems to be still very much in the programmatic stage, but it is certainly worth thinking about how this could work in other fields of inquiry.

Let us therefore narrow the focus by looking at discourse analysis, of media discourse, on the domain of politics, as in the contributions to this volume. By analysing and comparing genres, and within them certain discursive practices or linguistic devices, one can focus on a specific, narrowly circumscribed domain of a culture's media, and not on whole media systems. The focus is then on a phenomenon of a sub-culture, as it were. But this is the accepted method of linguistic and discourse analytic contrastive research already. One the other hand, one can ask if there are certain genres of political discourse in the media which are likely to be more resistant to transcultural influences, in contrast to others which are more likely to embrace them, and test this hypothesis by studying the differences between them. Parliamentary debates broadcast on the radio or on television, as well as Christmas addresses by heads of state may be cases of the first type. Political interviews, on the other hand, might be a genre that is more open to transcultural standardisation. One could also do a comparative analysis of one genre, say political interviews, in the media of "old" and "new" democracies. This approach should yield interesting results, if indeed the genres should prove to be comparable across the two domains. Lastly, one can transfer the Heppian paradigm to media discourse analysis and look at particular genres in national and international media. This will presumably yield differences between the two types-but can we draw conclusions from this to transcultural traces in the national media genres? What kind of comparative design might give us an answer to this question? Presumably it would be interesting to do longitudinal studies and to look at the changes within a genre in national and international media over time. Generally, ethnographic descriptions of the cultural and transcultural context should be part of any analysis, and an essential element of this should be the description of the discourse type to which the genres analysed belong. It is to this we turn now for the project pursued in this volume.

POLITICAL DISCOURSE IN THE MEDIA

Political discourse in the media is a complex phenomenon: it is institutional discourse, media discourse, and mediated political discourse. As institutional discourse, it differs from everyday conversation in being subject to institutional goals and procedures. As media discourse it is different from other types of institutional discourses by being, above all, public discourse addressed to a mass media audience. This sets it apart from the discourse of other institutions, such as medicine, the law, or education. As mediated political discourse, it is the outcome of the encounter of two different institutional discourses-those of politics and of the media. Just what constitutes the goals and purposes, subtypes, genres and discursive practices of this hybrid discourse, is the question pursued in political discourse analysis.

"Political discourse in the media" as a term is ambiguous in its referential domain: it can refer to the discourse *of* political agents in the media, or the discourse of journalists *with* politicians in the media, or to the discourse of journalists *about* politics and political agents in the media. Discourse *of* politicians or other political agents like spokespersons are for instance speeches on important issues and occasions, e.g. in parliamentary debates, at party conferences, summit meetings, etc., also statements, press conferences and the like. These events are embedded in journalistic news discourse and, in the case of the broadcasting media, maybe carried live, to be repeated as soundbites in later programming. Discourse *with* politicians and other political personnel are dialogic speech events in which political representatives interact with journalists in interviews. Focusing again on the broadcasting media, such interviews can take place in radio and television news, in news magazines or in talk shows, or they can be an event in their own right. They can be conducted on a one-on-one or a panel/ debate basis (Clayman & Heritage 2002). Discourse *about* politics and politicians is journalistic discourse in the genres of report, analysis, commentary, etc. by the speakers of news programmes, the anchors of news magazines, by studio experts and correspondents on location. This discourse *about* politics can, and usually does, embed other voices: In quoting the voices of politicians and spokespersons of diferent parties on an issue, journalists can create a debate that may not actually have taken place in this way. In interviewing the politicians themselves, they can monitor and critically observe the political process on behalf of the audience. In interviewing or quoting outside experts on the issue they provide explanations of what it means in the wider context of society. In asking ordinary people about their opinions, they demonstrate how it may concern the man or woman in the street. Vox pops can also be heard in audience participation programmes, through the voices of members of a studio audience, or by members of the home audience calling in, or sending faxes or e-mails.

Discourse *about* politics is thus the overarching category in which the others can be embedded. Various journalistic genres are involved; they can be monological, in which case the audience is addressed directly, or dialogical, in which case the participants address the audience via their interaction with their interlocutors. In the sense of Gofman (1974:539ff, 1981:137ff), media discourse belongs to what he calls *podium events*. These are defined as social events which are either addressed to or performed for a live or mass media audience (e.g. lectures, sermons, staged plays; radio and television news, interviews, talk shows).Te participation framework of political discourse in the media consists of journalists, as representatives of a media institution, of political actors as representatives of the institution of politics, of actors from other social institutions, of lay people as representatives of the world of everyday life, and the audience, as representatives of the public. Focusing on television, members of all of these groups can be heard and seen, but their importance and status are very different. Although political actors are the newsmakers of political discourse, so that the discourse is always *about* them, they do not necessarily have to be present. This is different for the journalists and the audience-both of them are constitutive for media discourse about any discursive domain. However, for the dialogical genre of political interview, political actors are, of course, necessary participants. Actors from other institutions can participate for analysis and commentary, but this could also be done by experts from within the media. The evaluations and other reactions from lay persons, the studio and/or mass audience likewise are not necessary but optional constituents of media discourse. There is a further distinction between the participants as to whether they are "on the podium", or in the audience. The first group can be called first-frame participants, the second, second frame participants. The conditions of participation are different for the diverse participant groups, and they are subject to the specific discursive practices within the institution of media discourse.

In comparison with everyday discourse, institutional discourse is therefore often looked upon as something artificial which adheres to its own regularities and discourse practices. From an analytic viewpoint, however, institutional discourse and everyday communication share all of the fundamental pragmatic premises for felicitous communication, but differ with respect to their instantiations in context. This holds for the conversation-analytic concepts of sequentiality and turn-taking (Fetzer & Meierkord 2002; Sacks, Schegloff & Jeferson 1974; Sacks 1992), for the interpersonal-communication concepts of face and footing (Brown & Levinson 1987; Gofman 1981), for speech-act theory's felicity conditions and the overarching pragmatic premise of intentionality of communicative action, with its subsequent differentiation between what is said and what is meant (Grice 1975; Searle 1975, 1995). The meaning of an interlocutors contribution may thus go beyond the level of what is said in both types of discourse. In both types of discourse, participants may flout conversational maxims in order to trigger conversational implicatures and to express conversationally implicated meaning (Grice 1975), and in both the communicative meaning of what speakers intend to communicate needs to be worked out by the addressees. Yet in institutional contexts, this meaning may not be freely negotiable due to constraints on possible participant roles and on the number of participants, as well as on the kinds of contributions, the turn-length and the kinds of sequencing expected or allowed.

Furthermore, the strategies of coding and interpretation are not just dependent on the type of institution, but also on the type of genre or activity type engaged in. This raises a problem for all general pragmatic principles, including Grice's (1975) system of conversational logic, for which Levinson (1979:376) offers two basic solutions for discussion:

> There are two ways in which the conflict between Grice's general principles of conversation and the particular expectations of specific activities can be reconciled. The first is to seek for a more sophisticated statement of Grice's principles that will allow differing degrees of application of each maxim and the corresponding adjustment of implicatures. The second is to accept Grice's maxims as specifications of some *unmarked* communication context, deviations from which however common are seen as special or *marked*.

If one opts for the second way of dealing with the problem, then the effort of institutional discourse analysis has to go into accounting for the parameters of markedness that distinguish types of discourses and their genres from the unmarked type of everyday conversation and its genres.

The most consequential feature of media discourse is that it is addressed to an absent mass audience and not to a group of co-present participants. The fact that media discourse is produced for such an audience influences both its content and its form. In the case of dialogic interaction being broadcast, the audience maybe directly addressed by the journalists and, in rare cases, also by their studio guests. As a rule, however, it will be in the position of a ratified overhearer (Gofman 1981), as for instance when journalists and politicians talk to each other in order to display their discourse to the audience. This has consequences for the way in which such discourse is constructed, as has been demonstrated for the news interview by analysts working within the framework of conversation analysis. In refraining from giving feedback to their interviewees, interviewers indicate that the interviewees' answers are not addressed to them but to the audience (Clayman & Hertitage 2002:120f.).

Another consequence of media discourse being addressed to an absent mass audience concerns the construction of meaning by the first-frame participants. Both in ordinary and in mediated face-to-face dialogues, participants may initiate repair sequences. In contrast to everyday discourse, however, there are constraints on the negotiation of meaning in mediated discourse. First, the length of a repair sequence is constrained by the programme's strict time schedule, and second, the audience cannot directly intervene in this process between the first-frame participants by asking clarification questions. It may, however, participate in a mediated manner if there is audience participation, or through other types of mediated discourse, for instance letters to the editor, phone-ins, email, chat, or through meta-discourse with other members of the audience. However, such attempts at the negotiation of meaning are always delayed or after the event.

The consequences for the first-frame participants are that they have to take particular care in recipient-designing their discourse for an audience that cannot intervene with comprehension questions. This holds equally for monologue addressed to the audience. The orientation to a heterogeneous mass audience whose members may have different stores of background knowledge leads to formal features of the discourse like the explanation of possibly unfamiliar referential terms, or the explication of inferences and jokes.

There is a connection between the features of recipient design of media discourse, its public character, and the rights and obligations of its participants:

...the design features... indicate that it is meant for reception by absent audiences. And this, in turn, establishes the intrinsically public nature of broadcast talk. Talk-in-public, especially political talk, is 'on the record' and this has consequences on what can and cannot be said and for ways of saying and not saying. (Scannell 1998:260)

So, in being produced for a mass audience, mediated discourse is necessarily public discourse. The public and mediated status of its participants and of the activity engaged in is one of the decisive factors which differentiate their rights and obligations from those of the participants of communicative events in other social domains. Thus interviewees are in a different position from, for instance, suspects being questioned by the police:

American citizens have a constitutionally protected right to remain silent in the face of police questioning, so that silence cannot be treated as incriminating in courts of law. But public figures have no such protection in the court of public opinion constituted by the news interview. (dayman & Heritage 2002:241)

This is why, if e.g. interviewees do not wish to answer a question, they are faced with a dilemma. Answering the question will lead to undesirable consequences. Yet there are strong pressures-from interviewers, the audience, and subsequent media exposure-to "just answer the question". In the political arena, politicians may chose, under specific circumstances, to explicitly opt out of the event (Lauerbach 2003b), but they do not have the right to remain silent and, should they decide to do so, this is generally used against them by portraying them as uncooperative, if not insincere (Fetzer 2002). Moreover, the silence is loaded with additional generalised and particularised inferential meaning: politicians are considered to not fulfill their obligation of informing the public and the electorate in an appropriate manner and, more specifically, to have a problem with the question asked.

Since media discourse is public discourse by definition, it is accessible to a general public, including other media, who have the right to comment on it and to recontextualize it, thus constructing intertextuality (Fetzer & Weizman 2006; Scannell 1998). And it is those intertextual references to "on-the-record" utterances and the subsequent construction of intertextuality which are at the heart of media discourse. This is reflected, for instance, in the genre of political interview in which politicians are challenged with prior statements and claims, and in the discursive practices of journalists in news programmes in which politicians' talk is explicitly taken up through direct and indirect quotes.

The absent mass audience that journalists, politicians and other participant groups of first-frame participants orient to is counterfactually conceptualized as an over-arching category for a more or less culturally homogeneous entity. But there is a tension here between the media publicly broadcasting to a mass of addressees who receive this discourse as individuals or small groups mainly in their private environment. Practices of audience address and occasional informal style show the media's orientation to this fact. Also, audiences are differentiated as to sub-cultural milieus, and first-frame participants may intend to address specific segments of the audience in particular, such as members of a political party in the context of a political interview or speech, the electorate in the context of a political interview or debate, and sometimes a nation, or a nation and its allies, in the context of a president's speech.

In international broadcasting, the multi-layered participant structure of media communication becomes even more complex. This is because the mass audience addressed in the second frame no longer represents a more or less culturally homogeneous group, and neither the first-nor the second-frame participants may orient to culturally shared background knowledge, value systems and discursive practices. In international broadcasting, the situation is also more complex linguistically. The broadcasters may e.g. use standard or regional varieties of English (or Spanish, or Arabic), interact with interviewees and other guests who speak the language used as a lingua franca, and the audiences addressed are at least bilingual and belong to different cultures.

Before being overly impressed by the challenge to international media that lies in recipient-designing their programme for such heterogeneous audiences, we should consider that the global media are no doubt also a factor in shaping their audiences' orientation to international media culture and in homogenizing their patterns of reception. Cameron (2003) has shown for a particular aspect of global business communication how such homogenization is achieved by strictly prescribing certain modes of interaction. In her study of global call-centre communication, she discusses prescribed scripted salutations, simulated friendliness and a relentless positive politeness. Similar manuals exist for the broadcasting personnel of international television companies to ensure consistent patterns of discursive behaviour which become, in turn, partially constitutive both of a channel's culture and of the reception habits of transcultural audiences. Such handbooks regulate the language varieties and formality levels to be used, the relation of image, text, and on-screen characters, the forms of audience address and of the address and referential terms for journalists and guest, etc.

Turning at last to political discourse in the media, we have seen that it is institutional, mediated discourse collaboratively produced for the major part by the interaction of the representatives of two macro-institutions of modern societies, of the institution of politics and of the institution of the media. It is the presentation of politics, not its production (see Section 2).

Politics has its events and genres within and through which it conducts its business, and the media have their events and genres within and through which they conduct theirs. Some political events occur independently of the media, such as party conferences, parliamentary debates, the reports of parliamentary commissions and election campaigns; some are events staged by the media or by the representatives of the political system, or both. They are staged to be carried live or to be reported on, such as national and other addresses, press conferences, or press releases on the part of politics, and interviews, talk shows, new reports, current affairs debates or news magazine portraits on the part of the media. However, the fact that political events may occur independently from media instigation does not mean that they are not shaped by the media. A good example are election campaigns or national holiday addresses (cf. Blumer & Gurevitch 1990,1995;

ben-Aaron 2005; Sauer, this volume). The goals of the institutions of politics and the media as well as their symbiotic relationship have already been remarked on in section two, as have as their respective and reciprocally influential practices of "boulevardization" on the part of the media, and of spinning and soundbite design on the part of politics. The fact that politics is interest-driven negotiation over limited resources within a society and across nations has consequences for the readings offered to a mass audience when its representatives talk to or talk with the media. One of the constitutive conditions of mediated political texts is that they are addressed to audiences whom their authors know to be divided as regards their interests and political affiliations, on most issues, and whom they will consequently try to persuade to stay within or to come into their camp. Thus political discourse in the media is persuasive discourse.

From a pragmatic angle, political discourse in the media can be conceived as communicative action (Fetzer & Weizman 2006). As in all types of persuasive discourse, and thus for the analysis of how politicians interact with the media, the contrast between perlocutionary act (Austin 1962) and perlocutionary effect (Searle 1969) deserves particular attention. The distinction is one of (1) intended versus achieved effects, and (2) between the audience as a whole, and subsets of hearers and audiences as its parts. The relevance of the intention/effect duality is explicitly highlighted by Chilton and Schäfner (2002:11), who draw the connection between a pragmatic approach to political discourse and media studies by pointing out that the concept of perlocutionary efect "is (...) of crucial importance in political discourse analysis in particular, because it points to the potential discrepancy between intended effect (that is, effect that some hearers may infer to be intended) and the actual effect on the hearer."

Here lies a particular challenge for political discourse analysis in that the heterogeneous audiences in mass-media discourse may comprise not only different national and international targets, but also different ideologically defined groups. This requires research on both the sides of the communicative process-of the practices of both production and reception. On the reception side, this means discourse analytic audience reception research, which is still in its infancy. What we can look for on the production side is the discursive traces of politicians' and journalists' orientation to multiple addressees with different, if not conflicting, interests and affiliations on the one hand, and with different (sub-)cultural backgrounds, on the other.

Just as other discourses of a society, the discourse of politics, and its ways of interacting with the discourse of the mass media, is subject to constant change. Such changes manifest themselves through the hybridization of its communicative genres-by incorporating features of one genre into another, and/or by a blending of generic styles, or by drawing on other or more discourses than before, e.g. by incorporating elements of economical, ecological and scientific discourse into political discourse (Fairclough 1995). The contemporary political interview in the Anglo-Saxon media is a particularly clear case of this happening. A particular kind of change has been triggered by a change in the participant structure of the political interview, or rather, in the status of the participating politicians. The arrival of grass-roots political movements and the appearance of their representatives in the public sphere have introduced a new type of politician to public interaction whose expertise may lie more in the fields of science and eco-technology than in politics. In dealing with professional politicians who have all present-day commodities and any possible personal and technical support at their disposal, and with professional interviewers who have the media know-how at their fingertips, they may be assigned therefore the status of partial experts, if not lay persons, and be treated accordingly. Present-day political discourse in the media thus has become hybrid in that it articulates together the orders of discourse of the political system (conventional, official politics), of the media, of science and technology, of grassroots sociopolitical movements, of ordinary private life, and so forth-but in an unstable and shifting configuration. (Fairclough 1998: 146f.)

Another change that can be observed is the incorporation of the familiar, "soft and feel-good" style of everyday conversation with its norms of politeness into the serious political interview:

Political interviews typically mix their genres and their discourses. In complex ways, politicians characteristically shift into conversational genre, and draw upon lifeworld discourses, in finding ways to address mass audiences who are listening or watching in mainly domestic environments. (Fairclough 1998:151)

The tendency towards everyday discourse holds for interviewers as well, but as yet seems to show itself more in the private than in the public media, at least in Britain (Lauerbach 2004). If hybrid genres can be considered indicators of social change in general, a particular composition of hybrid elements can indicate a particular state of social development:

> A particular articulation of genres and discourses within a generic complex is a particular effect of power corresponding to a particular state of hegemonic relations. It is also a potential focus for resistance and struggle. To take an example, not all professional politicians are willing to go along with more aggressive and contestatory styles of political interview which fit in with the media priorities to make programmes more entertaining by subordinating political discussion to gladiatorial contest. (Fairclough 1998:151)

However, the manner in which journalists define their roles and professional identities can vary across channels within one culture (for instance for professional interviewers in the British television channels BBC and ITV, cf. Lauerbach 2004). Variation across cultures, which is the focus of the papers in this volume, is of course to be expected all the more. For instance, in the participant structure of news programmes, in some cultures one prominent anchor who is in sole control maybe preferred, in others two or more anchors conversationally interacting as a team. Since cultures can differ in their preferred discourse styles for certain social domains, the conversationalization of institutional discourse and especially of media discourse, which has been found to hold for the Anglo-American context (Fairclough 1995), may not necessarily be found in other cultural contexts, such as the German, Flemish, Finnish or Swedish ones, or in those of the "new" democracies. And since discourse styles may also be evaluated differently across cultures, the Anglo-American phenomenon of conversationalization may, for instance, be interpreted as an appropriate style for political discourse in some cultures while it will be looked upon as a non-serious mode of communication in another one, where it may be appropriate for talk shows but not for news interviews. In a similar vein, what may be conceived of as a public domain in one culture, for instance a politicians family and their intimate interpersonal relationships, maybe conceived of as a private domain in another culture. The interesting point in comparative analysis comes when such features can be shown to cluster in a meaningful way, so that they support generalising interpretations.

Based on interviews with journalists in a media studies context, Köcher (1986) studied the self-images of British and German media professionals. Her results yielded roughly two groups: "bloodhounds" for the British media, and "missionaries" for the German ones. Twenty years later, and with the more finegrained methods of micro-level discourse analysis, such clear-cut categories are presumably not to be achieved, but the papers collected in this volume should nevertheless contribute to our understanding of how political discourse in the media can vary cross-culturally

THE CONTRIBUTIONS

The contributions in this volume fall in three parts. The papers in the first part start off from the textual micro-phenomenon of linguistic form and examine its functions in discourse, those in the second part employ a textual meso-perspective and investigate genre-specific discourse practices, and those in the third part are based on a textual macro-outlook and analyse political media events-national addresses, and the multi-generic macro-texts of election nights.

Part I, *From linguistic device to discourse practice,* comprises two contributions. Anne-Marie Simon-Vandenbergen, Peter R. R. White and Karin Aijmer's *Presupposition and 'taking-for-granted' in mass communicated political argument. An illustration from British, Flemish and Swedish political colloquy* examines to what extent taken-for-grantedness is used as a strategy in political media language as a genre across cultures, and whether it is characterised by similar choices at the interpersonal level. The data are taken from British, Flemish and Swedish radio and television interviews and debates. Rut Scheithauer's *Metaphors in election night television coverage in Britain, the United States and Germany* is based on Lakoff and

Johnsons (1980) cognitive-constructivist theory of metaphor. It presents a quantitative and qualitative analysis of the use of metaphors by nine television stations covering the British general election of 1997, the German parliamentary election of 1998 and the US presidential election of 2000.

Part II, *Discursive practice in political interviews,* contains four contributions. Annette Beckers *"Are you saying...?" A cross-cultural analysis of interviewing practices in TV election night coverages* employs an integrated framework informed by pragmatics, conversation analysis, and appraisal theory. It examines the form and function of question-answer-routines in political and expert interviews on the basis of data recorded during international and national coverages of the UK and German General Elections (1997/1998), and during the US Presidential Elections in 2000. Marjut Johanssons *Represented discourse in answers.*

A cross-cultural perspective on French and British political interviews examines the communicative function of represented discourse from a cross-cultural perspective in a dialogic framework by focussing on the different functions and contexts of use in French and English political TV-interviews. It compares and contrasts its descriptive and argumentative uses in the two sociocultural contexts. Anita Fetzer's *Challenges in political interviews: an intercultural analysis* is set in a sociopragmatic frame of reference. It examines language-and culture-specific preferences for communicating, interpreting and contextualizing challenges. The study is based on a corpus of British and German political interviews from the general elections in Britain (1997) and Germany (1998). Elda Weizman, Irit Levi and Isaac Schnee-baum's *Variation in interviewing styles: challenge and support in Al-Jazeera and on Israeli television* explores patterns of interviewers' challenge and support in TV news interviews conducted by two interviewers-Faysal al-Qasem in Arabic (on Al-Jazeera) and Ben Kaspit in Hebrew (Israel Television, Channel 1), focusing on topic introduction in the openings, explicit comments and elaborative reformulations in triadic interviews with two interviewees. It compares and contrasts symmetric and asymmetric confgurations in the two sociocultural settings and interprets the diferences in terms of challenge and support.

Part III, *Media events: from public address to election nights,* comprises three contributions. Christoph Sauer's *Christmas Messages by heads of state: multimo-dality and media adaptations* employs a frame of reference informed by functional pragmatics and critical discourse analysis. It investigates the multimodal quality of Christmas Messages by European heads of state on TV giving particular attention to the 'multimedia show' by the British Queen in 2003 and the 'sermon by the Finnish President in 2004, thus accommodating the complex relationship between what TV viewers see and what they hear. Raimund Schiefi's *Information meets entertainment: a visual analysis of election night TV programs across cultures* analyses the semiotic work, techniques and conventions used by TV stations to articulate the transitions between inside and outside and to produce a spatially fragmented yet coherent televisual text in the context of the broadcast studio. It compares and contrasts the techniques used by the stations BBC, BBC World, ITV, CNN International, CNN, NBC, ARD and RTL, and analyses their strategies. Gerda Eva Lauerbach's *Presenting television election nights in Britain, the United States and Germany. Cross-cultural analyses* examines the discursive practices with which presenters interact with various types of participants inside the studio and on outside locations. It focusses on the ways in which they construct from this a comprehensible and coherent text for the television audience. The data are national and international broadcasts covering the British and German parliamentary elections of 1997 and 1998, respectively and the US presidential elections of 2000.

2

Presupposition and Taking-for-granted

INTRODUCTION

Recent linguistic research on media political language, whether the concern is with the written or the spoken media, can roughly be divided into three groups of studies. In one type of studies the focus is on ways in which language reflects explicit or implicit ideologies. Typically these studies have aimed at laying bare the means by which speakers/writers convey political opinions regarding crucial societal issues such as class, gender or race relations. The linguistic framework within which most of these studies are carried out is critical discourse analysis in the broadest sense. The ultimate goal of this type of research is to raise awareness of language as an instrument of power and thereby to attempt to have an impact on power relations, to contribute to lifting inequality. These studies hence have a clear ideological starting-point and purpose. Examples are van Dijk (1998a, 1998b), Fairclough (1995, 2001), Wodak et al. (2000), Blommaert and Bulcaen (1997), and many articles in the journal *Discourse and Society*.

The second group of studies on media political language focus on the mechanisms of interaction and ways in which participants engage in talk. These studies are not so much interested in the ideologies of the speakers as in the way media interaction develops in different genres such as radio or television interviews and debates. The linguistic framework within which these studies are to be situated is typically conversation analysis in some variant.

Examples of such work are Great-batch (1992) and Clayman and Heritage (2002).

The third group comprises studies which take a functional approach to discourse in a broad sense and concentrate on the linguistic means, lexical and grammatical, of persuasion. The focus is on participants' rhetorical strategies by means of which they attempt to get their points across and reach their goals as political speakers. This type of research shares with the first group of studies its interest in the power of linguistic choices and with the second group its interest in the way speakers deal with the demands made by the various genres in which they are involved-for example how is it that speaker answer face-threatening questions, deny accusations or strengthen their own arguments. This type of research tends to go into detailed analyses of linguistic choices as rhetorical devices employed by political speakers to reach certain goals which are crucial in the presentation of themselves in the media. Examples are Harris's study (1991) on answering questions, Simon-Vandenbergen (1996, 1997) on image building, Lauerbach (2004) on political interviews as a hybrid genre.

The present article is to be situated within the third group. Its aim is to study strategic uses of lexicogrammatical means in an attempt to persuade. More specifically the focus is on the use of a set of resources which we see as construing 'taken-for-grantedness'-certain formulations by which propositions are treated as generally known or agreed upon, and hence as uncontentious and not at stake argumentatively Our specifc focus will be upon two modes of taken-for-grantedness-that associated with what the literature terms presupposition (see e.g. Bertuccelli Papi 1997; Cafi 1998; Lambrecht 1994) and that associated with meta-discursive locutions such as *of course* and its Dutch and Swedish equivalents *na-tuurlijk* and *ju* respectively. The research elaborates on previous work on the use of modality and evidentiality in British political discourse (especially Simon-Vandenbergen 1992) and on cross-linguistic research in this area (especially Simon-Vandenbergen and Aijmer 2005; Lewis 2004). Our goal is threefold.

The first aim is to look at taken-for-grantedness as a persuasive strategy in political TV debates. This paper builds on Sbisà (1999) and takes the argumentation further in the direction of finding an answer to the question why speakers find it useful to treat certain propositions as generally known or agreed upon or otherwise not at issue. It is often assumed that such formulations are used with the aim of making propositions unarguable, or at least with the aim of making them less accessible to argumentation. For instance, Cafi (1998) writes:

> Obviously, it is more difcult to question something that is communicated only implicitly rather than something which is communicated openly, if only because what is implicit must be recognized before being attacked. This is proved by the highly polemical and aggressive value underlying any attack to presuppositions; such an attack is seriously face-threatening. (f 998:753)

However, in the type of media data examined in this paper the taken-for-granted material does, at least with some regularity, get challenged. This finding forces us to look beyond some simple notion of unarguability in seeking to identify the rhetorical purposes which may be served by these formulations in the mass communicated political arguments which constitute our current data set.

The second aim of this paper is of a more general linguistic nature. Starting from the system of engagement as developed by Martin (1997, 2000) and elaborated by White (1998, 2000, 2002, 2003) we want to argue that presupposition deserves a place in that framework as one of the options. While a consideration of presupposition is absent in the model presented in White (2003), both White (2006) and Martin and White (2005) do discuss what is termed 'taken-for-grantedness' and in this context consider the potential intersubjective and rhetorical effects associated with the use of presupposing formulations. The account in this paper is generally supportive of the approach taken by White and by Martin and White but seeks to consider the rhetorical function of taken-for-grantedness in greater depth, and in the context of cross-linguistic comparisons.

Thirdly, the data are taken from political debates in three closely related cultural contexts, the British, Flemish and Swedish ones. We believe that by studying closely linguistic choices in similar data in different languages and cultures the resources which are exploited surface more visibly. Furthermore, if it appears that the choices are similar we can hypothesise that political discourse in these cultures relies on the same tactics. However, in order to reach this third goal of studying strategies from an intercultural point of view much more research is called for, on a larger amount of data from more widely different cultures. We therefore see this third goal as mainly exploratory in nature.

First we briefly introduce the framework we are using and its relevance for the data under consideration (Section 1). Section 2 discusses the data. We then outline our view of the rhetorical efect of 'taken-for-grantedness' as it operates in connection with the discourse marker *of course* and its Flemish and Swedish equivalents (Section 3). The use of presupposing constructions across the British, Flemish and Swedish data is dealt with in Section 4. Section 5 gives the discussion of and conclusions from the findings.

THE SYSTEM OF ENGAGEMENT

Various authors working within a functional approach to language have argued for a view of modality which goes beyond the formal categories of modal auxiliaries and epistemic adverbs to include a wide range of lexical and grammatical expressions of speakers' attitudes towards the truth value of their propositions (especially Stubbs 1986). In such encompassing defnitions of modality various systems which are kept apart in more formal approaches are brought together in that they serve similar aims in positioning the speaker vis-à-vis their utterances. These systems form a heterogeneous group including evidentials, hedges, concession, negation and others. From a rhetorical perspective it makes indeed good sense to treat choices from these diferent systems as working together to create semantic prosodies such as confdence and authority (Simon-Vandenbergen 1992, 1996, 1997). White (2003) and Martin and White (2005), elaborating the system of engagement as introduced by Martin (1997), accommodate these diferent types of expressions in an encompassing system of choices which all express the ways in which "the textual voice engages with alternative voices and positions" (White 2003:261). White's and Martin and White's contribution to the research on the functionality of modal and evidential expressions has been to draw attention to the fact that a primary functionality of these resources is to enable the speaker/writer to expand or contract the dialogic space available to alternative positions. In developing this argument, they have demonstrated that commitment to the truth-value of the propositions is to be seen as one factor but not the only one and ofen not even the most important one.

Within the model (White 1998; White 2003; Martin & White 2005) the main choice is between monoglossic and heteroglossic utterances, the former being bare statements whereby propositions are declared absolutely. For example,

(1) Two years on, the British government has betrayed the most fundamental responsibility that any government assumes-the duty to protect the rule of law. It is a collusion in an international experiment in inhumanity, which is being repeated and expanded around the world. *[Te Guardian,* January 10, 2004, leader pages-24]

Such utterances are seen as undialogic in that they ignore the backdrop of alternative viewpoints and other voices against which such utterances always operate, offering no recognition of these alternative points of view. In this they contrast with formulations which do recognize the communicative context as heteroglos-sic in that the speaker/writer is presented as responding to prior utterances, as positioning him-or herself with respect to other viewpoints, or as anticipating the responses of those to whom the utterance is addressed.

This is achieved through modalisation, attribution and a range of additional metadiscursive qualifers including negation, concession and the *of course* locutions which are our current concern. White claims that the contexts in which the barely asserted 'monoglossic' option is typically found are either those in which knowledge is established and therefore need not be argued for, or contexts in which the textual voice "constructs itself as being in solidarity with a readership which holds the same (...) views" (2003:264). In Martin and White (2005), the model is further developed to allow for a difference between bare assertions such as those just listed and those which involve presupposition, as the term has been defined in the literature. Presuppositions, of course, are those formulations in which the proposition survives even under negation. For example, the proposition that the Canadian government has betrayed its promises is presupposed in the following.

(2) After nine years of the government's betrayal of the promised progressive agenda, Canadians have a gut feeling that their country is slipping away from them.

Martin and White contend that un-presupposing bare assertions of the type listed earlier present the proposition as still in play argumentatively in some way, while the presupposing formulation presents it as a 'given' which puts nothing at stake argumentatively. (See Martin & White 2005: Chapter 3.) It is precisely this latter rhetorical effect that we are interested in this article and we shall come back to this monoglossic option in Section 3.

In contrast with the monoglossic utterance, the heteroglossic one is dialogistic in the sense that, as just indicated, it engages with alternative positions (White 2003:265). It can do so in two main ways, i.e. by expanding or contracting the space for other voices and alternative positions. The expansive options actively recognize alternative positions or allow for their possibility and hence lower the interpersonal cost for any who might advance such a viewpoint. For example, in the following two extracts, *it's possible, would, I believe* and *will* are dialogistically expansive in actively allowing for alternative dialogic possibilities.

(3) it's possible that a severe shake-up would bring your husband to realize how much you really mean.

The sad aspect of all this is that by giving support to this invasion Blair will be destroying the UN and I believe will have betrayed the British people.

In contrast, the contractive options operate to challenge, head of, deny or exclude dialogic alternatives, even while in some way allowing for, or engaging with these alternatives Thus negation is the archetypal dialogically contractive option in that, in denying some proposition, it necessarily invokes and hence allows for that contrary position, even while asserting that the denied proposition is unsustainable. The locution which is our current concern, *of course,* is included among these dialogically contractive options in that it (a) presents the speaker/writer as dialogically engaged with the putative addressee in anticipating that the proposition is something which will already be known or agreed upon, and (b) construes any contrary proposition as going against common sense or common knowledge. Under Whites engagement framework, it is classified as an instance of 'concurrence' in that it presents the addressee as inevitably sharing this piece of information or this viewpoint with the speaker/writer.

It is our proposal in this paper that even while presupposition is 'monoglos-sic' in Martin and White's terms and locutions such as *of course* are 'heteroglossic', they nonetheless do share one important aspect of their rhetorical functionality. Both formulations, in their different ways, present the proposition as a 'given', as informational or evaluative content which the speaker/writer is presented as taking for granted. In this we are extending Martin and White's notion of taken-for-grantedness, which for them is limited to 'monoglossic' presupposition, to include the heteroglossic concurring option of *course* (and related formulations.)

In Sections 3 and 4 we look at taken-for-grantedness as construed via formulations such as *of course* and at taken-for-grantedness as construed via presupposition respectively.

THE DATA

The British data used for this study are taken from the programme *Question Time* (BBC1 8 January 2004) and from a corpus comprised of some fifty episodes of the BBC radio programme, *Any Questions* (June 2003-December 2004), the Flemish data are from the programmes *Ter zake Zaterdag* (Canvas, 7 February 2003) and *De Zevende Dag* (Canvas, 8 February 2003). The data cover 6 debates. The Swedish data are from a debate on nuclear energy broadcast on 21 March 1980. These programmes share a number of features, including that the protagonists are politicians, that the topics are political issues, and hence that these are interactions which all fall under the heading of 'political discourse'. Further, in all cases the interaction is managed by an interviewer or moderator. Thirdly, in all cases these are broadcast programmes, whether on the radio or on television. For the purposes of this study the difference between radio and television programmes is less important. The crucial factor is that the discourse is political, the issues controversial, and the interaction takes place for an audience of viewers or listeners. On the other hand there are some differences between the genres which these data represent that may have an impact on the discursive choices, and thus potentially on the use of presupposition as a tactic. We shall briefly comment on these genres.

The English and the Flemish programmes belong to the genre which Great-batch (1992) and, following him, Clayman and Heritage (2002) call 'the panel interview'. According to Greatbatch, the advantage of panel interviews over one-to-one interviews is that the former solve the journalist's problem of having to reconcile combative questioning with the preservation of neutrality. By asking questions of two or more interviewees, typically representing different parties and viewpoints, the interviewer can provoke lively debate while maintaining neutrality. The liveliness results from disagreement among the interviewees. The disagreement can be voiced at different places in the turn-taking and can be addressed to the interviewer or to another interviewee. Greatbatch (1992) points out that the strength of disagreement in this genre increases with the abandonment of the expected question-answer format and with the identity of the addressee. The extracts given in the discussion will show that both the English and the Flemish data display the features of this genre. Not infrequently do interviewees address each other and in some cases they even deviate from the topic to become personal in an escalation of heated and unmitigated disagreement (see Clayman & Heritage 2002:313f. on the escalation from disagreement to confrontation).

The Swedish data are well described in Hirsch (1989). The genre is a formal television debate in which the turn-taking can be characterized as "mechanistic or almost completely predetermined" (1989:118). The debate in question took place in the last days before the referendum on nuclear energy in Sweden held on 23 March 1980. In this debate, the representatives of the three lines met. Line 1 is in favour of nuclear energy while line 3 wants to abolish it. Line 2 is a compromise, neither radically for nor against it. The three lines were represented by four speakers, and a well-known news broadcaster acted as moderator or "master of ceremonies". The primary goal of the activity was to influence the voting behaviour of the home audience. From the interaction point-of-view it is important to mention that the turns were very strictly timed, that claims made by one speaker are answered by another speaker only indirectly, and hence that there is no overlapping talk, no interruptions, no abandonment of "institutionalised footing" (Greatbatch 1992:287), no escalation of disagreement towards confrontation.

The passages given in the following sections as illustrations follow normal orthographic and punctuation conventions for readability's sake. We have opted against a detailed CA transcript for the sake of uniformity: while the Flemish data were recorded and transcribed by us, the Swedish data have been transcribed at the Department of Linguistics, Göteborg University and this transcription has been used here (although some conventions have been changed for the sake of consistency with the other data). The *Question Time* data were transcribed by us, while the data from *Any Questions* were collected from the BBC website at www.bbc.co.uk/radio4/anyquestions.shtml.

OF COURSE AND ITS EQUIVALENTS IN THE FLEMISH AND SWEDISH DATA

It has appeared from previous research that the adverb *of course* is extremely frequent in British political discourse. Both Simon-Vandenbergen (1992) and Lewis (2004) demonstrate that it fulfils some very useful rhetorical functions in this type of context. It is over-archingly a mechanism by which the speaker/writer announces that the current proposition is so generally known or so generally agreed upon as to be self-evident. It is thus a dialogistically anticipatory gesture in that either a state of knowledge or a value position is projected onto the audience. In English, *of course* shares this functionality of announcing self-evidence with a few other locutions, for example, *naturally, it goes without saying, needless to say, as you know* and *obviously.* For the purposes of this paper we have chosen to confine ourselves to *of course* (and its Dutch and Swedish counterparts) because it is overwhelmingly the most frequently used of these locutions in our data. For example, in our database of transcripts of the *Any Questions* programmes, *of course* occurs in all 55 transcripts at an average of 7 instances per transcript (373 instances in 55 transcripts) while *obviously* occurs 137 times in 48 transcripts and *naturally* only 7 times in 7 transcripts (and only half of those instances construe 'concurrence'). In the Dutch and Swedish data we have looked at *natuurlijk* and *ju* respectively because (a) they too are announcements of self-evidence and (b) as announcers of self-evidence they are the closest to *of course,* and (c) because, like *of course,* they are the most frequently occurring announcers of self-evidence. In the Dutch data *natuurlijk* occurs 24 times in 6 transcripts, i.e. with an average of 4 per transcript. In the Swedish data *ju* occurs 169 times in the 90-minute debate, while *naturligtvis* occurred only twice and the synonymous *förstås* and *givetvis* were not found at all. In a study of the translation equivalents of *of course,* Simon-Vandenbergen and Aijmer (2003-4) have found that the word *natuurlijk* was the prototypical equivalent of *of course* in all its functions. In Swedish, it is striking that the most frequent translations of*of course, naturligtvis* and *förstås* (as found in Simon-Vandenbergen and Aijmer 2003-4) were (almost) absent from the debate, which indicates that they do not have the rhetorical function of *of course.* Te frequency of *ju* is accounted for further in this section.

The rhetorical functions served by *of course* can be grouped together under two broad headings. In the first instance it can be seen as having a 'politeness' function. For example,

(4) DIMBLEBY (moderator)

Welcome to Petersfeld in Hampshire which is decked out for Christmas and where we're in St. Peter's Church, which is renowned architecturally for its fine Norman tower and socially for its concerts, plays, exhibitions and civic events, as well as being of course a place of Christian worship.

In such instances the announcement of self-evidence acts as a form of dialogic apology cum explanation which can be accounted for by reference to the Gricean maxim of'quantity' (Grice 1975). Since the informational content of the framed proposition is presented as being so widely known as to be self-evident, such formulations involve the speaker saying 'more' than is necessary. They are thus an apparent breach of'quantity'. The speaker indicates an awareness of the apparent breach, while at the same time signalling that there is some other good reason why he/she needs to announce information which the addressee already knows-for example, in order to foreground a particular piece of information, in order to put together all the steps in a chronology, to ensure that the addressee knows where the speaker is coming from argumentatively, and so on. When used in this way, then, *of course* can be seen as a signal of discursively necessary redundancy. In such cases, *of course* has *as you know* as its near synonym-i.e.

...we're in St. Peters Church, which is renowned architecturally for its fine Norman tower and socially for its concerts, plays, exhibitions and civic events, as well as being, as you know, a place of Christian worship.

In the above instance, the proposition at issue involved entirely uncontentious and uncontested informational content-that St Peter's Church was a place of Christian worship. Such uses are rare in our data and are not of major interest in the context of this paper's central concern with political argument and conflict. However, we also find this politeness-oriented, apparent redundancy signalling function in connection with evaluative or speculative, and hence potentially more contentious, propositions. Consider by way of example the following two extracts,

(5) a. If there is to be a war on terror, and perhaps there must be, because of course September 11th was an outrage b. I think the terrible thing is that you knew from the very first moment that it really didn't matter what anybody said or anybody did this unfortunate man was going to meet the most terrible death. A man obviously not involved in the day-to-day difficulties. And a man who had gone there to do a constructive job. So of course you think first of the family.

Here the signalled assumption is that all will share the speaker's view of the attack on the World Trade Centre in New York in 2001, and that all will respond in the same way to the news that Iraqi insurgents had executed the British man they had taken hostage during the US and British invasion of Iraq in 2004. Despite the material being evaluative rather than 'factual', the same apology cum explanation effect applies. Since these are value positions which are presented as self-evidently the case, their expression is, on the face of it, redundant. The speakers signal their awareness of this apparent breach of the maxim of quantity, alerting their listeners that there is, nevertheless, some good communicative reason why they are being told something they already know to be the case. Once again the *of course* functions as a signal of necessary redundancy. The ideological potential of such uses is obvious. Not only do they project particular value positions onto the putative addressee, but they also construe that value position as universally shared, thus positioning any who might dissent from the viewpoint as at odds with what is common knowledge or common sense. In such cases, *of course* has *needless to say lit goes without saying* as a near synonym. For example

If there is to be a war on terror and perhaps there must be because, it goes without saying, September 11th was an outrage
In the second instance, in contrast with this solidarity and politeness function, *of course* serves an oppositional function. Here the announcement of self-evidence acts as a dialogic 'put-down by which the speakers immediate interlocutor is presented as having dealt inappropriately with informational or evaluative material. The interlocutors have either shown themselves to be ignorant of, to have overlooked, or to have omitted to mention a point of some significance, or, alternatively, they have made too much out of some point, for example presenting it as argumentatively significant or crucial when, from the current speaker s perspective, it is too well known to have any such rhetorical potential. Consider byway of example the following extract. The current speaker presents the previous speaker s arguments in favour of a ban on fox hunting (then being proposed by the British government) as flawed in that the previous speaker has failed to take into account evidence against the pro-ban position provided by recent experiences in Scotland.

(6) JENKIN

Well I myself would never break the law but you've got a problem where so many people feel that a law is unjust. We've had chief constables speaking publicly about the huge amount of resources that are going to be necessary to police a ban on foxhunting and of course they've already tried to ban foxhunting in Scotland and the legislation is a complete nonsense because they carry on foxhunting and they just shoot the foxes at the end instead of catching them by hounds. The 'put-down effect applies here as this counter evidence is presented as universally known. In failing to take it into consideration, the prior speaker is construed either as grossly ill-informed (he is ignorant of what is commonly known) or as dissembling (he seeks to misrepresent the case at hand by suppressing common knowledge). There is also a further positioning effect by which the wider audience is presented as standing with the current speaker, and against the former speaker, in sharing this view of the significance of the Scottish experience. In such cases, *of course* has *as everyone knows* as its near synonym. For example,

We've had chief constables speaking publicly about the huge amount of resources that are going to be necessary to police a ban on foxhunting and, as everyone knows, they've already tried to ban foxhunting in Scotland and the legislation is a complete nonsense because they carry on foxhunting and they just shoot the foxes at the end instead of catching them by hounds.

Alternatively, *of course* is employed as the current speaker presents some key point of the prior speaker's argument as self-evident and hence not relevant or at issue in the current debate. Consider by way of example the following, in which the speakers are Dimbleby (D) and Bryant (B):

(7) D: What do you make then of the point that Peter Hitchens was making-making, to the effect that the marriage is fundamental to the belief of the church and fundamental to its identity, as he believes it also to be in a coherent civilized society? B: Of course marriage is absolutely essential to a coherent and a good society and for the vast majority of people it's the way they're going to live their lives but there are some people, like myself, who are gay or are lesbian who are never going to have the opportunity of marriage, who might want to live in long trusting loving relationships and I think the church should be helping people to do that rather than making it more difficult.

Here the current speaker (Bryant) doesn't simply concede the prior speaker's point about the social role of the family, but, via the use of *of course,* construes it as so evidently the case as to be irrelevant to the issues which are actually under consideration. With such uses of *of course,* it is usual for the locution to be followed by some adversative connective such as *but* or *yet*. Once again this is a use of *of course* by which the prior speaker is cast as either foolish (they have overestimated the significance of some argumentative point) or as rhetorically unscrupulous (they have sought to base an argument on a point they know to be irrelevant). And once again there is a positioning effect by which the current speaker is construed as aligned with the wider audience against the prior speaker. However, in this instance it is an assessment of the argumentative significance of some point which the current speaker supposedly shares with the wider audience. In such cases, *of course* has *it goes without say inglneedless to say* as its near synonym. For example,

It goes without saying that marriage is absolutely essential to a coherent and a good society...

In summary, then, of this section, we can say that in English all uses of *of course* are announcements by the speaker that they regard the current proposition to be so widely known or so widely agreed upon to be 'self evident'. Within this broader functionality, instances of *of course* may vary according to whether they are serving a solidary or an oppositional function. In the first instance they act as dialogic apologies cum explanations, as the speaker signals a discursively necessary redundancy. In the second instance they act as put-downs by which some prior speaker is indirectly accused of understatement (having ignored or failed to mention some relevant point) or, alternatively of overstatement (having made too much out of some essentially irrelevant point).

In Flemish *natuurlijk* can serve they same functions as *of course* in English as they have been outlined above. That is to say, it is an announcer of self evidence which can be either solidary ('apologetic' signal of necessary redundancy) or oppositional (a 'put-down'), and within the oppositional, it either implies 'understatement' (failure by the dialogic opponent to note some very widely known significant point) or 'overstatement' (making too much argumentatively out of some universally known point).[3] Its use is illustrated in the following extract.[4] The politician is Rik Daems (RD).

(8) I: Well, Mr Daems, what is Mr Van Rossem saying there? He says the executive board was perfectly aware of the

plans of the Swiss and apparently the VLD party chairman Karel De Gucht knew about it, too. Do you know about that scenario?

RD: Not at all. I think that the inquiry committee has revealed a number of things which are important. I think that we regrettably find that we have landed in a party political situation where some people have at particular moments stooped to personal attacks but if you distance yourself from that for a moment then I think that you find in the report a number of aspects...

I: Yes

RD:...mainly to well financially it was an enterprise in which a number of very bad decisions were taken, mainly under the impulse of the Swiss and what struck me especially is that now a few days ago it appeared from the Ernst & Young report in Switzerland that well in fact there had been premeditated deception

I: Yes and according to Mr Van Rossem...

RD: [overlap] which of course doesn't mean...

I:...according to Mr Van Rossem the executive board knew about this, some VLD people knew about it and nothing was done, he says.

RD: [overlap] Well, Karel De Gucht of course hadn't become party chairman by 1997 because that was the time of the purchase of those air buses...

I: Hmmm

RD:...so I think that things are being mixed up and that Mr Van Rossem...

I: Is he mistaken and talking nonsense, Mr Van Rossem?

RD: Well I think Mr Van Rossem of course now that he wants to become a politician is perhaps a little bit infuenced by that but the essence of the story, Mr Belet, is that you have to look at the conclusions of the report because what is important for me is that we have uncovered to some extent where the causes are of such a large company going bankrupt: bad management, wrong financial decisions.

In the above extract Rik Daems (RD), federal Minister of State

Enterprises is being interviewed on the bankruptcy of Sabena, the national airline company. The interviewer refers to Mr Van Rossem, one of the senior dismissed Sabena pilots who became the spokesman for the Sabena pilots at the time and accused the government of not having disclosed knowledge of the Swiss plans to stop their financial input. Van Rossem claimed the government had known about it for a long time and should have reacted. RD uses the word *natuurlijk* (the Flemish equivalent of *of course)* twice in this extract. The first time it functions to convey that 'as everybody knows' Karel De Gucht could not have been responsible as he wasn't party chairman at the time, in contrast with what Van Rossem claims. The implication is that the accusation of Van Rossem is therefore clearly unjustified and it is plain for everyone to see that. This usage of *natuurlijk,* then, clearly parallels the use of *of course* as an oppositional 'put-down' in English which we exemplified above. More specifcally, it is the first type of 'put-down where the dialogic opponent is construed as guilty of' understatement'. They are represented as either ignorant of, or as deceitfully failing to mention, some significant point which is known to the rest of us. As was the case with the equivalent *of course* in English, the adverb builds up a solidary relationship between the current speaker and the audience against the dialogic opponent.

The second occurrence of *of course* (source item *natuurlijk)* occurs in association with the dialogically expansive items *I think* and *perhaps.* The reason is that the interviewee is making a strong statement here about the dishonest intentions of the Sabena pilot but has no evidence for making claims about intentions. Therefore the accusation is hedged even though the word *of course* at the same time closes down the dialogue. Here we see the Flemish equivalent of English *of course* where the functionality is to signal necessary redundancy. That Van Rossem, as a would-be politician, might be expected to distort or misrepresent is construed as a proposition which is self-evident and which, accordingly, wider audience members will already know and take for granted. The speaker 'apologises' for proposing a point of which the audience is supposedly only too well aware, signalling that, despite this apparent redundancy, he still needs to make this point for the purposes of advancing his own argument. The effect, obviously, is highly ideological as the view that would-be politicians are by nature deceitful is projected onto the audience and construed as universally held. The speaker, in his capacity as an established politician, thus implicitly distinguishes between 'real' and 'would-be' politicians.

The above examples show *natuurlijk* as 'put-down (understatement) and as 'apology' (signalling of necessary redundancy). In the following passage *natuurlijk* functions as 'put-down (overstatement).

(9) VR: Yes, of course the threat of war is something terrible and we must do everything to forestall that. It goes without saying. The people want that. Of course we want that, too uhm but we must also have a consistent policy, I think. Uhm. Mr Michel was in New York at the end of January. He was impressed by what he heard there. He asked for an understanding of the American viewpoint. There was even mention of a U-turn. He has. he denied that. Uhm he comes back to Europe and then we adopt a viewpoint that is in fact completely in contradiction with the impression which he gave in New York.

The speaker, MP for the opposition, disagrees with the government's refusal to give defensive support to Turkey, as has been asked by the US. The government spokesperson in this interview argues that Belgium must do everything to avoid a war against Iraq. This is the point where the speaker in the above extract comes in with *of course,* which, while expressing agreement with the government's argument, presents it as an overstatement, which does not detract from the opposition's line of argumentation.

In Swedish political speech the word *ju* is extremely frequent (see Simon-Vandenbergen and Aijmer 2005). It clearly differs, however, from *of course* and *natuurlijk* in that it does not cover the same oppositional functions. Its function is mainly to mark self-evidence and to construe a relationship of solidarity. As shown in Simon-Vandenbergen and Aijmer (2003-4), it can be seen as a rhetorical equivalent of *of course* in that it also functions to announce self evidence and thereby to construe a relationship of solidarity between the speaker and their audience. In contrast with Dutch *natuurlijk,* however, it is not the most frequent translation equivalent of *of course.* However, just like *of course* and *natuurlijk* it represents the proposition as an undisputed truth and hence is used by political speakers as a ploy to create a power imbalance with the opponent. In contrast with English *of course* and Dutch *natuurlijk,* Swedish *ju* is a modal particle rather than an adverb. This means that it can for instance not be fronted or moved around and is much less salient. It can be said to have a 'sneaked in character. The following extract illustrates this use of *ju* (translated as *of course).* The speaker is Rune Molin (RM):

(10) RM: Why do we get such diferent contradictory messages? Of course it can't be demanding too much that the voters should get information about what is going to happen to the electricity supply how you are going to ration, how you are going to raise the prices and so on, because that is of course what is going to be the consequence when one is going to lower the electricity supply in the eighties. Dahleus is of course going to leave the scene himself afer the 23rd of March I have read in the papers, but could you not before that tell us who will carry out your political message?

In conclusion, it has appeared from recent research that at least in British, Flemish, Swedish and French (Lewis 2004) political discourse the rhetorical mode of 'concurrence' (White's term 2003) is favoured in contexts where speakers wish to contract the dialogue in the sense of making it difcult to challenge the proposition as it is presented as shared knowledge. The use of items indicating shared knowledge typically confrms solidarity in contexts where interactants already share a great deal of common ground and a common outlook (see Holmes 1988). Their use in contexts where very little is actually to be taken for granted, as diferences in opinion are the very 'raison d'etre' of the genre (political debate), is aimed at construing solidarity with those who need to be persuaded, i.e. the audience, against the opponent.

The use of presupposition as another tactic 5.1 The monoglossic statement.

It appears from the data in all three languages concerned that the concurrence strategy discussed in the previous section is just one of the more encompassing range of linguistic choices which in political discourse raise the interpersonal stakes for any who might want to question, challenge or reject a proposition being taken-for-granted by the speaker. In White's taxonomy (2003), the dialogic contraction devices, while being heteroglossic in recognising the theoretical possibility of alternative opinion, at the same time close down the dialogue by making challenges difficult. Such dialogic contraction is therefore closer to the monoglossic mode than the dialogic expansion devices. White points out that the monogloss option is also typically used where textual voice and audience either do share a common outlook or where the textual voice, for persuasive purposes, creates solidarity with a particular readership, who possibly hold an opinion distinct from other sections of the community. In Whites taxonomy it is the bare assertion which realises the meaning of the monoglossic mode.

It appears indeed that in the data political speakers do present highly controversial judgements in a monoglossic way by expressing them as bare unmodalised statements. Here is an example from the Flemish data. The speaker is a member of the opposition and criticizing the safety policy of the government. The oppositions viewpoint is that even though a lot of money is being spent on police reform, the result is less safety than before:

(11) VR: The central theme: safety. And they spend a lot more money to have fewer people who take care of safety. That's an incomprehensible story.

The strength of the argument lies in the juxtaposition of the different propositions. While the government cannot deny that money has been spent on police reform (objective fact), nor that the reforms involve a re-allocation of tasks so that there are fewer policemen on the streets (objective fact), the subjective elements in the utterance are the following: first, the vague quantifer *a lot more* is a subjective assessment; secondly, the presentation of having fewer people who take care of safety as the goal (in the form of a subordinated purpose clause) is the speaker's subjective assessment of the facts; thirdly, the nominal phrase *fewer people who take care of safety* to refer to policemen on the street is strategically chosen because it emphasizes the paradoxical situation. However, it expresses a contestable equation of the class of policemen on the street with the class of people taking care of safety. The evaluative comment *Tat's an incomprehensible story* merely sums up the argument: the government's policy has been presented by the speaker in a monoglossic way as indeed paradoxical.

However, there is another type of strategy which is at least as common as the bare statement to construe solidarity and to block dialogue. This is the presentation of material as presupposed. We want to argue that within the taxonomy of engagement modes it is the most dialogistically restrictive of all the engagement options, limiting the scope for dialogic alternatives even more thoroughly than bare assertions of the type just exemplifed. Under this option, the speaker does not simply decline to offer any recognition that the proposition is in some way problematic or subject to contestation (as is the case with non-presupposing bare assertions). They go beyond this to present the proposition as simply not at issue, as a proposition which can be assumed and hence need not be asserted. While a non-presupposing monoglossic statement presents at least part of the information as new, presupposition structures present the information as known. While monoglossic utterances do not build in the possibility of dialogic alternatives, they are nevertheless dialogically 'upfront in making a statement which can be affirmed or denied. Presupposed material, on the other hand, is 'sneaked in as it were. Not only does it not open up a dialogue but it definitely shifts attention away from the thus backgrounded material.

Presupposition takes many forms and has been widely discussed in the linguistic literature. It is not our ambition here to give an exhaustive account of the different types as they occur in the data. What we want to do by giving some examples of different manifestations of presupposition is to show that it is an important means of persuasion in political discourse. In the next section we specify the way in which we are using the notion in this paper.

THE TERM PRESUPPOSITION

The *terra presupposition* covers many different things. One important distinction that has been made is between semantic and pragmatic presupposition. According to Cafi (1998:752) "[t]he concept of semantic presupposition is quite clear". This is true to the extent that there are clear criteria which allow us to decide under what conditions we can claim that some material is semantically presupposed. Semantic presupposition is defined in terms of truth-conditions, as a subtype of entailment, in the sense that a proposition which is presupposed remains true under negation and questioning. The following example is from Bertuccelli Papi (1997). The sentence 'Sue is dancing a macarena' presupposes that there is a person named Sue and there is a dance which is the macarena. This type of existential presupposition survives even when the sentence is negated or turned into a question: 'Sue is not dancing a macarena' and 'Is Sue dancing a macarena?! Semantic presupposition manifests itself in various lexical expressions and grammatical structures, and Bertuccelli Papi (1997) gives the following list: definite descriptions (including proper names), factive predicates including epistemic verbs (like *know, realize)* and emotive predicates (like *be surprised, regret, forget, deplore, resent),* implicative verbs (like *manage, remember),* change of state, inchoative and iterative verbs (like *stop, start),* verbs of judging (like *accuse, blame, criticize),* clefing and pseudo-clefing, prosodic emphasis, temporal clauses, non-restrictive relative clauses and counterfactuals. Semantic presupposition is conceptually different from pragmatic presupposition, which is defined in terms of common ground or background knowledge. Lambrecht (1994) gives the following definition of pragmatic presupposition:

> The set of propositions lexicogrammatically evoked in a sentence which the speaker assumes the hearer already knows or is ready to take for granted at the time the sentence is uttered. (1994:52)

While this definition clearly distinguishes pragmatic from semantic presupposition, in practice it appears that the two concepts are hard to keep apart. The same types of lexicogrammatical structures are given for both types. In fact the distinction has, as Lambrecht points out (1994:61), "been all but abandoned in the literature", and Bertuccelli Papi remarks in the same vein that semantic presuppositions "have to be treated as pragmatic phenomena" (1997:11). The types of lexicogrammatical structures mentioned above are the ones we shall look for in the data at hand, even though what we are interested in are not the truth-conditions but the fact that these structures evoke situations, events which are presented by the speaker as background knowledge, propositions whose truth the speaker takes for granted. Thus when a speaker says *I regret that you told these lies* we have a case of semantic presupposition (the truth of the main proposition depends on the truth of the subordinated proposition, and the presupposition that 'you told these lies' survives under negation in *I don't regret that you told these lies*). However, what is more interesting from the point of view of interaction is that in uttering *I regret that you told these lies* the proposition 'you told these lies' is presented as common ground, while the assertion which is at stake is that 'I regret this'. Why is this the crucial point in interaction?

There are two reasons. One is that by encoding something as background, shared knowledge, the speaker at the same time presents a proposition as one whose truth is accepted by the hearer. In other words, pragmatically it is not the logical entailment which is of interest in the analysis of verbal interaction as much as the speaker's assumption of what can be taken for granted. Secondly, in terms of information structuring it is important that the presupposed material is backgrounded as old information, while the information in the assertion is foregrounded as new. Presuppositions in this way contribute to the structuring of the discourse, and "determine the point of view from which the text develops" (Bertuccelli Papi 1997:13). Both these factors play a role in the choices which speakers make with regard to what can be encoded as presupposed material.

The pragmatic view of presuppositions obviously entails that they are not static but are negotiated and interactively construed. But it also entails the possibility of exploitation. Bertuccelli Papi puts it as follows:

> It is therefore legitimate to wonder by whom pragmatic presuppositions should be taken for granted and by whom they are granted. The most plausible answer is that speakers treat presuppositions as noncontroversial, even though they may in fact be controversial and not taken for granted by the addressee. (1997:12-13)

Similarly, Lambrecht (1994:65) mentions the "conscious or unconscious exploitation of presuppositions for special communicative purposes". The reason why presuppositions are exploitable is that they are harder to challenge. As Lambrecht points out, the 'lie-test' shows that if the addressee wishes to challenge the 'old' information in the presupposition, he/she has to use other strategies than the straightforward 'That's not true'. For example, if the addressee replies *Tat's not true* to the utterance *I finally met the woman who moved in downstairs* she is challenging that the speaker met her, not that she moved in downstairs. If the addressee wishes to challenge the taken-for-granted nature of the presupposed proposition she would have to say something like *I didn't know that you had a new neighbour or What are you talking about?* (1994:52). In such cases Lambrecht demonstrates that presuppositions are based on the assumption of shared knowledge which is not put up for discussion. There is, however, also the cognitive principle of 'pragmatic accommodation' (Lambrecht 1994:66), which means that speakers frequently create a new presuppositional situation which can then be the starting-point for the further development of the conversational exchange. If someone says *My car broke down* this does not necessarily imply that the speaker thinks that the addressee knew that she has a car. Even if the addressee did not have this information she will accommodate to the new situation. Such cases of pragmatic accommodation are, however, to be distinguished from what Lambrecht refers to as "devious" cases of exploitation (1994:70). The difference lies in the effects aimed at: devious cases are not aimed at conveying information indirectly but at creating "a fictitious presuppositional situation" for certain rhetorical purposes. In this paper we shall examine which types of presuppositions are used by political speakers and for what purposes.

It is important to emphasize that, whatever the pragmatic effect in specific contexts, certain lexicogrammatical expressions by themselves trigger presuppositions. It is these expressions that we will examine. We shall, on the other hand, not be concerned with pragmatic presupposition in the very broad sense in which it has been used by some, to include all knowledge that language users have and which is brought into the production and comprehension of utterances. Kempson (1975:166ff), for instance, refers to the 'Pragmatic Universe of Discourse', defined as the "body of facts which both speaker and hearer believe they agree on" in a conversation. Mey (1998:186) claims that a "serious theory of pragmatic presuppositions (...) inquires *metapragmatically* into the ways in which an utterance is understood in the context of the language users' 'common ground". And Mey further points out that it is then important not only to inquire how people say things but why they say them at all (1998:187).

In this paper we are focusing on structures that are traditionally subsumed under semantic presupposition, while recognizing that they need to be studied from a pragmatic point of view, both in their exploitation and their understanding. We are not concerned with pragmatic presupposition in the broadest sense, which includes various forms of implicitness such as conversational implicatures (whether particularized or generalized).

PREVIOUS RESEARCH ON PRESUPPOSITION FOR PERSUASIVE PURPOSES: SBISA (1999)

Sbisà (1999) discusses the use of presupposition for persuasive purposes in the Italian daily press. One interesting question she deals with is why presuppositions should ever be persuasive, why there is "a default tendency" in the addressee to take the presupposed information for granted (1999:501). The answer, according to Sbisà, lies in the normative nature of presuppositions: they are to be defined not as shared assumptions but as assumptions that ought to be shared. This entails that speakers violate norms of interaction if they take for granted that information is shared while it is not. If therefore presuppositions are not satisfied, addressees will consider speakers as uncooperative. Thus, ideally, speakers should strive towards producing utterances which trigger presuppositions only when the "objective context" indeed contains those presuppositions. The reason why presuppositions are useful for transmitting ideologies is then that they tend to be left unchallenged, since they are backgrounded. Explicitation and challenging of presuppositions are options available to the addressee but, as Sbisa points out, dispreferred ones (1999:506).

The data examined in this paper differ from those discussed in Sbisa (1999) in several ways. First, they are spoken instead of written, and there is an interlocutor who has the option of choosing the dispreferred reaction. Studying the reactions of hearers adds an important aspect to the discussion of the motives behind presupposition. Secondly, it will be shown that the dispreferred reaction is not infrequent in this genre. While we notice that in our data there are instances of presupposition where the proposition is not challenged, it is significant that, where the presupposition involves currently contentious material, it was not unusual for the presupposed material to be rejected or otherwise challenged in some way. Here is an example from the British data, an exchange between Dimbleby (D) and May (M):

(12) D: Theresa May, why dump on returning officers? [presupposes that' dumping on returning offices' has taken place]

M: Well I'm not dumping on returning officers.

PRESUPPOSITION IN THE DATA

The following extract from the programme *Question Time* illustrates the type of structures and meanings that we are interested in. The issue of debate is the government's plans to introduce top-up fees for university students, for which they could get a loan. David Willits (W), Shadow Secretary voices the Conservative party's opposition to this plan. David Dimbleby (D) asks the question:

(13) D: David Willits, you were asked whether Tories will be voting in the lobbies for this because your position purports to be that you're against top-up fees. W: We are against them, we are against them and we're against them because we don't think we want to see our students any other perhaps on the latest proposals 23,000£ of debt when they leave university. I don't think that's the right way to go. And as a Conservative I want to encourage people to save and I hear Ministers in the areas that I debate particularly, pensions, things like that, say they've got to encourage people to save. I don't see how getting saddling young people with 23,000 pounds' worth of debt is gonna help them start off in their lives and we should remember how

> we got into this. We got into this because the government set a target, an arbitrary target for the expansion of universities, that they should reach this target of 50%. Well, I completely agree with what PhylisJames said, I don't think it's in the best interests of the people in this country, you do need a better education to set such a target, they need [interruption by moderator]

The first instance of a construction which exploits presupposition is 'I don't see how...'. This expression is synonymous to other expressions such as 'I don't understand how'. The proposition in the subordinated interrogative clause, in this case a *how-clause,* is in such structures presented as known information, since the only unknown element, the missing bit is the element in the *wh-word* (i.e. *how).* In this concrete example, the speaker presents as presupposed that the government is going to 'saddle young people with 23,000£ worth of debt'. The term *saddle* is evaluative, which means that the negative judgement is simultaneously absorbed in the message as presupposed and non-negotiable. We have a similar example in the expression 'we should remember', a factive verb. In the above instance, what needs to be remembered is that the government took the wrong decision ('bad for them'), and again an evaluative term, *arbitrary,* is smuggled into the presupposed material.

The next example is from the Swedish nuclear debate. The speaker is Per Unckel (a member of the Conservative Party and in favour of nuclear energy line 1). The addressee (Ulla Lindström) is a member of the Social Democratic party and is in favour of line 3 and abolishing nuclear energy.

(14) if Ulla Lindström does not trust lines one and two I suppose Ulla Lindström anyhow trusts the developing countries themselves when they shake their heads and wonder how we in Sweden can think about doing away with nuclear energy/when this implies that the pressure on scanty oil resources/which could be of use to the developing countries becomes still harder

The tactically relevant presupposed material in this passage is in the two *when*-clauses *when they shake their heads (...)* and *when this implies (...).* Te speaker first presents the disapproving attitude of the developing countries towards Sweden's plans to do away with nuclear energy as self evident by putting the proposition in a *when-clause.* Next, at a deeper level of subordination, the proposition that these plans would harm the developing countries by increasing the pressure on resources, is also presented as presupposed in a *when-clause.*

The following extract is also from the Swedish material. The speaker is Per Unckel (line 1):

(15) the election is about whether in addition to the global energy crisis we have already to a large extent been affected by we should place additional burdens which maybe too heavy for us

What is presupposed in the above utterance is that there is 'a global energy crisis'. Further, the comparative referential term *additional* is relevant here in terms of presupposition, since it presupposes the current existence of a burden (in the form of the global energy crisis').

Here follow some more examples of presuppositional structures from the Flemish and Swedish data.

(i) Factive predicates

The presupposition trigger of factive predicates can be illustrated with the following example from the Flemish data, from an interview with Jean-Luc Dehaene (DH), former Prime Minister of Belgium:

(16) DH: Well I call that continuing the debate after the elections and so I thought that this hype uh was unnecessary uh totally artificial uh and some people apparently did not see that they were thereby undermining the verve of the innovation...

I: Hmm

DH:...and and the campaign that should revolve around the innovation.

What is presented as new information is that some people apparently did not see something. That they were undermining the innovation is presented as to be taken for granted. The verb 'see' is indeed frequently used as an evidential and has a factive meaning: you can only see what is there. Another example from the same interview:

(17) DH: But when I see that this position uh damages my party, that through the way in which they handle this in my party they damage themselves, then I have to stop this.

The following is an example from the Swedish data, with Lennart Dahleus (LD) speaking:

(18) LD: Yes, Per Unkel knows of course that there are more possibilities for serious accidents than those we have discussed, steam explosions, and that nuclear power is a dangerous source of energy and that it contains enormous risks ranging from uranium mining to waste disposal that we probably agree on and that there are risks which have no equivalent in other sources of energy.

(ii) Relative clauses

Consider the following extract from the Flemish data:

(19) RD: This of course doesn't alter the fact that the government has approved an investment plan in the long term, a framework within which the NMBS [National Railways Company] must try to become healthy again, and one thing should certainly not be forgotten and that is a very important thing after all...

I: [overlap] Yes

RD:...in a few months the liberalisation of this goods transport starts and therefore...

I: [overlap] Precisely. Uhm.

RD:...we must really urgently take a number of measures which...

I: [overlap] Yes

RD:...in so many years were not taken because otherwise competition is going to hit very hard.

I: [overlap] Well, Mr Van Rompuy, it's the previous government's fault again.

VR: Yes, well, we're getting used to that.

On the face of it the relative clause gives information which is quite innocent: there would be no point in taking measures if they had indeed been taken before. The fact that the information is added at all raises the question of why it is added and why it is added in the form it is. The shared knowledge of the world which we need in order to explain the workings of this utterance is that 'in so many years' is a reference to the previous legislature, when the speakers party was in the opposition and his opponent in the debate was in the government. This utterance is a way of reversing the tables in holding the opponent responsible for 'what is bad! The next extract is an example from the Swedish debate. The speaker is Rune Molin, who represents line 2 in the referendum which was neither clearly for nor against nuclear energy.

(20) RM: It is self-evident that if we use our nuclear plants, the possibilities will increase considerably for cutting a dependence on oil which is wrecking the economy of the whole of Swedish society.

Below is another example from the Swedish debate. The speaker is Per Unckel (line 1):

(21) PU: In this nuclear debate there has been one feature which I myself have appreciated much//and this is a feature characteristic of many of those who still support line three/ /which implies a demand for a more tolerant society with room for more human concern and closeness/if it was this that this referendum was actually about/1 think that no one would have any doubts about its outcome.

The relative clause carries the presupposition that people in line three want a more tolerant society with room for human concern and closeness, which is obviously positively evaluated. However, the speaker draws attention to this as already known or old information in order to then foreground that this is not what the referendum is about. His own viewpoint is that this desire for a better society is actually a reason to use nuclear energy not to abolish it. What we have here is a 'put down of line threes position by presenting its argumentation as an overstatement, something everyone agrees on but which does not solve the problem. Similarly in the next example from the Swedish data, the addressee is obviously assumed to share the presupposition conveyed in the *which-clause.* The speaker is Per Unckel (line 1) and the addressee Lennar Daleus (line 3):

(22) PU: yes Lennart Daleus was surprised that I spoke about oil in a referendum about nuclear energy/the reason is of course that we have decided to use our nuclear reactors in order to open up the possibility of us being forced to reduce our dependence on oil, which is well on the way to getting out of hand

(iii) Conditional clauses

(23) VR: Do people feel safer?

RD: [overlap] Well of course if in politics, colleague Van Rompuy, you get important people such as Mr Dehaene is an important man, who want to create the impression among the population that unsafety increases...

VR: Oh, it's Mr Dehaene?

RD:...then I think that's bad. What m...

VR: Oh dear, Mr Dehaene creating unsafety.

RD:... what matters is reality...

VR: [overlap] Tat is that is...

RD:...and I'll give you another example.

VR: [overlap] very new to us, that is very new.

I: Yes, you must conclude, Mr Daems.

VR: [overlap] that is very new..

By presenting the contestable information in the conditional clause of an *if...then* structure which expresses a general truth that information is backgrounded as given and the focus is on the result, namely the value judgement 'I think that's bad'. It will be noted that the speaker makes use of several closing down strategies at the same time: *of course* (concurrence), subordination in an *if* clause in a general truth statement (presupposition), subordination in a relative clause (presupposition).

The following example is from the Swedish data (the speaker is Per Unckel, line 1):

(24) But it is clear that/if one now decides to demolish nuclear

reactors/which correspond to all the energy that we get from water power/then this cannot pass without a trace/ and line three confirms I suppose also this by claiming that there is no other country which is so dependent on nuclear power as Sweden

In (24) the speaker uses the conditional clause structure, which includes the relative clause with presupposed material, to convey the following message: 'if one decides to do away with nuclear energy, one does away with all the energy we get from water power'.

(iv) Existential structures

By 'existential structures' we refer in this context to structures with definite noun phrases triggering the presupposition of the existence of their referents. A very frequent type in political argumentation is an identifying clause with as subject 'the problem'. It is illustrated by the following example:

(25) RV: The problem of Mr Dewinter is that he only...

DW: It is linked...

I: [overlap] Yes

DW.:...to it.

RV:...looks at the past. And we want to do something...

I: [overlap] Okay

RV:...about the future and Mr Dewinter refuses to discuss that.

I: No, he has a clear thesis. His future is: full is full.

DW: [overlap] immigration stop.

The topic of discussion is immigration and Robert Voorhamme (RV, Socialist party) is attacking Filip Dewinter (DW, Flemish Bloc) for his thesis that the government policy does not work. He uses the expression 'The problem... is that...' In this type of structure two propositions are semantically presupposed, namely the identified and identifying elements. In this case these are firstly that there is a problem which the opponent has (the identifed element), and secondly that he only looks at the past (the identifier element). What is new information is thus that the problem is now identified as such. How do we have to understand the workings of this type of utterance? First, 'problem' is a judgement term: whether something is a problem or not is a subjective assessment of a state-of-affairs. Second, 'he only looks at the past' is pragmatically to be understood as a judgement as well, since our knowledge of the world tells us that politicians need to look at the future. This is indeed explicit in the contrast with the speaker's own party ('And we want to do something about the future'). Through this structure a negative judgement (a criticism of the opponent as a politician) is made into presupposed material.

(v) Pseudo-cleft structures

(26) DW: [overlap] What you are doing...

AD: [overlap] That's not possible, according to the law...

DW: [overlap]...by slowing down...

VR: [overlap] Mr Dewinter

DW: [overlap]...by slowing down integration...

AD: [overlap] human rights...

DW: [overlap]...is...

AD: [overlap]... says very clearly...

DW: [overlap] importing...

I: [overlap] This is incomprehensible. Let's...

DW: [overlap]... importing backwardness. And that is the wrong position.

There is a lot here which is presupposed in Filip Dewinter's (DW) statement: that the government is slowing down integration and that there is backwardness associated with the Islam culture. What is presented as new information is that this backwardness is imported. Again, value judgements are thus sneaked in as shared knowledge.

In the following example from Swedish there is a reversed pseudo-cleft summing up what has been presupposed in the preceding context. The speaker is Per Unckel (line 1):

(27) this is actually so self-evident that even line three ought to be able to agree//we can use nuclear power being certain that in spite of its risks/it is safer than any other alternative

which is at our disposal today//and this is what is most important

What is presupposed by the pseudo-cleft construction is that nuclear energy is safer than any other alternative type of energy. However the speaker cannot count on the audience's willingness to go along with the assumption that nuclear power is the safest source of energy and with the positive evaluation conveyed by the pseudo-cleft construction.

THE EXPRESSION OF DISAGREEMENT AND THE CHALLENGING OF TAKEN-FOR-GRANTEDNESS

In general, disagreement is dispreferred in interaction. It has been shown that in ordinary conversation speakers will avoid disagreement and when it does arise they will try to soften it in various ways, including the use of delay devices, prefacing the disagreement with agreement expressions, and hedges (see Pomerantz 1984). In contrast, Clayman and Heritage (2002:309f.) have shown that disagreement is characteristic of panel interviews. By bringing together speakers known to represent different viewpoints the genre by definition invites disagreement. Further, the interviewers themselves frequently elicit disagreement by phrasing and rephrasing arguments and confronting interactants with the oppositions viewpoints.

Also in contrast with ordinary conversation is the practice in panel interviews of voicing disagreements straightforwardly rather than hedgingly Mitigating elements are almost always absent. Clayman and Heritage also show that disagreement in that genre may easily shift into confrontation, and that such "escalation" is signaled by a shift from mediated address (through the interviewer) to direct address (Clayman & Heritage 2002:315). All of these features are indeed found in a very salient way in the Flemish data, which are from panel interviews.

The following extract illustrates such an escalation. The topic is the decision to put the former Prime Minister, Dehaene (Christian Democrats), who is not a candidate in the coming elections, nevertheless on the list because he is expected to attract votes. The exchange becomes heated, with a great deal of overlapping talk, and very personal:

(28) I: Yes, Mr Daems, this is embarrassing for the Liberal Democrats, isn't it?

He is not even on the list and yet he is in the limelight.

RD: Well let me first say something about that tremendous call for Dehaene. I understand that Mrs Schauvliege has opened a website and she wanted a hundred thousand signatures, well, she's got five thousand. So that's a tremendous call, if you ask me.

I: Yes, but in one week's time

RD: [overlap] But apart from that...

I: [overlap] That's in one week's time.

VR: [overlap] If you received five thousand if you received five thousand letters...

RD: [overlap] but apart from that...

VR: [overlap]... I would... I think you would...

RD: [overlap] Oh but...

VR: [overlap]... be happy with that.

RD: [overlap] But colleague Van Rompuy...

VR: [overlap] I think you would be happy with that.

RD: [overlap] About the internet...

VR: [overlap] I don't think you have recently received five hundred, have you?

RD: [overlap]... about the internet I know...

VR: [overlap] I don't think you have received five thousand.

RD: [overlap] You are extremely excited today, I think.

In the Flemish panel interviews disagreement is frequently voiced in very direct terms such as *that's not true, that's not correct,* or even *that's a lie.*

A similar situation obtains in the English data, where it is quite common for participants to forthrightly criticize, confront and nay-say each other. In the following extract, by way of example, the speakers, Scotland (S) and Howard (H) directly contradict and attack each other.

(29) S: But I think I want to add on to what David said because

of course one has to acknowledge that schools facing the challenging circumstances with which many do in London are two and a half times better off now than they were. The improvements in the figures coming out now is clear, that they're doing two and a half times better. So those schools are really moving forward. And just to remind everyone that the Prime Minister does send his child and his children to state comprehensive schools and he hasn't opted out of this system.

H: Before-before Patricia lets her imagination run away with her let's remember that one in three of every child-one in three of our primary school children leave primary school unable to read, write and count properly and under this government the truancy figures.

S: That's not true.

H:. and truancy-oh I'm afraid it's true, I wish it weren't true but I'm afraid it's true, I know it's hard to believe but it's true.

In the Swedish data there is less open disagreement. Only occasionally does the speaker accuse his opponent of not telling the truth:

(30) and when it is about oil Per Unckel says that it is quite clear that it is possible to replace the dependence on oil by nuclear power but to use your own words in an earlier context it is of course not true you know of course that in order to get rid of the total dependence on oil we would need fifty sixty power plants in this country (LD)

With regard to presuppositions, it has likewise been argued in the literature that interactants tend not to challenge them. Cafi points out that attacking presuppositions is not only difficult (because the implicit meaning must first be recognised before it is attacked) but also "highly polemical and aggressive" (Cafi 1998:753). Mey (1998:188-189) makes the same point in saying that in daily life we do not normally "go presupposition-hunting" and that we tend to take most presuppositions simply for granted. He goes as far as to claim that "metapragmatically questioning an interlocutor's presupposition is a dangerous sport, inasmuch as it may threaten the 'face' of my conversational partner" (1998:189).

Sbisa (1999), too, ascribes the usefulness of presupposition as a persuasive tactic to the dispreferred nature of explicitation and challenging and hence to the default reaction of acceptance. However, at least one reason why presuppositions are typically left unchallenged may be that speakers violate the norms of discourse if the presupposed propositional content cannot be assumed to be part of the hearer's knowledge. Sbisa puts it as follows:

> Moreover, it is among the speaker's responsibilities to issue an utterance containing certain presupposition inducers only if the objective context really contains the presupposition they trigger. Thus we are describing presuppositions as assumptions that the speaker ought to make, or, however, assumptions for which he or she is responsible. (Sbisa 1999:503)

On the other hand, hearers "accommodate" to presuppositions:

> If at time t something is said that requires presupposition P to be acceptable, and if P is not presupposed just before t, then-ceteris paribus and within certain limits-presupposition P comes into existence at t. (Lambrecht 1994:67)

This type of accommodation is, however, different from what takes place in the case of what Lambrecht refers to as "devious exploitation of presuppositional structure" (Lambrecht 1994:70). As shown in the above extracts, presenting controversial propositions as to be taken-for granted is a strategy in political discourse. Such expressions are indeed manipulable because speakers use them for presenting non-shared and even highly contested propositions as if they were shared knowledge. The effect is on the one hand that solidarity is confirmed with those who share the speakers' viewpoint and on the other hand that those who hold alternative opinions are put into a position where more interactive work needs to be done if they want to challenge the speakers views. The potential rhetorical usefulness of presupposition has been remarked upon by e.g. Verschueren (1999:157) and Cafi (1998:752). The question remains whether interactants in the types of data under investigation do make the efforts to challenge presuppositions.

It appears indeed that, in contrast with the rules of 'normal' interaction (cf. the "normative" nature of presupposition, Sbisà 1999:502) the rules of media political debate do allow for and indeed seem to dictate the challenging of presuppositions. The challengers are the interviewer/moderator as well as the opponent in the debate. In several examples from the Flemish data given in the previous section speakers do challenge the presuppositions. In examples (19) and (23) given above, the challenges are put in bold.

The speakers in the English data demonstrate a similar willingness to challenge presupposed propositions, at least when they involve a point which is significant attitudinally or ideologically. The following exchange is illustrative of this tendency. The speakers, Peter Hitchens (H) and Maude (M) are discussing the recent resignation of the highly infuential Conservative Party politician, Michael Portillo.

(31) H: Well I don't think it's a loss to the Conservative Party, in fact I wish he'd said it a long time ago because some years ago I suggested to the electors of Kensington and Chelsea that they should pick me instead because he wasn't-he wasn't a Conservative, which I don't think he is or was at the time. And what's interesting about Michael Portillo is this strange journey that he's been on for some time away from Conservatism ... turning the Conservative Party into New Labour with a blue T-shirt on. ...

M:...Peter makes his point, I've heard him make before, about modernisation is all about making us like New Labour, it isn't at all. I mean a Conservative Party has been in existence for 200 years, it is actually, as Michael Howard said the other day, it's the most successful, the longest standing political party in the history of democracy.

Here, via the nominal structure, 'this strange journey... away from Conservativism... into New Labour', the first speaker (Hitchens) presupposes that there has been a move, led by Portillo, to make the Conservatives more like the Labour Party. Despite the 'taken-for-grantedness' of the formulation, the second speaker unembarrassedly sets about turning an assumption into an arguable assertion and then forthrightly rejects it. Thus in his reply, he treats what was a presupposition as a 'point' which he asserts the speaker has made before. The challenging of presuppositions was also frequent in the Swedish data:

(32) RM: [with nuclear power] we would be able to provide forty thousand new beds/we would able to get a hundred thousand new day care centre vacancies we would be able to get thirty thousand new jobs in child care we can improve the schools/all this is something we will find it difficult to do during the 80s anyhow/but it will be still more difficult with the rapid winding-up and the costs you impose on the citizens with your policy LD: yes I really protest-the four hundred thousand billion that you mentioned are a sheer fabrication as well as the proportions of the crisis which you say will come about if we get rid of nuclear power

The relative clause in 'the costs you impose on the citizens with your policy' conveys the presupposition that 'the line 3 policy' of winding up nuclear plants will impose costs making reforms possible. This presupposition is challenged by LD (the line 3 adherent) who claims that the costs are imagined.

The occurrence of challenges in this genre can be explained from the nature of the event itself. The rules of interaction in a media political debate are completely different from those in ordinary conversation with regard to norms of politeness and what is considered to be face-threatening (see Simon-Vandenbergen 1992; Simon-Vandenbergen and Aijmer 2005). These diferences follow from more general diferences on a number of parameters. Using Hymes's framework for the analysis of communicative events (1968) we can establish major diferences along all parameters of the framework: setting and scene, participants, ends, acts, key, instrument, norms and genre. For instance, while conversations in daily life are geared towards creating and preserving solidarity and goodwill (Brown & Levin-son 1987), media debates are aimed at winning votes. The interaction is hence highly competitive and polemical. Further, participants in media debates are not speaking in their own name but as representatives of groups and exclusively acting as 'we' (though ad hominem arguments may for instance change the footing: the Flemish data contain a clear example of this (example (28) above), when one politician says to his opponent in the debate "You are extremely excited today I think"). This means that in Gofman's terms (1981:147) the speaker as 'principal' is communicating as a member of a political party and/or in a particular role (for instance as a government minister). One of the consequences of this is that the modesty maxim (Leech 1983) does not apply (Simon-Vandenbergen and Aijmer 2005). Another consequence is that attacks on the group are not felt as personal attacks. Further, the norms of interaction with regard to turn-taking, interruption and overlap are regulated by the interviewer/moderator but participants in their aim to persuade and score will frequently break them (cf. high frequency of overlapping speech). All such differences create a genre in which presuppositional manipulation is the rule, expected and recognized as such by the opponent. In contrast with conversational partners in daily life, political opponents do go 'presupposition-hunting' as part of the game.

Another question is to whether *of course* and its equivalents in the Dutch and Swedish data trigger any challenging. This would involve the denial by the hearer that the information is to be taken for granted, an explicit rejection of the 'obvious' nature of the statement. As pointed out above, the markers of 'to-be-taken-for-granted' are used in different contexts and with different functions. In most of these functions they are left unchallenged simply because the proposition is indeed not contested. These are cases where *of course* expresses agreement with the interactant or where it signals concession. In the example below, from the Flemish data, the interviewee uses *of course* ('natuurlijk') to convey agreement with the interviewer:

(33) I: Wouldn't it have been better if Mr Van Rossem had been heard in the commission of inquiry? He could have said it then, I don't know why...

RD: [overlap] Yes, as far as I'm concerned...

I: [overlap]... why

RD: [overlap] well...

I: [overlap]... he wasn't heard.

RD: Yes, as far as I am concerned I wasn't in charge of the workings of the commission so that...

I: [overlap] Would you...

RD: [overlap]... is his own affair.

I:... have found it a good thing if he had been heard?

RD: I certainly wouldn't have had a problem with that.

I: It's too late now.

RD: Yes, of course it's too late now. The commission of inquiry has finished its work but apparently Mr Van Rossem has still found other channels to vent his opinion.

The interesting cases are those where *of course* functions to convey concurrence on contentious issues. In such cases the speaker holding the alternative viewpoint will indeed deny the proposition, as in the example below. The speakers are Filip Dewinter (Flemish Bloc) and Robert Voorhamme (Socialist party, which is in the government coalition referred to as purple-green). The topic is immigrant policy:

(34) DW: Indeed, what Fortuyn said: full is full. And I don't think that we need still more new foreigners. No. We need to face the foreigners with the choice: adapt or return. In other words, a policy of integration for those who are here already. May I point out to you that for purple-green this is of course a bit of an alibi decree, isn't it? They have allowed 230 thousand foreigners to... RV: [overlap] Not true

In the Dutch data 5 out of the 24 occurrences of *natuurlijk* get challenged. These are all cases where the proposition qualified by *natuurlijk* contains contextually highly polemical material.

In the English data, speakers also demonstrate a willingness to resist the rhetorical effects associated with *of course* and hence to challenge attempts by other speakers to construe particular propositions as entirely unproblematic and universally agreed upon.

An example of such manoeuvring is provided in the following extract where the speakers, Phillips (P) and Oaten (O) are discussing a decision by the UN to end sanctions against Libya for the Lockerbie bombing, provided that compensation is paid to the victims' families.

(35) P: Now to get to the actual question-should Libya, for example, be exempted by paying money? Personally I think no, I think this is blood money and... I think it's all part of the way the West has over many decades now appeased terror, it's appeased terror by saying to the people who are committing terrorism-because you're committing terrorism we're now going to actually look at the root causes of this, we're going to have you to the UN, we're going to treat you as dignitaries, we're going to pay court to your cause. And that actually has incited more terror. And if one can say to people who have committed murder or have murder committed on their behalf-well all you have to do is pay a bit of money and then we can admit you to the family of nations, I think that is wrong, I think we would not do it, for example, if some body committed murder in our civil society-you wouldn't say pay money to the family and then we will admit you to the fact-to civilised society we will expunge it from the record, of course we wouldn't.... O:...if this situation that has emerged has meant that we now have Libya as part of the civilised world then this is a good thing. If this paying of the compensation is Libya's way of acknowledging that what happened was wrong this is a good thing. If it's a way of actually moving Libya forward in a positive way we have to accept this has to be on the whole a better thing than having Libya outside of the family of those civilised nations.

Here the first speaker employs *of course* to construe as 'taken-for-granted' that no-one in 'civilised society' would accept excusing murderers of their crime upon payment of money to the victim's family. The second speaker goes directly against this purportedly agreed-upon proposition as he develops his argument in support of excusing Libya.

Propositions with Swedish *ju* were not challenged to the same extent, probably because of the non-oppositional nature of this modal particle. On the other hand, *ju* itself was typically used to meet a challenge by explaining something as self-evident:

(36) PU: at last Lennart Daleus you still owe me the answer to the question/what governmental report was it that talked

> about the burning sun as an illustration of what you mean by nuclear power LD: you know that poetry of course uses a different language than we do in technical language for in the presentations we have made from the referendum we have prepared from the governmental reports which are the basis for the referendum

DISCUSSION OF THE RESULTS AND CONCLUSIONS

In this article we have shown that 'taken-for-grantedness' is frequently manipulated in media political discourse. In doing this we have adduced further evidence of its importance as a rhetorical strategy. The advantages of the strategy mentioned in the literature are its construal of solidarity with like-minded viewers and the difficulty of challenging by those who hold alternative views. However, it has been shown that this strategy is recognized by the opponent for what it is, i.e. as a rhetorical ploy, and hence that the announcements of self-evidence and the presuppositions do get challenged. The question we can ask then is why speakers go on using the tactic anyway. One reason is of course that the first advantage still holds, viz. that the solidarity with the like-minded is confirmed and strengthened.

It is the like-minded in the first place who are addressed as the electors. Further, there is always the possibility that the yet-to-be persuaded will not recognise the tactic of taking-for-granted tactic as such and accept the implication of general knowledge. Most importantly however, the tactic has value as a rhetorical device which creates a forceful utterance and as such contributes to the image which politicians wish to project for themselves, i.e. that of someone 'in the know' (cf. Simon-Vandenbergen 1996). As such, the strategy becomes a way of making strong value judgements, likely to be challenged but nevertheless giving the speaker a temporary advantage in the battle for scoring with the audience. We may therefore conclude that such tactics are part of the professional discourse, and hence that interpersonal meanings are as much part of the genre as ideational ones.

Secondly, we have suggested that the engagement framework as developed by White (2003) needs to diversify its monoglossic option to more clearly allow for differences in rhetorical effect between presupposing and non-presupposing bare assertions. Our discussion has demonstrated the importance of noting the difference between bare assertions in which some point of contention is presented as new information (the non-presupposing option) and those in which it is presented as background, common knowledge (the presupposing option). As such presupposition has tremendous manipulative potential. White (2006) does introduce the notion "explicit attitudinal assessments" and places these in the framework as "unarguable and monoglossic". Our findings are in agreement with this, but we would argue that the pragmatic context may overrule the default effect of unarguability The nature of media political debate reshapes presuppositional utterances into strong evaluative statements which cry out for challenging. As such presuppositions are two-faced in this genre. On the one hand, they present as presupposed judgements which the speakers know are not shared by their interlocutors and which they know will get challenged. The rhetorical effect is, however, in the saying itself. On the other hand, the presuppositions will work in the 'normal' way with at least part of the television audience, i.e they will simply be accepted.

Thirdly, we found that similar tactics were used in the British, Flemish and Swedish data. This suggests that the rules of interaction are largely similar in the genre in these cultural contexts. The Swedish data differed from the British and Flemish ones in that the debate was of a more formal and more strictly regulated type, and the rhetorical strategies differed accordingly. The similarities can partly be explained from similar views on linguistic ideologies and on how political debate works, what politicians are supposed to do and how the media handle political discussion. However, this aspect is in need of further study on the basis of more and culturally more varied data.

3

Metaphors in Election Night Television Coverage

INTRODUCTION

The purpose of this paper is to study the cross-cultural diferences in the meta-phorisation of elections in television discourse. Metaphors are a popular means of simplifying complex concepts. They enable us to make sense of abstract concepts by drawing parallels to concepts that are more easily accessible to us: "We typically conceptualise the nonphysical in terms of the physical" (Lakoff & Johnson 1980:59). In our data, elections are for instance conceptualised as JOURNEY (e.g. "Were you happy with the *way* the campaign *went* all the *way* through?"), as WAR (e.g. "This would be a complete *massacre* if these polls are correct"), or as SPORT (e.g. "No rest for the Vice President this afternoon despite a 30-hour campaign *marathon?).* Yet beyond achieving easy comprehension, the use of metaphors also suggests a certain view of elections in particular and of politics in general which audiences are invited to share. Are there intercultural differences in the channels' use of metaphors? Do commercial channels differ from public ones? Do national channels differ from international ones? Can metaphors from certain source domains said to be gender-biased, as suggested by Howe (1988)? These are some of the questions this paper addresses.

Analyzing the current British media culture, Cohen (1998:18) found that events are often presented as exciting, controversial and sentimental. Is this trend evident in the present American and

German media culture as well? Critical discourse analysts like Norman Fairclough have long pointed out that media texts of the informative genres increasingly contain elements of entertainment, incorporating features of conversation such as personalisation, dramatisation, emotion-alisation (cf. Fairclough 1995; also see Lauerbach 2004). Cohens excitement and controversy overlaps with Faircloughs dramatisation, Cohens sentimentality with Faircloughs personalisation and emotionalisation. Do metaphors personalise, dramatise and emotionalise television broadcasts of elections? Are there cross-cultural diferences in the ways this is done?

The remainder of the paper is organised as follows: Section 2 describes Lakoff and Johnsons cognitive constructivist model of metaphor and the functions of metaphor. It introduces the data and the context of the elections. Section 3 presents the findings of the qualitative analysis and compares how the various channels realise certain conceptual metaphors. It also provides a quantitative overview of the most frequent metaphor clusters. Section 4 discusses whether cross-cultural diferences can be discerned in the use of metaphor, addresses the special nature of the international channels, and compares commercial channels to public-service ones. It also deals with the question of gender-bias.

TEORETICAL FRAMEWORK

Cognitive metaphor theory

According to Eco (cf. 1984:87), the term 'metaphor' defes precise defnition. The difculty lies in distinguishing metaphors on the one hand from literal language and on the other hand from other tropes, e.g. from similes. Beardsley (1967) and Searle (1979) identify metaphors as those utterances that would clearly be false if taken literally. Black (1979:35) points out that this test fails because "the negation of any metaphorical statement can itself be a metaphorical statement and hence possibly true if taken literally." Levinson (1983:271) suggests that if the context blocks the literal force of an utterance, this constitutes a trigger, not a proof, that the respective utterance might be a metaphor. For the purposes of the present analysis, metaphors are taken to be those cases of figurative language in which one concept is understood in terms of another and in which features are transferred from one domain to another. In the phrase "I've *invested* many months in this", 'time' is conceptualised through 'money'. The feature that is transferred is that of a resource that is perceived as valuable and limited.

There are two major approaches to metaphor: the constructivist and the positivist approach. Constructivists presume that the objective world is only accessible to us by applying our knowledge about the world and expressing it via language. They see metaphors as cognitive instruments that *create* reality. Non-constructivists assume that reality exists independently of human language and knowledge and that the world can be described perfectly well with literal language without the need for figurative speech (cf. Ortony 1979:1-2). Some scholars of the positivist approach hold that metaphors can easily be replaced by equivalent literal language. This is known as the *substitution view* of metaphor. A special case of this is the *comparison view* of metaphor going back to Aristotle (cf. Malmkjaer 2002:352). According to the comparison view, a metaphor is an implicit simile, i.e. an implicit comparison. It is argued that the metaphor "Richard is a lion" hardly difers from the simile "Richard is *like* a lion." Proponents of the comparison view of metaphor claim that a pre-existent[1] similarity between the two concepts that constitute the metaphor is the grounds for comparison. Constructivists, on the other hand, maintain that this similarity is decisively *established* by the creation or use of a metaphor, i.e. the perceived similarity between "man" and "wolf" can be minor before they are combined in the metaphor "MAN is a wolf". This post-construction similarity opens metaphors, especially creative ones, to polysemous interpretation (see Section 2.2).

The analysis of metaphors presented in this paper is based on Lakoff and Johnson's (1980) ground-breaking cognitive constructivist study *Metaphors we live by*. They challenge the traditional view of metaphor according to which metaphors are mere rhetorical flourish, "at best ornamental, and at worst, misleading" (Malmkjaer 2002:350). Lakoff and Johnson demonstrate that metaphor is not

A metaphor consists of two subjects, the target domain and the source domain (Lakoff & Johnson 1980). In the metaphor "Man is a wolf", 'man is the target domain and 'wolf is the source domain. Through this metaphor, opinions shared by the members of our speech community about the nature of wolves determine our view of man. The metaphor thus *highlights* the features stereotypically perceived to be shared by both subjects and *hides* features of the target subject that the source subject does not have, or is not generally known to have.

Lakoff and Johnson distinguish between two levels of metaphor: metaphorical *concepts* that exist on the cognitive level, and metaphorical *statements*, i.e. linguistic surface realisations on the utterance level. Moreover, they diferentiate between three main types of metaphors: (i) *orientational* metaphors with a spatial orientation, (ii) *ontological* metaphors in which abstract concepts such as events, activities, emotions or ideas are experienced in terms of concrete entities, substances, containers or persons, and (iii) *structural* or *conceptual* metaphors (cf. Lakoff & Johnson 1980:14-32). "I'm feeling *up* today", a linguistic realisation of the concept HAPPY IS UP,[2] is an example for an orientational metaphor. "His ego is very *fragile*" (MIND AS A BRITTLE OBJECT) is an ontological metaphor. For the present study structural metaphors are the most important type of metaphor.

They "use one highly structured and clearly delineated concept to structure another" less clearly delineated, more abstract concept (Lakoff & Johnson 1980:61). When underlying metaphorical concepts materialise in many linguistic surface realisations pertaining to one semantic domain, we have a metaphorical *cluster*. For instance, "The exit polls can be two percent out *in either direction*", "Those results are about to *come* in" and "Were you happy with the *way* the campaign *went* all the *way* through?" are all realisations of the metaphorical concept ELECTION IS A JOURNEY. The terms 'metaphorical concept', 'conceptual metaphor' and 'structural metaphor' are used interchangeably throughout this paper.

Functions of metaphor

Contrary to the positivist belief (cf. 2.1), metaphors far exceed the ornamental function. They can be powerful rhetorical tools. It seems that it is ofen via analogy that we extend our understanding of the world. Just as stereotypes function by categorising people to reduce the unmanageable complexity of everyday life, metaphors are capable of boiling elusive matters down to a handy expedient level. Analysing conversation, Levinson observed that speakers adhere to a *maxim of minimization,* i.e. they tend to "produce the minimal linguistic clues sufficient to achieve" their ends (Levinson 1987:169; quoted in Wilson 1990:124). Metaphors are linguistically very efcient: They communicate a lot with minimal linguistic efort, whereas attempts at literal paraphrases are ofen lengthy, clumsy and graceless.

The extensive use of metaphors in the present data indicates that metaphors are easily understood without the need to clarify meaning. This is indispensable because mass media communication is essentially one-way: no interactive negotiation and clarifcation of meaning is possible (cf. Wilson 1990:125). However, as audiences are always heterogeneous, television channels have to allow for more than one understanding of their message in order to leave space for deviant, contrary interpretations. Fiske (1987:40) proposes irony, jokes and contradictions as devices which open a text to polysemous readings (cf. Lauerbach 2004). As metaphors, especially innovative ones, may not trigger exactly the same connotations with everyone, it would seem that they are another device to allow for varying interpretations.

The American channel NBC talks about New Hampshire having "changed its political *DNA*" from Republican to Democratic. Depending on a viewers political leanings, this could either be interpreted positively as ofering better evolutionary chances for survival or negatively as serious genetic malfunctioning. New, original metaphors might appeal to the recipient, but relax control over interpretation. Conventional metaphors, on the other hand, monotonous and uninspiring as they might be, are unambiguous, i.e. they prevent polysemous reading. It seems that the media have two ways of dealing with this dilemma: either (i) choosing conventional metaphors from diferent semantic domains to appeal to various sections of the audience, or (ii) striving for a balance between conventional and creative metaphors. An example of (i) is the way in which the American channel CNN depicts 'organised labour. It is referred to firstly as the Democrats' "biggest *weapon*", secondly as a flexing "*muscle*" and thirdly as the "key *engine*" of Democratic turnout. In contrast to the *weapon* and *muscle* metaphors, the *engine* metaphor gives greatest credit to the unions as organisations in their own right. The *muscle* metaphor and especially the *weapon* metaphor might appeal more to conservative viewers, the *engine* metaphor more to lef-of-centre viewers.

As visualised in Figure 1, metaphors have a wider range of meanings on the 'live', creative side of the continuum, i.e. polysemous readings are possible. The number of interpretations is restricted firstly by the local frame of the individual text and secondly by the global discourse environment, i.e. by the typical rhetoric

employed by the speaker or institution in question. Conventional metaphors are located on the right side of the graph. They have a narrower range of meanings. The interpretation at the 'dead' end of the continuum is so habituated that such metaphors are perceived as 'literal'. Idioms are classical cases of'dead' metaphors that allow for only one interpretation. Contrary to Wilson, Lakoff and Johnson (1980:55) hold that metaphors are no less alive if they are conventional, i.e. they can infuence our perception of the target domain, in our case elections, just as or even more powerfully than creative metaphors.

PREVIOUS STUDIES OF METAPHOR IN MEDIA DISCOURSE ON POLITICS

In the past two decades, several studies have investigated metaphors in the domain of politics. Examining the metaphors used in the 1987 British general election, Montgomery et al. (1989) noted that ELECTION is mostly presented as WAR. Besides WAR, Howe (1988) and Beard (2000) found POLITICS ofen depicted as SPORT. Wilson came to the conclusion that single, isolated instances of metaphor do not afect our perception of reality. However, frequent repetitions of metaphorical concepts within and across local discourse practices are "directive evidence" (cf. Wilson 1990:130) to the recipient for adopting the view of politics which the media are presenting. It is the task of critical discourse analysis to uncover processes of suggesting preferred interpretations, as attempted in the present paper.

DATA

For the present study, the opening sequences of the coverage by BBC, ITV and CNN International of the 1997 British general election, the coverage by ARD, RTL, BBC World and CNN International of the 1998 German parliamentary elec-tion, and the coverage by NBC and CNN of the 2000 US presidential election were analysed. The opening sequences are approx. 20 minutes long. BBC1 and IT V are the leading British television stations. In the US, CNN was at the time the leading 24-hour news channel, and NBC a leading mixed channel. In Germany, RTL has been the market leader since 1993. ARD is the larger of the two German public channels (cf. Schulz 2004:176-178). BBC World and CNN International are international 24-hour news channels. ARD and BBC are public-service stations, whereas the others are commercial.

All three elections led to a change in government: In the 1997 general election in Britain, 'New' Labour under Tony Blair ended eighteen years of Tory rule under Margaret Thatcher and John Major. Labour's victory had been predicted by the opinion polls but its extent came as a surprise. Similarly, the victory of Gerhard Schröder and the Social Democrats in the 1998 parliamentary elections in Germany put an end to the conservative Kohl era and shifed the majority in parliament to the 'Neue Mitte' (comparable to Blair's 'third way'). In the 2000 US presidential election campaign, then Vice President Al Gore, the Democratic candidate, was struggling not only against his Republican competitor George W. Bush, but also with the legacy of then President Bill Clinton who had been-unsuccessfully-impeached, charged with perjury and obstruction of justice in investigations of his relationship with White House intern Monica Lewinsky.

The analysis focuses on discursive contributions under the immediate control of the channel and its representatives, i.e. anchors, studio personnel and external reporters, but also takes into account contributions from the channels' interview partners.

THE MOST FREQUENT METAPHOR CLUSTERS

A large proportion of all linguistic surface metaphors involve a rather small number of conceptual metaphors. This suggests that those metaphors are not arbitrary but systematic uses. The following metaphor clusters were the most frequent in the data: ELECTION IS A JOURNEY, ELECTION IS WAR, ELECTION IS CONTEST, ELECTION IS SPORT, ELECTION IS NATURE, ELECTION IS BUSINESS, ELECTION IS DRAMA, ELECTION is LAW and ELECTION is RELIGION as well as the meta-discursive DRAMA and COVERAGE is SPORT. Metaphors from source domains that occurred only with very few isolated surface realisations were not considered in the analysis because they might arise from a speaker's idiosyncrasies whereas the large number of surface realisation from the above-mentioned source domains are assumed to be intentional and systematic uses.

Rut Scheithauer

The semantic categories are all conceived in a relatively wide sense. For example, the category BUSINESS includes economics, sales, trade and consumer terms; DRAMA embraces drama and other types of fiction; NATURE comprises matters of life and death, parts of the human body and natural phenomena; JOURNEY comprises various modes of transport and movement; and RELIGION comprises all matters metaphysical. If peaceful coexistence of political parties is doubted by the speakers, the underlying assumption seems to be that ELECTION (POLITICS) IS WAR.

Within each section (3.1-3.8), the findings are presented in chronological order, i.e. the 1997 British election first, then the 1998 German election, and finally the 2000 US election. Within each election, the national channels precede the international channels. The findings are visualised per metaphor cluster in Tables 1-12 for each individual channel. An overview of national, international and overall averages is presented in Table 13 in Section 3.9.

Election is a journey

ELECTION IS A JOURNEY is the most frequent conceptual metaphor across all analysed channels. Despite little pre-metaphorical similarity, it seems that ELECTION IS A JOURNEY (just as LIFE IS A JOURNEY) is so frequent because travelling, no matter how short the journey, is a universal experience that everyone can easily make sense of. 'Going' is so pervasive that (i) it has acquired an additional meaning, namely'happening', as in "there was a lot of tactical voting *going* on", and (ii) it has even been grammaticalised in the *going to-*

future. Its meaning has expanded from a movement in time *and* space to a development in time only. JOURNEY metaphors are very common and as such not restricted to political or media discourse. They do not seem to lend themselves as much to sensational reporting as WAR or DRAMA metaphors.

In the BBC's coverage of the British 1997 elections, "We *set out* to winning those ninety seats", stated in an interview by Deputy Labour Leader John Prescott, is one of the clearest cases of describing a political activity as a journey. The metaphor "the exit polls can be 2 percent out *in either direction*", voiced by election analyst Peter Snow, is another example. The verbal metaphor in Snow's question "How many seats will the parties get in that contest to *cross* Downing Street and *open the door to* Number Ten?" is visually reinforced by a simultaneous animation which takes the viewers into Number 10 and through the door to a virtual picture gallery of previous prime ministers.

Remarks such as "The exit poll is in line with what the national polls have been giving us right the *way* through the campaign" made by ITV's political editor Michael Brunson are both literal and metaphorical because a campaign actu-ally involves physical touring of the candidates around their constituencies. However, whereas in many journeys travelling or arriving at the destination are ends in themselves, the ultimate aim of elections lies beyond the end of the campaign. For the government-to-be, another long journey starts only once they have won ofce. Other examples of highly conventional journey metaphors are ITV anchor Jonathan Dimbleby's comments "If this exit poll is correct, it really is the most astonishing *turn-around*", "We will *explore* all this on the assumption that the exit poll is right" and "The counting is about to get *underway*?

CNN Internationals anchor Richard Blystone announces that the first results of the British election will not be "*coming* in for another hour", thus personifying the results as if they were on a little journey of their own. Correspondent Chris-tiane Amanpour states that the old ideological divides have "*gone*".

On public-service channel ARD regarding the 1998 German elections, Green politician Kerstin Müller states that her party wants "den *Atomausstieg*" (to *get out of* nuclear energy) as if nuclear energy was a vehicle they wanted to get off before it crashed. Presenter Marion von Haaren asks SPD politician Christine Bergmann: "Mit wem werden Sie denn in Zukunft *zusammengehen?"* (With whom will you *'walk* together' [down the road of governing] in the future?) Phrases such as "Die CDU *kommt* auf 36%" (Te CDU *arrives* at...) and "in den Bundestag *kommen" (enter* parliament) are very typical of both German channels.

By saying that the Green Party is not a *"steuerungsfähige* Fraktion" *(steerable* group), RTL's political expert Johannes Grofi implies that party members should be manageable like a vehicle that does not have a mind of its own. He thereby depersonalises the MPs. Grofi acknowledges that the Social Democrats did well in the election because they followed "einem *gradlinigen* Plan" (a *straight* plan).

On BBC World, political guest expert Heinz Schulte uses the phrase "coalition with the SPD in the *driving seat"* which highlights the fact the SPD will be in control of the coalition-vehicle. The metaphor hides that the junior coalition partner will not be a passive passenger but demand their share in the decision-making process. Reporter Angus Roxburgh refers to the CDU's poll results, which improved during the campaign, as *"creeping up".*

CNN International's anchor Bettina Lüscher asks what *"went* wrong at the CDU". By campaigning in a certain way, the German conservatives made a mistake, they took the wrong road. "Either *way* it looks as if Mister Kohl is out of a job."

In their coverage of the 2000 US elections, CNN's political expert William Schneider explains that Americans "want a change of *leadership* but not a change of *direction".* Senior political correspondent Wolf Blitzer is *"following* two congressional races"

NBC reporter Tim Russert states that if Bush can win certain states, he will be *"on his way towards"* 270 electoral votes. Anchor Tom Brokaw notes that the states on the map have _*"so far [...] gone* the *way* we expected them to". Simultaneously, there is a caption on screen showing the words "Te *Road* to 270" together with a picture of the White House. Tis visual element reinforces the verbal message. Correspondent Katie Couric reports that "voters who were most concerned about honesty and strong leadership *went* heavily for Bush."_ Curiously, they went both literally to the polls to vote for Bush, as well as metaphorically choosing the Republican over the Democratic way of governing.

As Table 1 illustrates, journey_ metaphors are particularly abundant in the German coverage while their number is somewhat lower for the British channels and considerably lower for the American channels.

Election is controversy war, _sport_ and _contest_ metaphors share one salient characteristic: they all highlight controversy. _Terefore, metaphors from these domains are grouped in a more generic super-category labelled *controversy.* controversy_ metaphors dramatise elections beyond their inherently exciting nature. In reality, however, political cooperation, consensus and compromise are possible, necessary, and especially in multi-party systems indispensable. As Howe (1988:99) and Beard (2000:22) have demonstrated, these aspects of politics are ofen concealed by using sport and war metaphors. However, it has to be pointed out that the media only *intensify* the antagonistic nature of elections by using confrontational metaphors; they do not *create* it. Given their long-term consequences, elections really *are* very exciting moments in politics. Before turning to the aggregate _fgures for the super-category controversy, the fndings for the three sub-categories are presented.

Election is war: Tere is a certain connection between the domains of politics and war. In practice, war is an instrument for solving international confcts when diplomacy has failed, and it is politicians who decide about going to war. _war metaphors paint a violent, destructive, uncompromising picture of elections.

In their coverage of the 1997 British elections, the BBC uses notably more war metaphors than any other channel under investigation. Calling the passive process of being elected to "*occupy* Number Ten"_ suggests a very hostile act, the use of military force by the Labour Party. It hides that the electorate is the decisive actor on election day. Similarly sensational is interviewer Jeremy Paxman's description of politicians as "*victors, vanquished* and *walking wounded*" and anchor David Dimbleby's saying that Peter Snow "will illustrate what's happened on the *battlefeld!'* Later during the night, the BBC visualises the battleground metaphor by blowing up building blocks representing target seats to the sound of explosions (cf. Schiefi, this volume). The intensifcation through the visual metaphor makes the verbal metaphor all the more drastic. The other channels use less confrontational terms like 'critical', 'core' or 'marginal' constituency instead of the dramatising 'battleground' metaphor. The frequent use of the 'battlefeld' metaphor by the BBC shows how high a premium they place on controversy (cf. Section 1).

IT V reporter Adrian Britton states that the returning ofcer in a Scottish constituency has been "*rallying the troops* saying [...] we've got to *beat* the English" in declaring the result first. In the same context, "*Brave Heart warrior spirit*" is not only a WAR metaphor but also an allusion to a Scottish national hero in Scotland's historical battle against the English. Moreover, there is talk of "*fghting* spirit" and "political *bloodshed*". The high concentration of five WAR metaphors within one minute of coverage is a strong indicator that irony is used here to open the text to polysemous interpretation (cf. Section 2.2).

On CNN International, correspondent Siobhan Darrow calls the Conservatives' loss of seats a "complete *massacre*" among Tory MPs. This is one of the sharpest metaphors in the entire data. It suggests that the electorate ruthlessly slaughtered the Tories. Anchor Richard Blystone declares that "you could make *enemies* but no friends" with the topic 'Europe' during the campaign. Here it is the voters who are depicted as the enemy, not the opposing party as is the case with most WAR metaphors.

Both in the English and German language the preparation for elections is referred to in WAR terms: English uses the word 'campaign' and German 'Wahlkampf' (election fight). ARD anchor von Haaren's question to Green politician Kerstin Müller if they would endure a coalition with the Social Democrats "*im Frieden*" (in peace) reveals the common notion that politics is a war-like pursuit in which peace is the exception. Apart from the harmless JOURNEY metaphor 'ins Parla-ment *kommen* (to *enter* parliament), both ARD and RTL use the military phrase 'in den Bundestag *einrücken/einziehen* (to *march* into parliament).

RTL anchor Peter Kloeppel dramatically refers to the German election as "die *Schlacht der Schlachten*" (the *battle* of *batties*). "Eine

Schlacht an der Wahlurne" (a *battle* at the polls) inadequately suggests that voters are fighting each other in the polling stations.

BBC World uses the metaphor *"alliance"* to refer to (i) the permanent CDU-CSU union and (ii) the coalition of these two with the FDP, the German liberals.

CNN International uses the less militaristic term *"coalition"* to refer to the same fact. BBC World reporter Angus Roxburgh's feeling that the election was very much *"a fght* between two big personalities" personalises the election and hides how important party loyalties are in German voting.

In their coverage of the 1998 elections in Germany CNN International's reporter Jim Bittermann describes Helmut Kohl as "one of the longest *serving* democratic leaders in history". The parallel between soldiers serving in the army and politicians is that they both serve their country. *Serving,* however, is not unambiguously a WAR metaphor. It could alternatively be understood in the non-ideological sense of *working for* or *waiting on* the people (as in a restaurant). Reporter Jonathan Mann and anchor Bettina Lüscher recount that Schröder has a *"commanding* lead" over this party which hides that party members are not as obedient as soldiers.

While the BBC uses the *most* WAR metaphors, CNN uses the *fercest* ones of all analysed channels. Their political expert Jeff Greenfeld reports that the Democrats *"dispatched"* advisers and supporters as if they were troops. CNN also talks about a party "carrying]" or "tak[ing]", i.e. conquering a state. As so ofen in the data, the active-passive role distribution of politicians and voters is reversed by such phrases. Correspondent Candy Crowley's claim that the Republicans have *"zeroed in on* Florida" depicts Florida as a target they want to hit. With regard to electing a Democratic speaker of the House of Representatives, Stuart Rothenberg calls some Democrats "possible *defectors"* who betray their own side and help the enemy.

NBC reporter Tim Russert suggests that elections are a matter of life and death by reporting that a candidate is *"fghting for his life"* or that "John McCain *shot* George W" in the primaries. As usual, it is the opponent that is presented as the agent although it is of course the electorate that is responsible for the outcome of the election. Most strikingly, in an interview Harvard historian Doris Kearns Goodwin quotes John F Kennedy as describing the signifcance of victory on election day in 1960 by saying that "at least it's not how the soldiers felt on D-Day It's not of that dimension!" This statement puts the import of elections and war into perspective.

Election is sport: Elections and sport do not seem to have much in common at first glance. Sport metaphors convey an image of a game that may be highly signifcant for individual sports people and their fans but remains without serious consequences for the society at large. Voters are much more powerful in democratic elections than a referee or an umpire in sport: They are the sovereign; they are the players, not the audience. Nonetheless, the competitive nature of both elections and professional sport seems a sufcient basis for frequent metaphorisation of elections through sport. Howe (1988:95) observes that in contrast to WAR metaphors, SPORT metaphors suggest "fair play" and the chance for "peaceful resolution". The most frequent SPORT metaphor found in our data is 'race/running'. The reason for this could be that 'running' is the most basic, prototypical sport of all, as well as being one of the most straightforward forms of motion in general. There is little evidence in our data that sport metaphors difer substantially cross-culturally according to the types of sport most popular in each country.

The BBC's sport metaphors are unusual in that they refer to boxing, a very tough, aggressive confrontation between two individuals. Presenter David Dim-bleby has "watched the politicians *slugging it out* together". Boxing metaphors like that hide that it is the electorate who are decisive on election day. ITV anchor Jonathan Dimbleby introduces the competition between constituencies to declare their results as a "*race* to be first". ITV correspondent James Mates replies that election aides in Sunderland are determined to be the fastest ever "*beating a record* set in Billericay back in 1959 of 57 minutes."

Referring to the expected struggle for Tory leadership afer the projected defeat of the Tory party, CNN International's anchor Richard Blystone states that "that *race* is just about on."

The ARD's SPORT metaphors are mostly race-related. They talk of a *"Kopf-an-Kopf-Rennen" (head-to-head* race) and of *"Hürden* für die Volksbefragung sen-ken" (lowering the *hurdles* for referendum). Apart from the chess metaphor *"em Patt" (stalemate),* RTL's sport metaphors are also race-related.

BBC World anchor Nik Cowing states that there is "resentment against Chancellor Kohl and all [...] those who have been *running* the country." The concrete 'running' seems to be preferred over the abstract 'governing' or 'ruling'. In their programme on the election in Germany, CNN International use five 'running' metaphors, the non-specifc *"scoring"* and the wrestling metaphor *"locked* in a campaign".

Reporting on the US election, CNN use only three metaphors that are *not* race-related, one of them being the baseball term "home base". This reference to one of the most popular American sports occurs only once in CNN's opening sequence and is as such far from being *a* tyical, let alone *the* most typical SPORT metaphor. Not surprisingly in view of the frequent race metaphors, the candidate for the American vice presidency is called "running mate", a metaphor originating from horse racing[3] that has been lexicalised. CNN's most arresting race metaphor, however, is calling Gore's campaign a *"marathon"*. A marathon runner evokes awe and admiration, i.e. positive connotations which are ofen absent in the context of professional politics.

All but one of NBC's sport metaphors are instances of racing. The frequent phrase 'a *race* that is *too close to call'* refers to the finish of a race which is so close that it is impossible to say who has won.

Election is contest: This category includes metaphors that pertain neither clearly to the domain of WAR nor SPORT but have in common that they highlight and intensify the confrontational nature of elections-and thereby hide the potential and need for cooperation in politics. A contest between two adversaries, a fight between good and evil, between right and wrong simplifes such a complex process as politics.

Reporting on the 1997 British elections, BBC election analyst Peter Snow describes the Liberal Democrats as *"chasing"* seats. Once again, the party is portrayed as the decisive actor instead of the voters. Snow goes on to depict the election as a "*contest* to cross Downing Street". There are also many other parties "*contesting* this time like the Referendum Party." ITV anchor Jonathan Dimbleby envisages that Labour will "*win* with a massive majority of 159 seats."

The author of this paper feels that the terms 'winning' and 'losing' are metaphors in the context of elections; they are already an interpretation of the most neutral way of referring to the results, i.e. getting' a certain percentage of the vote or a certain number of seats in parliament. To say that then Foreign Secretary Malcolm Rifind faces a serious "*challenge* from Labour" hides that it is the electorate who are the decisive actor, not the opposition.

CNN International's Ṡiobhan Darrow depicts then Defence Secretary Michael Portillo as a potential "big *contender*" for the Tory leadership-a fairly mild term compared to 'opponent', 'challenger' or 'adversary'.

ARD anchor Marion von Haaren portrays the German Social Democrat Gerhard Schröder as *"Herausforderer" (challenger)*. Exit poll analyst Ulrich Deppen-dorf depicts the parties in terms of physical strength: "die *stärkste* Partei" (the *strongest* party). This common way of presenting election results in German is somewhat diferent from presenting the strongest party as the *winner* in countries with majority voting systems. Both German channels talk considerably less about *'winning'* and *'losing'* than their British and American counterparts.

RTL's political expert Grofi presents the campaign as a "reiner *Personalwet-tbewerb* zwischen den beiden Spitzenkandidaten" (a mere personality *competition* between the two top candidates). This hides the fact that party afliation may have played a central role for many voters. This verbal metaphor is visually mirrored in RTL's title sequence: Schröder and Kohl are shown on a split screen as opposing poles without mentioning parties (cf. Schiefi, this volume). It would seem that the major parties in Germany and Britain have, at least up to the 1990s, had a fair percentage of loyal supporters whereas in the US the candidates' personalities seem to be more important. The "*Personalwettbewerb*" metaphor suggests that similar forces are at work in German politics, too. RTL anchor Peter Kloeppel further personalises the election by calling it a

"*Duell* zwischen diesen beiden *Kontrahenten*" (a *duel* between these two adversaries).

Reporting on the German elections, BBC World uses the lowest number of CONTEST metaphors of all analysed channels. Reporter David Shukman thinks that the Conservatives will try to "*challenge*" the political dominance of Gerhard Schröder afer the election. CNN International's anchor Bettina Lüscher uses a metaphorical mix from the domains of WRESTLING, WAR and CONTEST: "Kohl has been *locked* in a tough *campaign* with [...] *challenger* Gerhard Schröder."

Regarding the elections in the US, CNN correspondents Candy Crowley and John King talk about the parties having a state "*in the bag*"-a hunting metaphor based on the fact that the prey, once killed, is put in a bag for the ease of carrying it home. The analogy holds in so far as hunters (presidential candidates) compete against one another for the highest quantity of prey (number of electoral votes); hunting the largest quantity is rewarded with the highest prestige; and the hunters are traditionally men. One might argue with Howe (cf. 1988:92) that depicting elections in terms of the male-dominated activity of hunting denies women fair and equal participation in and experience of elections. On the other hand, 'having something in the bag' has become so conventional that it is not necessarily associated with hunting anymore. It has come to mean 'having achieved, secured something'. However, the hunting analogy ultimately fails to hold in the domain of elections because voters are the decisive actors in democratic elections, not politicians.

Apart from 35 uses of'winning' and 'losing' in NBC's opening section, correspondent Katie Couric and anchor Tom Brokaw refer to the election as a "*contest*" and a "hotly *contested* race".

We now return to the super-category CONTROVERSY and its aggregate figures for the sub-categories WAR, SPORT and CONTEST. As Table 5 shows, the US channels use by far the most CONTROVERSY metaphors. One possible reason for the many controversy metaphors in the American data is the use of the majority voting system in the US. Majority voting systems (also called first-past-the-post or winner-take-all) tend to be two-party systems. As in the prototypical war and in many sport encounters, there are two parties opposing each other. Under majority voting systems, victories tend to be clearer than under proportional representation. If governments were formed solely on the basis of proportional representation, parties might be seen less as opponents and more as co-operators becoming part of one team. However, although the British electoral system is also a majority voting system, the CONTROVERSY total of BBC and especially of ITV is considerably lower than the American average.

Election is nature

It lies in the nature of nature that it has positive as well as negative efects on people-just as elections. Accordingly, nature metaphors are used both positively and negatively the latter ofen being catastrophe-like.

Frank Skinner, a well-known stand-up comedian hired by the BBC as a roving reporter for comic relief (cf. Schiefi, this volume), exemplifes what it means to open a text to polysemous reading by saying that he is "gonna supply a sort of *lowbrow,* down-at-heel counterpoint to your intellectual analysis in the studio." Some people will be more attracted by the intellectual analysis in the studio, others less so.

BBC anchor David Dimbleby refers to the election result as a *"landslide"*. Later during the programme, this verbal metaphor is visually reinforced through computer animations "that bury hapless candidates" (Schiefi, this volume). ITV uses slightly more dramatic nature metaphors than BBC, for example *"ero[sion]"*, *"flooding"*, *"tremor"*, *"seismic shift"* or *"disaster"*. Such catastrophe metaphors hide the fact that elections do not just occur; they are deliberate man-made decisions by the electorate.

CNN International refers to the Tory defeat as a *"melt-down"*, thus equating it with the potentially disastrous melting of fuel rods in a nuclear power station. By saying that Blair has realised that it is time for the Labour Party to "adapt or *die*", correspondent Christiane Amanpour also makes elections a matter of survival. Andrew Neil, editor of *The European,* states on CNN International that John Major was going to put Britain in the *"heart"* of Europe but that it is "nowhere near the *heart,* [it is] not even the big *toe*". This neatly exemplifes how elusive concepts like European politics can be boiled down by using analogies to the human body that are immediately accessible to everyone. The "toe" metaphor is a playful, creative extension of the very conventional "heart" metaphor.

The German channels ARD and RTL use very few nature metaphors: ARD uses none at all and RTL just two. RTL reporter Carsten Mierke refers to the conservatives' defeat as "*Erdrutschartigkeit*" (like a landslide), which is more of a simile and thus milder than the outright "landslide" metaphor used by BBC and ITV. BBC World uses some very positive and some fairly mild nature metaphors. The dominant position of the conservatives "is *evaporating*" especially in the East because the "*blooming* economy" that Chancellor Kohl promised has not materialised. Compared to the high number of nature metaphors in their coverage of the British election, CNN International use very few in their reporting on the German election. Jonathan Mann states that many SPD supporters feel that Kohl has become "*tired*" afer 16 years as chancellor.

Christian Coalition President Pat Robertson states on CNN that "the moral *climate*" of the nation was the decisive factor in the 2000 US election, thereby making it sound natural that the Republicans should do well-and hiding that the electorate makes a calculated decision. CNN correspondent John King quotes Al Gore's father saying that his son was "*born* to be president". Of course, this is impossible in a democracy but we infer that being the son of a "legendary Tennessee senator" gave Gore a head start into politics.

NBC anchor Tom Brokaw says that New Hampshire has "changed its political *DNA*" from a faithfully Republican state to one in which the Democrats have a true chance. This suggests that voting patterns are biologically determined, and not ideologically, psychologically, economically or socially.

If New Hampshire's change of DNA is interpreted as a mutation, it carries ambivalent associations, either of serious genetic malfunctioning, or of better evolutionary chances for survival. How it will be interpreted depends on the political preferences of the audience. It is thus another example for opening a text to polysemous reading.

Election is business

The spheres of politics and business are linked through a government's interests in a nation's economic well-being and through companies' dependence on an administration providing a necessary minimum framework to do business, and last but not least through old-boy networks. The world of business is complex, but apparently perceived to be less abstract than politics; otherwise it would not be illuminating to depict elections in terms of business.

There are hardly any business metaphors in the British and in the US data. The BBC talks about "a busy night in *store*" for the returning ofcers. Similarly, ITV has a "huge night of drama in *store*". Reporting on the UK election, CNN International's anchor Richard Blystone states that "people are going to want their *pay-off* and that according to John Major, Blair would "*sell* British sovereignty" in Maastricht. The illuminating aspect about the pay-off metaphor is that it highlights that the electorate does not vote for a party out of altruism but because they expect something in return, just as you have the right to good service in a business transaction.

ARD and RTL '*rechnen* mif (literally: *calculate* ('reckon) that there will be) certain majorities. This highly conventional metaphor is also used a lot in everyday talk. RTL moreover refers to political agreements between coalition partners as "*Geschafte*" *(deals).* In their coverage of the German election, BBC World refers to politicians "*deliver[ing]* promises" and doing "a *deal*" with a coalition partner. Similarly CNN International talks about a "tall *order*" being difcult to "*deliver*" for Schröder.

CNNs metaphor about Al Gore "looking for one last *promotion* afer eight years in the House, eight in the Senate, and eight as the Vice President" is an analogy to a common business process which is ofen dependent on performance. As opinion polls showed, capability was not the decisive quality for the majority of voters in the 2000 US election, but that might not always be the case in business promotions, either.

NBC presenter Tom Brokaw reports that both parties made an enormous "*investment*" in Florida-which is certainly literally true but has an added metaphorical truth to it, as financial commitment alone does not ensure success on election day. Correspondent Katie Couric describes the voters as consumers by saying that "according to the exit poll, neither candidate was a *complete package* voters really wanted." Although this metaphor depersonalises the candidates, it adequately refects who makes the decision on election day: the people.

As shown in Table 7, the international and the German channels use more business metaphors than the British and US channels. This is counterintuitive as the free market economy is commonly associated with Britain and the United States. However, the figures might be misleading due to the low absolute number of business metaphors in our data.

Election is drama

Elections and theatre have little in common-unless you believe that all the world is a stage. The decisions of politicians have far more serious consequences for the well-being of the country and the international community than those of actors. What politicians and actors have in common, however, is that their success is determined to a large extent by how much people like and support them.

Out of all examined broadcasters, ITV uses the most DRAMA metaphors to sensationalise elections, e.g. "the *drama* of election night", "the election *story*" and "*subplots* in the election". The BBC uses only one drama metaphor. During CNN International's 1997 broadcast, interviewee Ian Hargreaves, editor of the *New Statesman* magazine, talks about Britain becoming "an active negotiator on the European *stage*". The German ARD does not use any drama metaphors at all. RTL uses the highly conventional "(k)eine *Rolle spielen*" (to play a (or: no) role), which is also used by BBC World. Referring to the presidential election in the US, Jeff Greenfeld from CNN's election desk states that there is something about long-term senators that does not "*play* on the presidential *stage.*" NBC anchor Tom Brokaw announces that "a late and unexpected development [...] adds to the *drama* of this evening."

As Table 8 shows, the number of drama metaphors in the data is fairly low. However, it seems that the commercial channels ITV and RTL use more drama metaphors than their public-service counterparts BBC and ARD. ELECTION IS DRAMA is the only category where tendencies towards entertainment and dramatisation seem more pronounced with the commercial than with the public-service stations (cf. Section 1). However, due to the low absolute number of drama metaphors in the data, these findings should not be overinterpreted.

Election is law

The domains of politics and law are linked through the legislative process. LAW metaphors hide the fact that there can be (and frequently are) more than two parties running for presidency or for seats in parliament, whereas in court, there are always only two sides to the argument: prosecution and defence. However, under the British and American majority voting system, and for that matter also under the German mixed system, only two parties stand a true chance of making their leader head of government.

The LAW metaphors used by BBC are remarkable, particularly as they are hardly used by the other analysed channels, and when used by the latter, they are not very illuminating. BBC anchor David Dimbleby opens the programme by announcing that we are about to hear "the voters' *verdict*". In an interview with the BBC, Tory Chairman Brian Mawhinney declares that they put their "*case* to the people" and refuses to speculate about the outcome of the election because nobody knows what "*judgment" the* people "*have passed*". Unlike SPORT or WAR metaphors, these metaphors give just credit to the peoples vital role in the electoral process.

Jonathan Dimbleby invites viewers to "*witness*" one of the great moments in British post-war politics on ITV. This does not only refer to the election itself but also to IT V s reporting about it. Secondly 'witnessing' history does not have quite the same legal force as 'judgment' or 'verdict'.

During CNN International's coverage of the British election, Andrew Neil, editor of *The European*, talks about Labour MPs who might "not *sign on* to the Blairite view" and Blair not "*sign[ing]* on" to the French and German way with regard to European afairs. In both contexts, 'signing' does not entail a iegal obligation but a political commitment. Reporting on the US elections, CNN correspondent John King likewise describes the election day as "a *signature day* in the life" of Al Gore. This metaphor suggests that Gore himself can decide whether to 'sign on to an existence as president, but it is the voters who make that decision.

ARD does not use any LAW metaphors. RTL's political expert Johannes Grofi explains Schröder's attractiveness for the voters by saying that he has one *"Tatbes-tand"* (aspect; literally: *element of ofence)* speaking in his favour: his age. *"Tatbes-tand"* is an odd and possibly unintentional lexical choice and should therefore not be overinterpreted.

BBC World reporter David Shukman states that there is not much *"precedent"* in post-war German electoral history for the exit poll being wrong. Though chiefly used as a law term, 'precedent' has long found its way into everyday talk In our context, it would not have any legal relevance even if there *were* a precedent for an exit poll being wrong. "Unprecedented" is used in a similar way by CNN correspondent John King who states that organised labour showed "an *unprecedented* turnout drive" in support of the Democratic Party.

By speculating whether Bush can *"steal"* away Tennessee and Arkansas (the home states of Al Gore and Bill Clinton), NBC reporter Tim Russert implies that these two states belong to the Democrats and that a Republican has no right to win there. Another possible interpretation of "stealing" is that it is really clever of Bush to be able to do so, i.e. "stealing" allows for diverging interpretations. Moreover, as so ofen, the candidates are assigned the active role by this metaphor which the electorate actually has.

Election is religion

Today, the domains of politics and religion are far less closely related in most contemporary Western societies than in the Middle Ages. But still nowadays, religious and moral issues cannot be ignored by candidates running for high political ofce. In some countries they can even decide elections.

The BBC uses no religion-related metaphors at all. ITV, BBC World and CNN International reporting on the German election use RELIGION metaphors that can be considered equally relevant to all faiths and thus do not put viewers from any religious community at a disadvantage. Metaphors such as "a *ritual* part of the drama of election night" (ITV anchor J. Dimbleby), the *"fate"* of fellow candidates (ITV reporter Caroline Kerr), and *"destined* for many years in opposition" (BBC World reporter David Shukman) are culturally impartial in that they are not restricted to the Christian faith. Such neutrality is particularly important for international channels addressing trans-cultural audiences with viewers of many diferent creeds.

During CNN International's coverage of the British elections, interviewee Andrew Neil, editor of *Te European*, puts Blair on a par with Jesus by saying that the election result would allow him to *"walk on water"*. This metaphor (afer the Bible, Matthew 14) magnifes how extraordinary the election result is and that it will give the Prime Minister superhuman powers. It thus personalises, dramatises and emotionalises the coverage.

ARD reporter Wolfgang Kenntemich quotes Hans-Olaf Henkel, President of the *Bundesverband der deutschen Industrie* (Germany's Federal Industrial Association), as hoping that "der *Kelch* Rot-Griin an uns voriibergeht", i.e. that the country be spared the ordeal (literally: the *cup)* of a coalition between Social Democrats and the Green party. The phrase "der *Kelch I* the *cup"* is originally from the Bible (Matthew 26) where Jesus, worried that he might be killed, prays: "My Father, if it be possible, let this cup pass from me." Although originating from the Bible, "der *Kelch I* the *cup"* has long been conventional in everyday talk.

NBC anchor Tom Brokaw also uses a metaphor deeply ingrained in the Christian faith when asking "whether Governor Jeb Bush in Florida is *his brother's keeper"*. Curiously, the phrase is used afrmatively by Brokaw, while originally in the Bible (Genesis 4) it reads: "I do not know, am I my brother's keeper?" This is what Cain replies to God's question about his brother's whereabouts who he has just slain. With hindsight, in view of the Florida recount, the metaphor gains a certain delicacy; on election day it was probably no more than a pun.

JOURNEY is not only the most frequent source domain for ELECTION, but also for COVERAGE, JOURNEY metaphors are mainly used to give the floor to other speakers, but also to tell the audience how the programme continues, e.g. *"Stay* with us-we're about to *take you on an exciting and bumpy ride"* (Tom Brokaw, NBC). BBC election analyst Peter Snow promises to illustrate "this battle for power in a more adventurous and inventive *way* than we've ever done before."

In English, the transition between anchor and other channel staff is commonly achieved via JOURNEY metaphors as in 'Let's *go* to...' or '*Joining* us now...'. 'Let's *go* to...' *in*cludes the viewer in the process. In German, turn-taking is handled via the plain ontological metaphor "und jetzt *geben* wir *zurück* ins ARD-Wahl-studio" (literally 'we *hand* [the floor] back to the studio). The term 'zuriickgeben' *ex*cludes the viewer from the action. Yet sometimes phrases similar to the English JOURNEY metaphors are used in German, too: "weiter mit Marion von Haaren" is short for "weiter*geht* es mit..." (we *go on* with...). The German channels use only one COVERAGE IS JOURNEY metaphor each while the British and American stations use a lot more. Twelve minutes into their coverage, RTL "*schreite[t]* zu unserer ersten Prognose [...] dieses Abends" (*proceed[s]* with our first exit poll of the night). By using the elevated term "*schreiten*" rather than the plain "weiter *geht* es mit..." or "Wir *kommen* jetzt zu" (We now *go* on with), RTL makes itself part of an important political ritual. ARD has invited "hochkarätige Gäste" (high caliber guests) into the studio who will "*begleiten*" (accompany) them through the election night.

NBC uses noteworthy COVERAGE IS JOURNEY metaphors that imply the need to guide the audience through the complicated events of the election night. Tom Brokaw invites the audience to travel through the night with NBC by saying teacher-like "We'll *take you through* what it all means" and tourist guide-like "We're about to *take you on an exciting and bumpy ride*" Especially the latter is a clear move towards exciting politainment.

Coverage is war: The only channels that use COVERAGE IS WAR metaphors are BBC, IT V and NBC. By talking about "two *battle-hardened* correspondents back at the *frontline*", the BBC makes itself part of the election battle. Anchor Tom Brokaw calls two NBC reporters "*veterans* of the long *march* of the *campaign*". Likewise, ITV presenter Jonathan Dimbleby introduces election analyst David Butler as "a *veteran* of programmes like this"

Coverage is business: RTL is the only channel that talks about their coverage in business terms: „Haben wir noch 'ne Variante *auf Lager?"* (Do we have another variant in *store?)*, and "eine Einstellung *liefern*" (to *deliver* a shot). It seems quite apt for a commercial channel to present its coverage aș business. What is RTL if not an enterprise selling its product? Such metaphors only hide that RTL is not selling messages to an audience but audiences to advertisers (cf. Lauerbach 2004).

Coverage is drama: ITV is the only channel that depicts its coverage as drama. Anchor Jonathan Dimbleby declares that "part of the *drama* of election night is to see how close our forecast is to the actual results." ITV is also the channel that uses the most ELECTION IS DRAMA metaphors.

Coverage is sport: CNN is the only channel to describe its coverage in sport terms. Anchor Judy Woodruff is "gonna *touch base*"with outside reporters. This is the second baseball metaphor used by CNN (cf. Section 3.2.2).

Quantitative overview

Table 12 presents an overview of all conceptual metaphors per channel. It should be pointed out that the findings have not been tested for statistical signifcance because the number of channels is too small to calculate the standard deviation. Given that previous studies of metaphor found politics depicted mostly in terms of war (and sport), it is important to stress that in our data election is most frequently conceptualised through the far less sensational journey metaphors-at least if the sub-categories war, contest and sport are considered separately (the sub-categories are indented for ease of reference in Tables 12 and 13). Across all channels, 25% of all metaphors are journey metaphors. They are followed in frequency by war, contest, sport and nature metaphors. Journey is also the most common meta-discursive conceptualisation of coverage.

What could be the reason why we counted so many journey metaphors in our data while Howe, Montgomery et al, Wilson and Beard found politics mostly metaphorised as war and sport? Given that journey metaphors are very frequent in everyday talk (e.g. life is a journey, love is a journey), it is almost hard to imagine that texts comparable to ours should not use any journey metaphors at all. One possible reason why war and sports metaphors were discussed more in previous studies could be exactly the frequency of journey metaphors in everyday conversation. journey metaphors are so conventional that they may not catch the eye quite as much as the ofen very striking and sensational war and sport metaphors.

Table 13 presents the national averages, i.e. the British average (BBC and ITV), the German average (ARD and RTL), the US average (CNN and NBC), the average of all national channels (i.e. BBC, ITV, ARD, RTL, CNN and NBC), the average of all international channels (i.e. CNN Int. UK 1997, CNN Int. FRG 1998, and BBC World), and the overall average of all channels.

DISCUSSION

This section addresses the questions if there are (i) cross-cultural diferences, (ii) diferences between national and international channels and (iii) between public-service and commercial stations in the use of metaphors. (iv) Finally it is discussed if the metaphorical concepts that were identifed are gender-neutral.

Great similarities across cultures

There is a notable similarity in the use of metaphors across channels and cultures in the analysed data. Not only do the same metaphorical concepts occur with all channels; also the quantities are alike in a lot of cases. The super-category controversy is by far the most frequent. If the sub-categories are considered individually journey metaphors are the most frequent with an overall average of 25%, closely followed by war (19%), contest (18%) and sport (13%). journey metaphors are the only meta-discursive metaphors that occur across all channels.

The fact the metaphorical concepts and even their quantities are remarkably similar across all investigated channels and cultures maybe explained by the fact that all channels are based in post-industrial western societies with similar cultural identities rooted in Christianity, a lot of common history and high economic interdependence. Furthermore, English and German are closely related languages that express many concepts including highly idiomatic metaphors in very similar ways. You could reasonably expect greater diferences of linguistic features if you compared election night broadcasts from a European or western culture to those from Asian or African cultures, which also difer greatly on a socio-cultural level. For instance, Wei's (2003) analysis of metaphors in Taiwanese election campaign discourse shows not only the use of metaphors from domains she calls costume and financial transactions, the latter being close to our category business, but also that election is frequently presented in terms of the compromise-oriented domain of marriage. Wei (2003:128) explains that, unlike in western culture, marriage does not "stress free will or the maximization of individual satisfaction" in Chinese culture. Rather "the primary importance of marriage is the fulflment of obligations to ancestors by ensuring the continuance of the family" (Tornton & Lin 1994:36; quoted in Wei 2003:129). marriage metaphors in Taiwanese politics reveal the expectation that even conficting political parties are obliged to resolve tensions and friction cooperatively (cf. Wei 2003:127-128).

Across all channels, a considerable number of metaphors reverse the active-passive role distribution between politicians and electorate. As if politicians did not have enough power once elected into ofce, they are presented as the key players even on election day on which they cannot do much apart from passively awaiting the electorates decision. This reversal may arise partlybecause candidates provide a face to abstract party politics, whereas the electorate are an anonymous, intangible mass. The active-passive reversal occurs mostly with metaphors from the domains of war, contest and sport: Parties having a state *"in the bag"*, parties *"carrying"* or *"taking"* a state, John McCain *"shooting"* George W. Bush-all these metaphors hide that voters are the decisive actors in democratic elections. When elections are portrayed as drama (see Section 3.5), and politicians are presented as actors on stage, this turns the electorate into mere spectators-another distorting twist. Bush *"stealing"* Tennessee and Arkansas from Gore is the only law metaphor in the data that reverses the role of electors and elected. Other law metaphors such as 'the people's *verdict*' or 'the people's *judgment*' as used by the BBC, seem to be the only metaphors that give just credit to the people's vital role on election day. IT V's nature metaphors *(erofsion], flooding, tremor, seismic shif, disaster)* do not reverse the active-passive roles, but hide that election results are deliberate decisions by the voters.

However, there are also some diferences between cultures. Both US channels use by far the most sport metaphors, namely 22% compared to the low German average of 6% and a British average of 10%. The US channels (66%) also clearly outnumber the German (48%) and British ones (45%) in the use of controversy metaphors. The German channels (40%) use a lot more of the non-sensational journey metaphors than the British (23%) and US (13%) channels. nature metaphors are used much more frequently by the British channels (13%) than by the German (2%) and US (5%) channels.

Clear diferences between national and international channels

As Table 13 shows, the international channels (35%) use considerably fewer controversy metaphors than the national channels (55%). The fact that across all channels 49% of all metaphors are controversy metaphors clearly demonstrates that harmony is generally not newsworthy. On the other hand, the *international* average for non-sensational metaphors such as election is a journey (international average 31%, national average 23%), election is nature (int. average 13%, nat. average 7%) and coverage is journey (int. average 11%, nat. average 7%) is much higher than the national average.

It is suggested that these diferences maybe explained by the fact that international audiences are usually not directly afected by election results in other countries, which in turn reduces the pressure on the international channels to spice up their coverage with sensational metaphors. National audiences, on the contrary, who presumably overlap to a very large extent with the electorate, have a high stake in the election result as they are immediately afected by it. The national channels may compete more directly against each other than the international stations amongst each other, the former trying to attract larger audiences by using highly confrontational metaphors to make their coverage captivating.

Minor diferences between public-service and commercial channels: Contrary to what intuition may have suggested, it is not discernible from the examined data that tendencies towards controversy and entertainment are generally more pronounced with the commercial channels than with the public-service ones. If anything, the BBC places a higher premium on controversy and excitement than commercial ITV through its numerous war and contest metaphors. The German public-service channel ARD is hardly less controversy-oriented in its use of metaphor than RTL.

Are some metaphors gender-biased? Following Howes (1988) postulation that the depiction of politics through war and sport denies women equal participation in and experience of the political process, the present analysis looks at whether the metaphors found in our data are gender-neutral. Compared to past decades and centuries, there might be more women in law, business, sport and even the military nowadays, but these are still male-dominated social domains. Likewise, open competitiveness (category contest) is stereotypically associated with male rather than with female behaviour. Metaphors from these domains could therefore be considered gender-biased. journey, nature and drama, on the other hand, seem gender-neutral source domains the use of which should make the election coverage equally accessible to both sexes. With metaphors from the realm of religion, the case is not so clear: while positions in the church hierarchy are mostly held by men, faith can be expected to be practiced more or less equally by women and men.

Counting war, sport, contest, business and law metaphors as potentially gender-biased, the following picture emerges: As shown in Table 14, the overall average of all channels' gender-biased metaphors amounts to 55%, ranging from a low 38% on BBC World to a high 75% on NBC. Both US channels use considerably more gender-biased metaphors than all other channels, which leads to a US average of 70 % (CNN 65%, NBC 75%). The British and German averages are 52% and 54% respectively. Given the large number of controversy metaphors within the category of gender-biased metaphors, the diference between the national and the international channels is similar to the that of the controversy metaphors, the international channels using far less gender-biased metaphors (42%) than the national channels (60%). For reasons of scope, the question of gender-bias can not be discussed exhaustively here. One example shall sufce to demonstrate what is meant by gender-bias: Anchor Tom Brokaw refers to NBC reporters as "*veterans* of the long *march* of the *campaign*". For men-at least for those who have served in the army-it will be much easier to identify with those veterans than for women who have not.

The question arises if the frequency of gender-biased metaphors is in anyway related to the sex of the anchor. As shown in table 14, six out of the nine investigated channels employ male anchors to present such high-profle events as election nights. Like the predominantly male professional politicians, male anchors have the opportunity to perpetuate traditional power structures by the frequent use of metaphors from traditionally male-dominated social domains. The two broadcasts presented by women-on ARD and CNN International covering the German election-use a below average percentage of gender-biased metaphors. Marion von Haaren hosts ARDs election night-53% of their metaphors are gender-biased, which is only just below the overall average of 55%. CNN International's coverage of the German election is presented by Bettina Lüscher; their gender-biased metaphors add up to 45%. CNN has a mixed anchor duo, Judy Woodruff and Bernard Shaw: An above average figure of 65% of gender-biased metaphors occurs in their programmes opening sequence. This is a high figure, but still 10 percentage points lower than that of their national rival NBC, whose election night is hosted by Tom Brokaw. However, it has to be said that the three broadcasts with the lowest percentage of gender-biased metaphors are presented by men: BBC World by Nik Gowing (38%), IT V by Jonathan Dimbleby (42%) and CNN Int. UK 97 by Richard Blystone (44%). This suggests that the percentage of gender-biased metaphors and the sex of the anchor are not related.

CONCLUSION

The analysis of metaphors during television election nights reveals that there are remarkable similarities across channels and cultures regarding metaphorical concepts and their frequency. The use of metaphors does also not difer very much between public-service and commercial channels, i.e. the diferences between the British BBC and IT V and between the German ARD and RTL are minor. The study also reveals that across all channels a fairly large number of metaphors portray the politicians as the decisive actors on election day and thus reverses the active-passive role distribution between electors and elected. There is a large percentage of metaphors across all channels that is perceived to be gender-biased, but no relation can be established between the number of gender-biased metaphors and the sex of the anchor. The most striking diference among the investigated channels arises in the super-category CONTROVERSY: the average of the national channels (55%) is considerably higher than the average of international channels (35%).

Across all channels, nearly 50% of the detected metaphors fall into the super-category controversy. This shows that metaphors contribute considerably to the tendency of increasingly dramatised infotainment observed by Fairclough (1995) and indicates that Cohens (1998) finding that the media currently place a high premium on controversy is not only true for the British media culture but also for the German and even more so for the US channels. However, the single most frequent metaphorical concept in our data, i.e. election is journey (overall average 25%), does not dramatise events at all, on the contrary it rather sofens them. The same holds true for the less frequent election is nature metaphors (8%) and coverage is journey metaphors.

As has been demonstrated, a fair number of metaphors allow for more than one interpretation. Our hypothesis that metaphors may serve as a device which opens a text to polysemous readings has thus been confrmed.

In future research, it would be interesting to investigate whether the use of metaphors difers with regard to the various political parties, i.e. whether conservatives are depicted diferently from liberals. More attention could also be paid to the distinction between creative and conventional metaphors. No figures have yet been established for the active-passive role reversal between the electorate and the elected politicians; this would be another area for more in-depth analysis. Moreover, it might prove fruitful to investigate the efects metaphor usage in more detail.

4

A Cross-cultural Analysis of Interviewing Practices in TV Election Night Coverages

During election night coverages, TV channels make extended use of talk-in-in-teraction through interviews with politicians and experts. This paper examines and cross-culturally compares the form and function of question-answer-routines in political and expert interviews. The methodology employed is informed by pragmatics, conversation analysis, and appraisal theory. The study shows that the choice of linguistic strategies is closely connected to the function of an interview within the overall context of the media event. This can be observed across cultures.

INTRODUCTION

Election night broadcasts on television usually contain a multitude of monologic genres, such as reports, and dialogic genres, such as interviews. In *Te Media Interview: Confession, Contest, Conversation,* Bell and van Leeuwen (1994) outline the general role of the interview in the broadcasting media as follows:

The interview has become a dominant mode of conveying information in the broadcasting media. Much of our news and current afairs show us, not what happened, but what people say about what happened (or might have happened, or will happen), and makes us eye-(and ear-) witnesses, not of events that would have occurred if no microphones and cameras had been present, but of events specially created for the purpose of being reported, such as press conferences and interviews. (Bell and van Leeuwen 1994:1)

Within their election night broadcasts, television channels stage a vast array of news genres, including interviews, for the above-mentioned "purpose of being reported" (Bell and van Leeuwen 1994:1). In doing so, they present the process of nation-wide decision-making as a dynamic live event. Interviewing practices play an active part in the discursive construction and reproduction of a channel's identity. Generally interviews conducted within election night broadcasts belong to two distinct sub-genres. Depending on the social and discursive identities of the interviewees, these two sub-genres are, firstly interviews with politicians and, secondly, interviews with experts. This paper combines qualitative and quantitative methods for a cross-cultural analysis of British, German and U.S.-American interviewers' questioning practices. Data is taken from the videotaped and transcribed opening phases of nine national and international election night broadcasts.[1]

TEORETICAL BACKGROUND

Research from various disciplines such as sociology, critical discourse analysis and pragmatics has shown that it is advisable to adopt a dynamic view on cultures. Cultures can be interpreted as sets of practices shared by members of a society, or members of a social group. Most of these practices are discursive in nature. Speakers and writers employ them in order to produce or exchange meanings. (Hall 1997) Producing and exchanging meanings also includes the discursive production and exchange of social meanings, such as interpersonal relationships. Across cultures, discursive practices may vary considerably. Such diferences are one of the main concerns of researchers from cross-cultural pragmatics and contrastive discourse analysis (e.g. Blum-Kulka, House and Kasper 1989; House 1996). Within critical linguistics and pragmatics, discursive practices have also been described as rhetorical styles (Fairclough 2000), or as communicative style (Selting 1999). For instance, Fairclough (2000:96) observes that "(a) rhetorical style is not an invariable way of using language, it is rather a mixture of diferent ways of using language, a distinctive repertoire". This "mixture" is not at all at random. Speakers and writers choose between linguistic options in a purposeful, goal-oriented way. As Selting (1999:1) suggests, styles are "meaningful choices made in order to achieve particular efects or to suggest particular interpretations". In spoken communication, the choice between styles is at its most dynamic: i. Tis paper is part of the research project "Television Discourse", supported by the German Research Foundation (DFG) and directed by Gerda Lauerbach. The goal of the project is a comparative discourse analysis of election night (and, in the case of the US presidential election of 2000, post-election night) television coverage in the United States, Great Britain and Germany. For more information, see http://web.uni-frankfurt.de/zenaf/projekte/TVdiscourses/lauerbach. htm.

Styles in spoken natural language have been shown as having the following properties: Rather than simply applying pre-fabricated styles, speakers actively construct communicative styles as dynamic, flexible and alter(n)able linguistic structures, i.e. styles of speaking and styles of conversation. These styles are constructed and interpreted as contextualisation cues in relation to contextual stylistic norms and expectations as well as to fit the recipient design for the particular recipient(s) and their reactions in the context of social interaction. (Selting 1999:2)

However, as mentioned above, choosing between stylistic options is not merely a matter of individual taste:

In relation to an activity type or genre that can be kept constant as tertium com-parationis, meaningful diferent ways of constituting this activity type or genre can be described as diferent communicative styles. Styles suggest additional social or interactional meanings which ofen have to do with self-presentation, defnition of the situation, defning of the relationship between speaker and recipient, framing of activities and situations, etc. (Selting 1999)

When examining communicative styles in media interviews, one has to bear in mind that such media interviews belong to the realm of what is known as "institutional talk", a term introduced by researchers from Conversation Analysis (CA). Most CA studies set off institutional talk against ordinary conversation. (e.g. Drew and Heritage 1992) This is criticised by authors like McElhinny who warn against constructing an ideologically biased dichotomy between ordinary and institutional talk (McElhinny 1997, quot. in Thornborrow 2002:3). Therefore, Thornborrow (2002) formulates a more neutral defnition of institutional talk:

1. Talk that has diferentiated, pre-inscribed and conventional participant roles, or identities, whether it takes place in a school classroom, in a TV or radio studio or in a police interview room (...).
2. Talk in which there is a structurally asymmetrical distribution of turn types between the participants such that speakers with diferent institutional identities typically occupy diferent discursive identities; that is, they get diferent types of turns in which they do diferent kinds of things (for example, interviewers conventionally ask questions, interviewees answer them; teachers nominate which pupil will speak next, pupils respond).
3. Talk in which there is also an asymmetrical relationship between participants in terms of speaker rights and obligations. This means that certain types of utterances are seen as legitimate for some speakers but not for others (...).
4. Talk in which the discursive resources and identities available to participants to accomplish specifc actions are either weakened or strengthened in relation to their current institutional identities.

In short, institutional discourse can be described as talk which sets up positions for people to talk from and restricts some speakers' access to certain kinds of discursive action (Tornborrow 2002:4).

All these criteria are valid for election night interviews on television, too. But how can the discursive practices employed by interviewers from diferent cultural backgrounds be analysed and compared in more detail? For the critical analysis of discourse in general, various researchers have argued in favour of multi-disciplinary approaches (cf. e.g. the contributions in Wodak and Meyer 2001). Within such multi-disciplinary approaches, linguistic analysis is seen as one important tool among others. However, it has been suggested that linguistic research itself should be multi-dimensional. As to the linguistic analysis of political discourses,

Chilton and Schäfner (1997) postulate that "(a)n analyst of political discoursé needs to refer to:

1. *pragmatics* (interaction among speakers and hearers)
2. *semantics* (meaning, structure of lexicon)
3. *syntax* (the internal organisation of sentences) (Chilton and Schaffner 1997: 214)

Observations on these linguistic levels should be linked to the strategic political functions of "coercion, resistance, opposition, protest, dissimulation, legitimisa-tion and delegitimisation" (Chilton and Schäfner 1997:226). News interviews have been analysed from various theoretical perspectives such as pragmatics (Jucker 1986) and Conversation Analysis (Clayman and Heritage 2002). Other forms of interviews have been examined as well (e.g. Stax 2004). Cross-cultural analysis of news interviews may yield valuable insights as to how diferently interviewers and interviewees construct and negotiate their discursive identities within various sub-genres of interviews and their hybrids (cf. Lauerbach 2004; Becker 2005). While no approach, be it mono-disciplinary or multi-disciplinary, will be fully able to analyse all these aspects in depth, it has proven fruitful for the cross-cultural analysis of TV election night interviews to combine tools from diferent research perspectives, and to evaluate the results quantitatively, as quantitative methods have yielded valuable insights for the analysis of linguistic resources within other genres as well (cf. Ford and Thompson 1996; Reaser2003). The dimensions of communicative style examined for this paper are outlined in Section 4 "Method and Analysis" below, following a brief survey over the data in Section 3 "Data"

DATA

Data for the analysis presented in this paper is taken from the videotaped and transcribed opening sections of six national and three international TV election night broadcasts from the 1997 U.K. General Election, the 1998 German *Bund-estagswahl* (Parliamentary Election), and the 2000 U.S.A. Presidential Election: BBC, IT V and CCN-I on the U.K. General Election; ARD, RTL and CNN-I on the 1998 German *Bundestagswahl;* and NBC and CNN on the 2000 U.S.A. Presidential Election. Opening sections are defned as the first approximately 20 minutes of an election night broadcast. Within these 20 minutes, all channels introduce their studio, their most important studio personnel and their most relevant external reporters e.g. in the party headquarters. As national and international channels difer signifcantly in their choice of either politicians or experts as interviewees, these two sub-sets of data are examined separately for each channel.

National channels usually interview representatives of as many political parties as possible. During the opening sections of their election night coverages, they tend to concentrate on representatives of the most relevant political parties, depending on the election system. For instance, afer the 1997 U.K. General Election, anchor David Dimbleby from the BBC interviewed only representatives from the two major parties during the opening section of the election night broadcast, whereas German ARD also conducted several brief interviews with representatives of the minor parties who may, due to the German election system, substantially infuence the outcome of a German *Bundestagswahl.*

International channels tend to concentrate on interviews with political experts. Many of these experts are professional journalists themselves. Information delivered by such experts ofen supplies background explanations about facts that are possibly unfamiliar to an international audience. For instance, in the opening section of the German election night 1998, anchor Nik Gowing from BBC World extensively interviewed expert Heinz Schulte about the complicated German voting system.

During the opening sections of the nine election night broadcasts analysed for this paper, 11 television journalists interviewed nine politicians and seven experts. Two channels showed two diferent interviewers. Seven channels showed only one interviewing person. On all channels, the anchors themselves did at least some if not all of the interviewing. The majority of interviewees was interviewed only once. One of the politicians was interviewed twice, and one of the experts was interviewed four times. All in all, 11 interviewers conducted 19 interviews, nine with politicians, ten with experts. The number of interviews within an opening section varied from one to four. Interviews contained between two and seven questioning turns. The total number of interviewing turns per opening section varied from two to 20. Politicians were interviewed by four out of six national channels, and not at all by the international channels. BBC, ARD and CNN showed interviews with politicians only, ITV interviewed one politician and one expert, RTL and NBC and all international channels only interviewed experts. Figure 1 illustrates the nine channels' choices of interviewees.

All interviews were transcribed and analysed firstly qualitatively, then quantitatively as outlined in Section 4 "Method and Analysis"

METHOD AND ANALYSIS

This paper seeks to cross-culturally compare aspects of communicative styles that are characteristic of individual television channels. Therefore, the analysis of interviews with politicians and experts focuses on discursive contributions under the immediate control of the channels and their representatives, i.e. on interviewers' linguistic strategies for the construction of interpersonal meaning. For this analysis, the framework outlined in Becker (2005) was slightly modifed. 65 questioning turns from the opening sections of nine election night broadcasts were qualitatively analysed with respect to *addressee orientation* (Section 4.1), *complexity* (Section 4.2), *question type* (Section 4.3), *appraisal* (Section 4.4), and *discursive functions* (Section 4.5). The results were evaluated quantitatively, and represented in bar charts for a preliminary comparative overview. The most frequent patterns of *feature combinations* were evaluated separately (Section 4.6). The analysis of both single features and feature combinations was summed up in nine preliminary channel profles (Section 5). These profles are, in the long run, to be worked out in more detail on the basis of a larger data corpus with interviews from the entire national and international election night broadcasts. Therefore, the analysis based on the openings of the election night coverages also serves as a test run for this combination of qualitative and quantitative methods. For the sake of clarity, the presentation of results proceeds from macro to micro and back, starting with the discursive construction of interpersonal relationships (Section 4.1 "Addressee Orientation").

Addressee orientation

How do speakers establish their interpersonal relationship in discourse? As House (1996) observes, English and German native speaker discourse tends to show characteristic phenomena in five central dimensions of cross-cultural diference:[2]

This paper combines the dimensions of "Orientation towards Other/Self" and "Orientation towards Addressees/Content", distinguishing between *high, medium and low addressee orientation.* These three categories were developed by Becker (2005) to faciliate cross-cultural empirical analyis regarding the degree to which interviewers linguistically orient towards their addressees, which is indicated by their use or avoidance of *nominal* or *pronominal terms of address* in their questions. Jucker and Taavitsainen (2003) defne terms of address as follows:

Terms of address are linguistic expressions that speakers use to appeal directly to their addressees. In English, for instance, Sir is used in addressing only, but other words used in addressing like you, Helen, daddy, darling or Professor Braun have other functions as well as they are used to talk about other persons rather than talk to them, and you can be used generically Address terms can take the form of pronouns, nouns, verb forms and other afxes. (Braun 1998:2; see also Braun, Kohz and Schubert 1986:xv-xvi)

House (1996) uses the term 'English' with reference to British English.

Pronominal forms of address ofen distinguish between a familiar or intimate pronoun on the one hand and a distant or polite pronoun on the other. (...) Brown and Gilman (1960:254) introduced the conventions of using T and V to talk about the choice between these two pronominal forms of address in many European languages. (...)

Nominal forms of address include a wide range of nouns. Typical examples are names (Peter, Sally), kinship terms (mom, granny), titles, (Sir, Your Excellence), military ranks (ofcer) and occupational terms. (teacher). (...) Terms of address may difer according to the formality of the situation, the social relationship between the speaker and the addressee, the politeness or deference that the speaker wants to extend to the addressee, to name a few of the most important underlying motivations for choosing an option. (Jucker and Taavitsainen 2003:1-2)

Becker (2005) assumes that *high addressee orientation* is represented in discourse by both nominal and pronominal forms of address, as highlighted in (1):

(1) Well, Mr Prescott, it looks as though you've done it this time! [UK 1997, BBC, anchor David Dimbleby in his first questioning turn addressed to John Prescott, Labour Deputy Leader] Similarly, the term *medium addressee orientation* is associated with either nominal reference (2) or pronominal reference (3), i.e. only one of the two reference types relevant for high addressee orientation:

(2) Doris, this is almost a mirror image because, in that race, it was Richard Nixon who closed fast at the end. In this race, it does appear that Al Gore has been closing some at the end. [USA 2000, NBC, anchor Tom Brokaw in his first questioning turn addressed to Doris Kearns-Goodwin, expert on history]

(3) First reaction! What do you think of the numbers? [FRG 1998, CNN-I, anchor Bettina Lüscher in her first questioning turn to political expert Stefan Baron] Finally *low addressee orientation* is associated with the lack of any kind of address terms (4):[3]

(4) Die Zukunft für die Koalition sieht nicht gut aus nach dieser Prognose. (Te coalitions future does not look good, according to this forecast.) [FRG 1998, ARD, interviewer Wolfgang Kenntemich in his first questioning turn addressed to Jürgen Rüttgers, the CDU's former Minister of Future]

Figures 2a and 2b show the distribution of the diferent types of addressee orientation exhibited by journalists interviewing either politicians, or experts. "Total" refers to the percentage of turns carrying a particular feature within the 30 questioning turns addressed to politicians (Figure 2a), and within the 35 questioning turns addressed to experts (Figure 2b).

As these figures show, interviewers used high addressee orientation slightly more frequently when interviewing politicians (37%) than when interviewing experts (31%). Middle addressee orientation was used in nearly equal frequency (questioning turns addressed to politicians: 33%, to experts: 35%), whereas low addressee orientation was used more frequently with experts (34%) than with politicians (30%).

At first sight, this might lead to the hypothesis that interviewing politicians generally involves more face-work than interviewing experts, either because a larger social distance has to be bridged, or because such interviews are ofen about potentially face-threatening topics, like losing an election. At the same time, as the number of politician interviews analysed for this paper was higher than the number of expert interviews, one might interpret the correspondingly higher number of sequence-initial turns as a motivation for the higher frequency of high addressee orientation, because in these turns the interpersonal frame (Scollon 1998) is established.

But, apparently, this is not the case in the three of the four channels covering the German election 1998. On the ARD, low addressee orientation is used in more than half of the interviews with politicians (54%). This is only surpassed by the share of low addressee orientation in the expert interview broadcast by German RTL (67%). Interestingly, the proportion of low addressee orientation on BBC World is above average, too (40%). At first sight, one might be tempted to assume that this might suggest a kind of accommodation process (Giles, Coupland and Coupland 1991) for the communicative style an interviewer from an international channel chooses when interviewing native speakers from another country, as it is the case here. Findings from the examination of other linguistic features seem to corroborate this hypothesis, such as the distribution of diferent types of turn complexity (Section 4.2). However, taking a closer look at the discursive functions of the turns containing low addressee orientation reveals that there are other relevant factors determining this choice. This will be discussed in Sections 4.5 and 4.6. All in all, the results of the qualitative and quantitative cross-cultural analysis of addressee orientation in election night interviews with politicians correspond closely to Houses findings: Both British and U.S.-American interviewers oriented more explicitly towards their political interviewees than German interviewers, using more high and middle instead of low addressee orientation.

In the expert interviews, a slight majority of interviewer turns was uttered with medium addressee orientation (35%), closely followed by low addressee orientation (34%), whereas high addressee orientation was used in 31% of the turns. This is mainly due to the striking frequency of low addressee orientation in the German channel RTL (67%), and in BBC World on the German election (40%), as interviewers from the other channels tend to prefer middle addressee orientation, or a combination of middle and high addressee orientation. Thus, both the results from interviews with politicians and interviews with experts correspond closely to Houses (1996) observations regarding an English tendency in favour of "Orientation towards Other" and "Orientation towards Addressees", and a German tendency toward "Orientation towards Self" and "Orientation towards Content".

Regarding Houses observations on directness, or indirectness, the question arose how these two criteria could be efectively coded for empirical evaluation. Politeness theory suggests that directness and indirectness are closely related to the amount of linguistic efort put into an utterance (Brown and Levinson 1978). Therefore, Section 4.2 examines the dimension of *complexity.*

Complexity: Qu-stioning activities within turns may come singly or in a series. They may be prefaced and/or postfaced. For the purpose of this analysis, the terminology of Linell, Hofvendahl and Lindholm (2003) was adopted. They distinguish between *single-unit questioning turns* as in (5) and *multi-unit questioning turns* (MUQTs) as in (6):

(5) Heinz, what do these figures now tell us? [FRG 1998, BBC World, anchor Nik Cowing to Heinz Schulte, political expert]

(6) Looking back on the campaign, Dr Mawhinney, were you happy with the way it went all the way through, are there things you like to have done diferently? [U.K. 1997, BBC, anchor David Dimbleby to Brian Mawhinney, Conservative Party Chairman]

MUQTs are defned as a family of turn types that fulfl the following conditions: Firstly, they consist of "two or more turn-constructional units (TCUs), which are delivered together, either in one single turn or in a close-knit turn sequence with no intervening substantial responder" (Linell, Hofvendahl and Lindholm 2003:540). Secondly, "one or more of the TCUs are formally designed as questions, or, more precisely, interrogatives, that is, such a TCU is marked by one or several interrogative indicators" (Linell, Hofvendahl and Lindholm 2003:540). The structure of MUQTs may vary considerably. MUQTs may consist of various combinations of interrogative and non-interrogative elements, such as a series of interrogatives, or prefaces and/or postfaces to interrogatives. Sometimes, like in (6), it is hard to impossible to decide whether a MUQT is to be interpreted as a series of interrogatives, or as prefaced/postfaced. Therefore, this analysis distinguishes only between single-unit questioning turns and multi-unit questioning turns, assuming that the use of these turn types corresponds to Houses dimensions of "directness" and "indirectness".

Research from Conversational Analysis suggests that the choice between single-unit questioning turns and multi-unit questioning turns may serve as a strategic linguistic option for both confrontational and cooperative goals:

dayman and Heritage (2002) argue that in the sometimes confrontational context of press conferences, single-unit questioning turns are neutral and information-seeking, whereas MUQTs are assertive and opinionated. Yet, the distribution of MUQTs is similar in the maternal health care encounters of Linell and Bredmar (1996), which is a conversationalized and cooperative activity, in which parties seek to develop mutual rapport. Here too, new agenda points are preferably delivered in multi-unit designs, whereas other information gathering questions are single-unit turns. (Linell, Hofvendahl and Lindholm 2003:541)

Multi-unit questioning turns ofen serve to accomplish conficting communicative goals at the same time (for details see Linell, Hofvendahl and Lindholm 2003). For instance, communicative efort of this kind may serve to mitigate the negative impact of a face-threatening-question (Brown and Levinson 1978;

Fraser 1990; Eelen 2001; Watts 2003). Further major functions, especially in media interviews conducted with an overhearing mass audience, are the contextualisation of an interviewer's question, e.g. by the more or less neutral rendering of background information, or the more or less subtle suggestion of candidate answers. In expert interviews, interviewers ofen use multi-unit questioning turns to collaboratively co-construct the news story. Quantitative analysis shows that most multi-unit questioning turns appear in expert interviews (Figure 3b), whereas most interviews with politicians make use of both types (Figure 3a).

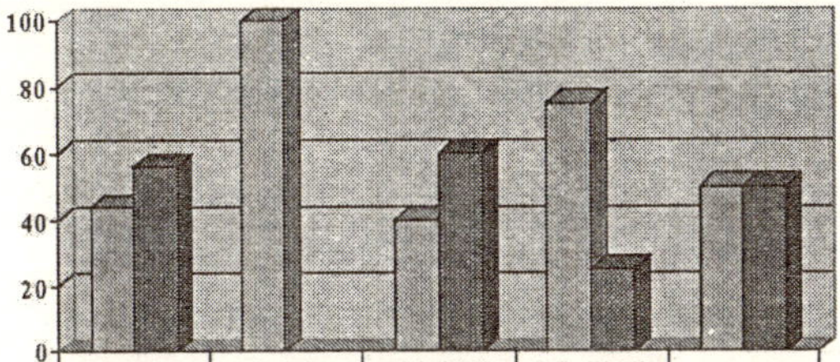

	UK-1997-BBC	UK-1997-ITV	FRG-1998-ARD	USA-2000-CNN	Total
single-unit	44	100	40	75	50
multi-unit	56	-	60	25	50

Figure 3a. Complexity-Interviews with politicians [in %]

In interviews with politicians, single-unit turns and multi-unit turns appear in equal shares, whereas the majority of questioning turns addressed to experts are multi-unit turns (74%). ITV is the only channel that uses single-unit turns throughout. BBC World is the only channel using both single-unit turns and multi-unit turns in its expert interviews. This may lead to the rash conclusion that interviewers generally put more quantitative communicative efort into their questioning turns addressed to experts, whereas less communicative efort is invested in interviews with politicians. However, one must not overgeneralise the neutrality of seemingly straightforward *single-unit turns.* In all kinds of turns, interviewers also strategically employ further discursive resources to control an interviewees answers. One of their most important linguistic means of control is the choice of *question type* (Section 4.3).

Question type: All types of questions aim at answers of a particular kind. Whereas closed questions like *yes-no-questions* (7) and *alternative questions* (8) only allow for a limited range of answers, open questions like *wh-questions* (9) seek to elicitate more elaborate answers (cf. Quirk et al. 1985; Friedrichs and Schwinges 1999; Beard 2000; Rost-Roth 2003):[4]

(7) Frau Müller, Gleichstand Bündnis 90/Die Grünen mit der F.D.P., theoretisch kann es jetzt sein, dass Sie mitregieren werden. Sind Sie denn bereit? (Ms Müller, a tie between the Green Party and the F.D.P., theoretically you might now be in the government. Are you ready for that?) [FRG 1998, ARD, anchor Marion van Haaren to Kerstin Müller, speaker of the Green Party]

(8) Well, Heinz Schulte, what about the reasons why chancellor Kohl has done much worse than anyone would have expected? Can anyone put their fingers on-you are a political analyst-and say "was it his arrogance, was it his belief in himself, was it the fact that he didn't take the party with him" or just simply that he was out of touch afer sixteen years in the chancellery? [FRG 1998, BBC, anchor Nik Gowing to Heinz Schulte, political expert]

(9) Was hat dieser Schröder, was Kohl nicht hat? Was macht ihn so attraktiv für die Wähler? (What has this Schröder got that Kohl lacks? What makes him so attractive for the voters?) [FRG 1998, RTL, anchor Peter Klöppel to Johannes Gro6, political expert]

More than half of all questioning turns directed at politicians and experts were closed questions of the yes-no-type. Experts were asked a comparatively high share of wh-questions as well (37%), whereas politicians were asked the highest share of yes-no questions (67%). Alternative questions were asked only by BBC,

ARD and BBC World. Apart from these quite explicit means of discourse control, interviewers frequently used various kinds of *appraisal resources*, as explained in Section 4.4.

Appraisal theory is a theoretical approach developed during the last fifteen years by systemic-functional linguists, and one of the theoretical orientations of the Frankfurt TV Discourse Analysis Project. *Appraisal theory* seeks to describe the linguistic resources speakers or writers use for evaluative purposes, always bearing in mind at least one real or virtual person as a co-active recipient. Central to *Appraisal theory* is the Bakhtinian perspective that all texts, either written or spoken, are dialogic in nature. This dynamic perspective has been adopted amongst others by Eggins and Slade (1997), Martin (1992, 1997), and White (2001a, 2001b). As *appraisal theory* is constantly being cross-checked against empirical data, it is currently undergoing noticeable changes (for an overview and recent updates see White 2002; Martin 2003; Martin and White 2005). This paper analyses how interviewers make use of the three main systems of appraisal resources as outlined by White (2001a, 2001b). These are *engagement* (4.4.1), *graduation* (4.4.2), and *attitude* (4.4.3).

The appraisal system of *engagement* "includes values which have been analysed in the literature under headings such as attribution, modality, hearsay, concession, polarity, evidentiality, hedges, boosters and metadiscursives" (White 2001b). "Engagement covers resources that introduce additional voices into a discourse, via projection, modalisation, or concession; the key choice here is one voice *(mono-gloss)*, or more than one voice *(heterogloss)*" (Martin and Rose 2003:54). Originally, these categories were developed for the analysis of monologic genres, not for dialogic genres like interviews. However, questions are not per se heteroglossic. When interviewers use declaratives as questions, they choose between increasing (10), or limiting the number of voices in the discourse (11):

(10) Well, Mr Prescott, it looks as though you've done it this time! [UK 1997, BBC, anchor David Dimbleby in his first questioning turn addressed to John Prescott, Labour Deputy Leader

(11) Sie wählen Schröder. (You will vote for Schröder.) [FRG 1998, ARD, anchor Wolfgang Kenntemich to Heidi Knake-Werner, PDS Parliamentary Party Deputy Leader] Only a "'bare' declarative" (White 2001a/b) as in (11) is labelled as *monoglossic.* This option was chosen very rarely within the corpus, as Figures 5a and 5b show. Monoglossic engagement only appears in the ARD interviews with politicians and in the BBC World expert interviews. This maybe interpreted as an accommodation process (Giles,

Coupland and Coupland 1991) as outlined in Section 4.1 "Addressee Orientation", an adaptation of German discursive strategies with their bias towards the direct and straightforward (House 1996). In both *monoglossic* and *heteroglossic turns*, interviewers may choose to further modify their questions by using resources from the *appraisal system* of *graduation* (4.4.2).

Graduation: If a question is modifed by items like 'a little' or 'certainly', this belongs to the appraisal system of *graduation*. Graduation refers to "[v]alues by which speakers graduate (raise or lower) the interpersonal impact, force or volume of their utterances, and by which they graduate (blur or sharpen) the focus of their semantic categorisations" (White 2001b). This appraisal resource was only coded as being either activated (12) or neutral (13), but without any further diferentiation regarding its subtypes.

(12) Mike, if this exit poll is correct, it really is the most astonishing turn-around.[U.K. 1997, ITV, anchor Jonathan Dimbleby to Michael Brunson, political expert]

(13) Heinz, what do these figures now tell us? [FRG 1998, BBC World, anchor Nik Gowing to Heinz Schulte, political expert]

Graduation was used to a higher extent in interviews with experts (54%) than in interviews with politicians (30%). This parallels roughly the distribution of single-unit turns and multi-unit turns as outlined in Section 4.3 "Complexity". Whereas graduation can be seen as a mainly quantifying resource, qualitative evaluations, on the other hand, are the objectives of the appraisal system of *attitude* (4.4.3).

Attitude: Attitude is concerned with evaluative positioning on an ethical, aesthetic, or emotional level. The corresponding sub-types of attitude are labelled *judgement, appreciation,* and *afect*.

Judgement is associated with the evaluation of persons and their actions according to normative values. *Appreciation* refers to the evaluation of objects or facts according to aesthetical values, whereas *afect* is a resource for expressing subjective emotional reactions to either persons or facts (White 2001a, 2001b). For this paper, the appraisal resource of attitude was only coded as being either activated (14) or neutral (15), but without any further diferentiation regarding its three subtypes.

(14) On these voter guides, have you put to rest peoples criticism that you're violating campaign law? [USA 2000, CNN, anchor Bernard Shaw to Pat Robertson, Christian Coalition President]

(15) 1st das Thema Beteiligung an einer SPD-Grünen-Regierung ein Thema für die F.D.P.? (Is the topic of participating in a SPD-Green government an issue for the F.D.R?) [FRG 1998, ARD, anchor Wolfgang Kenntemich to Jörg van Essen, Parliamentary Executive Director]

These figures show that more than half of all questioning turns contain some kind of evaluation to which a reaction is sought, with a slight majority on the side of the questioning turns addressed to politicians (60%). And again, BBC World seems quite "German" in its profle, with a striking parallel in the 1998 election night broadcast by CNN-I.

So far, analysis has concentrated on potential features of interviewer turns taken out of their discursive contexts. Within their discursive contexts, interviewer turns may have several *discursive functions.* These are explained in Section 4.5.

Discursive functions

Strategic sequencing of questioning activities is an important discursive resource for interviews (Lauerbach 2001; Clayman and Heritage 2002). It is also explicitly recommended in handbooks for journalists by authors like Friedrich and Schwinges (1999). Within a sequence of questioning turns, turns are used to accomplish diferent goals. Most questioning activities within the corpus were *questions* in the sense of "[a]ny topic-initiating turn by IR, asking for information or yes-no-response" (Lauerbach 2001:201) It is important to state that the term question is used strictly functionally here, not in a grammatical sense. Questions usually take the grammatical form of an interrogative as in (17), but other grammatical forms are possible as well, e.g. declaratives such as in (18):

(17) Frau Bergmann, noch steht das Ergebnis nicht fest, aber es sieht alles danach aus, dass es einen Regierungswechsel

geben wird. Hatten Sie mit einer so deutlichen Fiihrung gerechnet? (Ms Bergmann, there is no result yet, but a change of government is apparent. Did you respect such a clear leadership?) [FRG 1998, ARD, anchor Marion van Haaren to Christine Bergmann, SPD]

(18) Well, Mr Prescott, it looks as though you've done it this time! [UK 1997, BBC, anchor David Dimbleby in his first questioning turn addressed to John Prescott, Labour Deputy Leader]

Follow-ups are requests for clarifcation, or interviewer activities "[continuing" (Lauerbach 2001:201) or elaborating a previous question on a topic (19):

(19) Frau Bergmann, die wichtigste Frage in diesem Zusammenhang ist ja, mit wem werden Sie denn in Zukunf zusammengehen? (Ms Bergmann, the most important question in this respect is, who are you going to co-operate with?) [FRG 1998, ARD, anchor Marion van Haaren to Christine Bergmann, SPD]

Formulations are used by interviewers to "preserve relevant features of a previous utterance while also recasting them" (Heritage and Watson 1979:129) Thus, they provide "a candidate reading for a preceding stretch of talk" (Heritage and Watson 1979:138) and may serve as an efcient tool "to control the direction of the talk" (Tornborrow 2002:97) (20):

(20) Are you saying you accept that Labour has won? [U.K. 1997, BBC, anchor David Dimbleby to Brian Mawhinney, Conservative Party Chairman]

Like formulations, *challenges* are also responding turns, with the interviewer "questioning aspects of IE's response" (Lauerbach 2001:201).[5] This is typically indicated by discourse markers like 'but' (21):

(21) But are you saying you think there's a chance Mr Major has won, surely your own polls are telling you that's not possible, are they? [U.K. 1997, BBC, anchor David Dimbleby to Brian Mawhinney, Conservative Party Chairman]

Within the corpus, only politicians' answers are either formulated or challenged. This suggests that, generally, interviews with politicians tend to be more confrontational, whereas expert interviews are conducted in a more co-operative way. Is it possible, then, to identify any generally preferred feature combinations for either sub-genre? Section 4.6 discusses four patterns that indeed appeared most frequently.

Feature combinations

Out of 579 potential feature combinations, a small group of only four patterns occurred in 24, 62% of the 65 questioning turns. These patterns were grouped into Type 1 and Type 2. Type 1 (13,85%) refers to questioning turns in which an interviewer exhibits high addressee orientation in a multi-unit turn which contains either a yes-no question (10,83%) or a wh-question (4,62%), heteroglossic engagement, elements expressing graduation and elements expressing attitude, and is used in the discursive function of question (22).

(22) Dr Mawhinney, er, its not a very good exit poll for you, it does look as though you've lost. [UK 1997, BBC, anchor David Dimbleby to Brian Mawhinney Conservative Party Chairman]

Type 1 shows up to five of the five features identifed by House (1996) as typical of "English" communicative style, namely indirectness, orientation towards other, orientation towards addressees, implicitness and verbal routines.

Type 2 (10,77%) refers to questioning activities in which an interviewer exhibits low addressee orientation in a single-unit turn which contains either a yes-no question (7,69%) or a wh-question (3,08%), heteroglossic engagement, but no markers of either graduation or attitude, and is used in the discursive function of follow-up (23):

(23) From East Germany? [FRG 1998, BBC World, anchor Nik Gowing to Heinz Schulte, political expert]

Type 2 shows up to four out of the five features identifed by House (1996) as typical of "German" communicative style, namely directness, orientation towards content, explicitness and ad-hoc-formulation.

Interestingly, data shows that both types of feature combinations mainly appear in characteristic discursive contexts, and almost regardless of interviewers' nationalities, with only a slight tendency towards House's (1996) observations on English and German conversation in general. The majority of Type 1 questioning turns occur in sequence-initiating or topic-initiating turns of interviews with either politicians or experts on the British and German public channels BBC and ARD, as well as in the interviews with the German expert on BBC World, and also twice in sequence-initiating or topic-initiating turns of the debate-agenda interview which CNN-I conducts with two opposing British political experts. As to Type 2, all questioning activities of this type occur in non-sequence-initiating and non-topic-initiating turns, mainly in the four interviews with the German expert on BBC World, but also once in one of the politician interviews conducted by the ARD. Hence, one should be wary of jumping to conclusions concerning cross-cultural diferences, or cross-cultural accommodation processes.

But what is it, then, that infuences interviewer's linguistic choices most strongly? Analysis has shown that there is a highly complex interaction between the infuences of cultural styles in general and discursive goals, both institutional and individual. More ofen than not, at least in the data, institutional and individual discursive goals openly outweigh what is generally seen as culture-specifc at least for ordinary conversation. And what about the diferences between public and commercial channels? Does the analysis of interviewers' questions yield any results that correspond to the much-quoted diference in seriousness versus sensationalism?

Summing up the results from quantitative and qualitative analysis presented in Sections 2 to 4, Section 5 "Channel Profles" attempts to formulate preliminary profles for the interviewing strategies practised by the nine channels.

CHANNEL PROFLES 5.1 NATIONAL BROADCASTS

UK 1997-BBC: Of all interviewers, BBC anchor David Dimbleby shows high addressee orientation most frequently, i.e. three times within the question-answer sequences of his three politician interviews. As he does so each time within the initial turns of these sequences, this can be interpreted as his strategy for the opening, or re-opening, of interpersonal frames (Scollon 1998). This is corroborated by the observation that two out of three sequence-initial turns are of the Type 1 pattern which is frequently found in sequence-initial turns of interviews with politicians. Dimbleby s ratio of single-unit and multi-unit questioning turns corresponds to the average, as does his choice of question types. All his questions are heteroglossic. Graduation and attitude are employed more frequently than average. All four discursive functions are used. All in all, the BBC interviewing practices can be seen as prototypical examples of what House (1996) has identifed as British English style.

UK 1997-ITV: The British commercial channel IT V is the only national channel which shows interviews with both an expert and a politician. Both interviews are conducted with medium addressee orientation in their sequence-initial turns and low addressee orientation in the subsequent turns. They both contain only single-unit turns, an equal share of yes-no and wh-questions, and heteroglossic engagement throughout. Whereas the politician interview contains no resources of graduation, the expert interview shows an equal share of turns with and without graduation. At the same time, all turns addressed to the politician contain resources from the appraisal system of attitude, whereas there is an equal share of turns with and without attitude in the expert interview. This corresponds to the discursive structure of these interviews. The politician is asked two separate questions, whereas the second question to the expert serves as a follow-up to the first question-answer exchange. The second question does not introduce new resources of graduation or attitude but draws implicitly on resources previously used, as this is frequently the case in follow-ups. In spite of this, the interviewing practices of the commercial channel ITV appear in general to be more direct, more content-oriented and more explicit than the practices of the public channel BBC.

FRG 1998-ARD: The German public channel ARD is the only channel out of all channels which employs two diferent political interviewers during its opening section. In turn, a male interviewer and a female interviewer question five German politicians from the three major and two smaller political parties. At first sight, nearly all linguistic features analysed correspond to the average found in interviews with politicians. But closer inspection reveals that the male interviewer displays e.g. signifcantly lower addressee orientation than average.

He is also the only national interviewer who uses monoglossic engagement. His style could be regarded as prototypical German style in the defnition of House (1996), other than the female interviewer's style. She counterbalances her colleague's ratio in low addressee orientation and monoglossic engagement by frequently using medium and high addressee orientation and heteroglossic engagement throughout. This could (and should) also be discussed from a gender perspective (Giora 1995; Mills 2003).

FRG 1998-RTL: The German commercial channel RTL is one of the two national channels which do not interview politicians in their opening sections. In this respect, RTL has more in common with the U.S.-American channel NBC than with the German public channel ARD. Addressee orientation in the expert interview is quite German, i.e. signifcantly lower than the average. Graduation and attitude are more predominant, whereas all other features are within the range typical of expert interviews.

USA 2000-NBC: In his only expert interview during the opening section, the anchor of the U.S.American channel NBC uses middle addressee orientation, multi-unit turn structure, heteroglossic engagement and graduation as well as attitude throughout. In its use of appraisal resources, this channel shows signifcant parallels to German commercial channel RTL, and even more so to CNN-I 1997. All turns are questions. Due to the high amount of interviewer talk, this interview can be interpreted as a typical example of a co-constructed news story.

USA 2000-CNN: In the opening section of the US.-American channel CNN, a politician is interviewed with a mix of linguistic resources ofen found at the more confrontative end of this sub-genre. Addressee orientation is middle to high, yes-no questions and wh-questions appear in equal shares, engagement is heteroglossic, but turns are mainly single-unit and spiced with resources from graduation and attitude. In contrast to the NBC anchor in his expert interview who uses only single questions, the CNN anchor also uses the strategic discursive resources of follow-ups and even formulation, just as BBC and ARD do in their interviews with politicians.

International broadcasts

UK97-CNN-I: In its coverage of the 1997 U.K. General Election, CNN-I is the only channel which shows a so-called debate-agenda interview. Both interviewees are professional journalists from the U.K. As they are not only there to co-operatively enrich the news story with their expertise, but also to utter their opposing views, it is not surprising that this expert interview difers from the other expert interviews in that it shows several features more typical of interviews with politicians than of expert interviews. The high share of turns with high or medium addressee orientation or turns bearing the Turn 1 pattern is clearly motivated by the interviewers communicative task to explicitly select the next speaker afer an interviewees answering turn. Multi-unit turns prevail. Graduation and attitude are used in all turns. All in all, this interviewer's style shows some similarities to the CNN interviewer's style described in 5.1.6, but also to the style of the BBC interviewer. This suggests an accommodation process towards the style associated with the interviewees' culture.

FRG98-CNN-I: Afer the German election in 1998, CNN-I does not aim at confrontation, which is rather a British delight, but, at the interpretation of current tendencies and the forecast of potential coalitions. A German expert is invited and interviewed in a co-operative but at the same controlling manner, with the anchor delivering most of the relevant information herself. Addressee orientation is middle to low. All turns are heteroglossic multi-unit turns in the discursive function of question. The share of wh-questions is higher than average in expert interviews, the ratio of graduation and attitude is lower.

FRG98-BBC World: The four BBC World interviews with a German expert are possibly the expert interviews stylistically closest to interviews with politicians, and, at the same time, the interviews with the highest degree of accommodation towards the native expert's national style. Like in CNN-I, all three types of addressee orientation are used, possibly also because of the recurring need for next speaker selection. There are more single-unit turns than in most expert interviews, whereas the distribution of question types corresponds to the average. The BBC World interviewer is the only international interviewer who uses monoglossic engagement, just as the German ARD interviewer is the only national interviewer using this kind of engagement.

Graduation and attitude are lower than average. This maybe due to the fact that the share of follow-ups is higher than average, as follow-ups ofen implicitly refer to the resources of graduation and attitude in the previous utterances (cf. 5.1.3).

In fact, the share of follow-ups is second highest of all nine channels. The only interview with a higher share of follow-ups is the political interview conducted by the national channel CNN. All in all, the expert interviews by BBC World on the 1998 German *Bundestagswahl* have structurally more in common with the politician interviews by German ARD during the same election, or with BBC's political interviews during the 1997 U.K. General Election, than with CNN-I's expert interviews during these two elections.

CONCLUSION

Cross-cultural qualitative and quantitative analysis of interviewing practices from the opening sections of nine election night broadcasts has shown that there is no such thing as a clear national interviewing style, at least not in the examined data corpus. Firstly, interviewers' stylistic choices depend strongly on the sub-genre.

Sub-genres are defned by the social and discursive identities of interviewers, i.e. by their social and discursive roles as politicians or experts. Secondly, within sub-genres, channels' interviewing practices sometimes difer more strongly within the same culture than across cultures, depending on whether a channel is public or commercial. For instance, the German commercial channel RTL seems to have more in common with CNN and CNN-I than with the ARD. Thirdly, even within channels, and even within the same election night broadcast, there maybe diferent interviewing styles, depending on an interviewers' sociocultural identities, e.g. on factors like gender. And, last but not least, data from the international broadcasts suggest that international interviewers tend to accommodate their interviewing style towards a tacitly assumed native interviewee's style. This means, indirectly, that it is highly probable that the same interviewers might use other communicative styles in other contexts. Still, it is not recommendable to refrain from attempts at cross-cultural comparison altogether and to concentrate on single interviewers' styles instead. There is no such thing as an invariable individual style. Even if such an individual style could be identifed, critical linguistic research would try to measure it against styles already known. All in all, the combination of qualitative and quantitative methods for the analysis of a small set of data has proven a useful tool for cross-cultural comparison of interviewing practices in televised election night interviews and for the formulation of first hypotheses. In a next step, the relationship between forms and functions shall be investigated in more depth and on the basis of a larger corpus. Fairclough's observation that "(a) rhetorical style is not an invariable way of using language, it is rather a mixture of diferent ways of using language, a distinctive repertoire"

5

A Cross-cultural Perspective on French and British Political Interviews

This contribution examines the communicative function of represented discourse from a cross-cultural perspective in a dialogic framework. It focuses on its diferent functions and contexts of use in French and English political TV interviews, where it is used in diferent contexts: French speakers prefer descriptive settings while British speakers prefer an argumentative setting. In the British data represented discourse is used as a device to construct an opposi-tional stance in negatively loaded contexts. In the French data, it is used to give an opinion and to construct agreement. Thus British political discourse seems more polarized, focusing on the process and on the products of decision-making, while its French counterpart concentrates on description and explanation, thus embedding their political action in a wider public context.

INTRODUCTION

In recent studies of *reported speech* a new perspective has emerged, especially in analyses concentrating on spoken language or interactional talk. From traditional lexico-grammatical approaches to diferent *forms* of reported speech-direct, indirect or free indirect speech-there has been a shift in various aspects of its use. When examining the *functional aspects* of reported speech, several factors can be considered: contextual, cognitive, textual, discursive and evaluative, to name but a few. These factors can be investigated in various types of situational contexts as well as in various genres (Linell 1998b; Holt 2000; Sakita 2002). At the same time, the term used to designate this linguistic object has changed in a number of studies: it maybe referred to as *voice, reporting discourse* or *represented discourse* (RD). In this contribution, the last term has been adopted.

In this chapter the functions of RD are studied in one interactional media genre, namely the *political interview.* Politicians are speakers who frequently quote their colleagues, opponents, supporters-and, not least, themselves. In previous studies of this phenomenon (Johansson 2000, 2002), the functions of RD were found to be linked to the diferent textual and discursive functions of talk. Politicians use RD when they are engaged in cognitive-discursive activities, such as telling, describing, and in particular explaining or arguing. In these various linguistic contexts, instances of RD can have diferent functions. These vary considerably: from anchoring a topic from public debate to an ongoing interaction, to introducing a point that allows the development of a counter-argument (ibid.). In studying the occurrence of RD in a politicians responses in an interview, the interactional organization of this activity type (Levinson 1992) is an essential issue.

In the political interview the main relationship between the social actors-the journalist and the politician-is asymmetrical: the institutional power to organize the talk is held by the interviewer (IR) in the first frame interaction (Fetzer 2002). While the starting-point is based on questions, and the interviewee (IE) has a genre-specifc constraint to answer them, s/he may have a certain freedom in answering and developing the topic-or s/he may seize it.

In the second frame interaction both speakers orient themselves towards the audience, but their goals difer: the interviewer is trying to reveal interesting information, while the politician seeks to infuence and persuade (Charaudeau & Ghiglione 1997). In other words, the way the politician tries to position her/himself in this social context is a result on the one hand of how the politician presents her/his experience and values and imposes a certain vision of the social world, on the other of how these are shared with her/his discourse community (cf. Charaudeau 2002:162).

The approach I adopt here is based on distinctions between diferent types of contexts and on the meaning of RD in them. In this study, instances of RD will be examined in four diferent contexts: cognitive, linguistic, social and sociocultural (Fetzer 2004). First, it is in the cognitive context that the basic type of RD can be determined (see Section 4.2). Secondly, the RD is used in linguistic and social contexts: this genre and activity type follow genre-specifc constraints of turn-taking, and certain genre-specifc cognitive-discursive activities are carried out by the speakers which unfold in certain types of textual sequences (see 4.3). It is the way in which the speaker constructs her/his talk and how s/he contextualizes the RD that reveals how RD represents, or refects, the sociocultural context of her/his discourse community (see Section 3).

The object of the study is to contrast instances of RD in the answers of French and British politicians in political TV interviews. In other words, the social and linguistic contexts of the political interviews are similar, but the sociocultural contexts difer. The objective is to find out what the functions of RD tell us about sociocultural diferences. My main research questions are based on the axes of similarity and diference:

1) What are the functions of RD in linguistic context?
2) What are the diferences between instances of RD with regard to sociocultural contexts?

The political interview is a genre in which the construction of meaning occurs at the intersection of two institutional discourses, both of which are culturally produced: the discourse of the media and that of politics. A certain variation is therefore to be expected regarding the functions of RD. I base this hypothesis on a pilot study (Johansson 2005), focusing on the functions of RD in a narrative linguistic context that can be characterized by causal and temporal markers. In the French data, almost all narrative RD appeared in stories that focused on confictual issues where the politician had to explain some questionable action of her/his own. In the British data, occurrences of RD were more problematic to categorize: they contained narrative features, i.e. temporal or causal characteristics, but they were not used to tell stories; rather, they were embedded in diferent types of textual sequences, for instance argumentative ones. In other words, their use was more incidental and hybrid.

In this chapter, I first present the data and a description of the instances of RD in the corpus (Section 2). I then discuss the perspective of cross-cultural pragmatics in Section 3 and defne the notion of RD in Section 4. The analysis is presented in Section 5.

DATA AND METHOD

Political interviews

The data are derived from British and French political TV interviews. In compiling data for intercultural comparisons, one has to ensure that the situations to be analysed are comparable (Traverso 2000b: 34). The case studied here is a single genre, namely the political interview. The French and British political interviews examined belong to diferent sociocultural contexts, but share features of the same activity type. In the data investigated, all the interviews are dyadic. The data was collected during approximately the same time period, and in fact some of the topics discussed are the same: social exclusion and the European Union.

The French TV interviews used here were recorded at the end of the 1980s and in the mid-1990s. These political interviews are from programmes called *Vheure de vérité* (Moment of truth) and *7 sur 7* (Seven days a week), both produced by French public broadcasting. These programmes were very popular; the French TV audience watched them for over a decade. *Vheure de vérité* was on for thirteen years, from 1982 to 1995; *7 sur 7* started two years later in 1984 and was broadcast until 1997.

The broadcast formats of the French interviews, however, were diferent. Normally, in both *L'heure de vérité* and in *7 sur 7* one politician was invited at a time. The diference was created by the interviewers. In the former there were three journalists, who took turns interviewing the guest for ten to twenty minutes each. In *7 sur 7* there was only one interviewer, Anne Sinclair, who talked to her guest-a politician or other celebrity-throughout the programme. The politicians interviewed in the present data represented diferent political parties, but all had occupied the position of minister in the past. The politicians were Martine Aubry (MA), Jack Lang (JL), Michèle Barzach (MB) and Bernard

Tapie (BT). All the politicians who appear in these interviews share the same political position: they were in the opposition at the time of the interview.

These data will be contrasted with four British interviews with the leader of the Labour Party, Tony Blair, interviewed by diferent interviewers on diferent programmes, such as *On the Record* and *Newsnight* on BBC.[1] The first of the programmes, *On the Record,* is a political one, while *Newsnight* presents various topical issues in the news and in interviews. In these interviews, Tony Blair is interviewed by David Dimbleby, David Frost, Jonathan Dimbleby and Jeremy Paxman in 1997 and 1998.

In other words, the corpus consists of four French and four British interviews. The length of the French interviews varies from 36 to 47 minutes; the British interviews are somewhat shorter, from 24 to 30 minutes. In presenting the data a minimum of transcription conventions is used. Excerpts from the French material are presented side by side with an English translation made by the author. The translations have been made in order to help the reader follow the argument, and do not include the transcription conventions.

Description of the data and method

The analysis of the instances of RD starts with identifcation of the linguistic object by its formal features: the syntactic form of direct or indirect RD and the explicit voice. The syntactic forms taken into consideration here are direct and indirect forms. In the examples, the underlined words refer to the introductory part and the words in italics to the recontextualizing part:

i. I thank Anita Fetzer for the use of her data.

(1) direct form

IE: vous l'avez rappelé a l'instant.. You recalled that a moment ago

deux fois cinq ans ministretwice the period of fve years as a minister

(2) indirect form

IE: euh il a dit *que c'était abominable* Uh he said *that it was horrible that it que ça ne correspondait pas du did not correspond at all to the facts tout aux faits*

In the direct form, the introductory and recontextualized parts are linked without any specifc linguistic element at the boundary between the parts. In spoken language, however, there maybe some kind of extralinguistic marking, as in example (1) above: the introductory part is followed by a fairly long pause marked by two dots (..). The indirect form is identifed by the inclusion of connector *that* in English or *que* in French as in example (2).

By *voice,* I mean a proper or common noun that refers to a person or group of people or to the source of the voice *(Jacques Chirac, the specialist, the Conservatives, a rumour).* In the examples, the voice is marked in boldface as in the cases above (1-2). According to these criteria, there are 53 instances of RD in the French data and 43 in the British.

In the analysis the context of emergence of RD was examined. This was done first along two main lines of *sequentiality,* namely *turn-taking* and *topic progression.* The main examination focuses on the *textual sequences* of answers and the speaker activity in them. In other words, the positioning of RD in answers was examined, together with the kinds of textual sequences in which RD emerges and how speaker meaning is constructed in a linguistic context. The notion of *textual sequence* is used here in the sense defned by Adam (1992) (see Section 4.3 and 5.1-5.2). As some of these instances have already been examined in narrative sequences (Johansson 2005), in this study the functions of RD are investigated in sequences that are descriptive, explanatory and argumentative. Secondly, the functions were investigated in order to find diferent sociocultural functions (5.3).

PERSPECTIVE OF CROSS-CULTURAL PRAGMATICS

Point of departure

In the field of pragmatics, a number of diferent terms are used to label approaches that focus on the cultural dimension or on cultural diferences in communication. However, there are few very signifcant diferences between the more traditional terms *contrastiveness, cross-linguistic, cross-cultural* and *intercultural.* In order to clarify their meaning, I discuss these next.

Contrastiveness is a term that has been used especially in translation studies in comparisons between two languages that start with description, juxtaposition and end up with comparison (Krzeszowki 1989:57). According to Chesterman (1998:54-61), *comparison* usually starts with a perceived similarity of some kind between languages and leads to a problem that can be formulated as follows: what is the nature of this similarity? In pragmatic studies a broad variety of diferent types of pragmatic categories have been studied, such as requests, apologies, complaints and invitations. But, as Verschueren (1996) says, they are not stable phenomena and there is no fixed form-function relationship. In this sense this analysis is also contrastive as it starts with *cross-linguistic* diferences between two languages: that is the linguistic forms of RD in French and in English.

In this study, the meaning of *cross-cultural* and *intercultural* is understood to be the same. Hinnenkamp (1995:2) sees intercultural- or cross-cultural-communication as a broad relation between language and culture, which focuses on "the confrontation of one language-culture link with another".

Scollon and Scol-lon (1995:123) share this view of the term 'intercultural' as referring to cultural diferences in communication and the problems that arise from these diferences. In these defnitions a broad perspective is adopted, but the focus is placed almost exclusively on problems of communication. Traverso (2002:322), in contrast, distinguishes two major types of study in the field of intercultural studies of interaction: on the one hand there are analyses that take as a starting point interactants who belong to diferent cultures and who are involved in interaction with each other (Traverso 2000a: 5-6), on the other hand studies that focus on one culture in a given situation and compare it to the same kind of situation in another culture (ibid.). In such cases the approaches postulate a linguistic element and examine similarities and diferences in its use in diferent cultural contexts (Traverso 2002:323).

The second view mentioned by Traverso is the same as that in cross-cultural pragmatics. In approaches like Wierzbicka's (1991) or that of Blum-Kulka, House and Kasper (1989), the starting point is the above-mentioned linguistic element; in other words, the comparisons in these studies are usually between diferent expressions and speech acts. This is my starting point as well; to my mind, however, comparison-or contrastiveness-has to be understood in a very broad sense.

Contextual approach

Here the focus will be on language users in certain linguistic and social contexts and how they relate to the sociocultural context. The *linguistic context* has to be understood as certain contextual constraints and requirements of an activity type and a genre: the way the activities take place in it (Fetzer 2004:6). The *social context* is not only that of the situational speech event. In this case, it is a question of the political interview as an institutional and media genre that designates certain genre-specifc institutional roles to the participants. In this the participants have their own objectives in relation to the audience (Johansson 2006). The social context is also that of the co-construction of the meaning between the speakers. In this it is important to analyze the complex and multiple ways by which the speakers display their interactive and discursive roles, not to mention their identities (Fetzer 2004:7). Fetzer (2004:9) sees the social context as the default one and the sociocultural context as a marked type of context. Instead of speaking of the cultural context, as is done in several cross-cultural approaches, I prefer to use a more precise notion of sociocultural context, as seen from a certain perspective on culture (ibid.) and examined through socially and culturally situated human (verbal) interaction. Moreover, here it is a question of the French and the British political discourse-two diferent discourse communities of sociocultural contexts.

The approach will not be contrastive in traditional terms, as Krzeszowki (1989:5) describes it, concentrating solely on similarities and diferences between two languages. Rather, as explained above, the approach adopted has to be understood as pragmatic, focusing on the use and functions that are being compared between the sociocultural contexts.

REPRESENTED DISCOURSE

Defnition of represented discourse

In my previous work I have studied speech and thought representation in interaction (Johansson 2000). For these, I proposed the notion of *represented discourse,* for the reason that this approach integrates several dimensions of analysis. How does this notion difer from reported speech? In order to understand this, the notion of reported speech has to be examined critically. It has been adopted as such in many recent studies on various types of spoken language or interaction, where it is used to investigate its functions. Despite this widening of its application, and even though these studies shed light on this linguistic phenomenon in language use, to my mind this does not change the meaning of the concept. Ontologically, it is derived from traditional literary, grammatical and context-independent approaches to language, in which it is seen as *reproducing* something, usually *spoken,* from previous speech situations and giving it a fixed meaning designated by the term 'reported speech. The notion thus refects the monologic and unidirectional theories of language and communication on which it is based; therefore, it is in my view inadequate for a dialogical approach to language. Some studies have suggested ways to overcome its shortcomings: Tannen (1989), for instance, proposes *constructed dialogue* and Sakita (2002) *reporting discourse.*

The notion of RD is based on a diferent theoretical framework, namely on dialogical, cognitive and pragmatic approaches to language and communication. In other words, there is a signifcant change in the conceptual basis and meaning compared to reported speech, in that the notion refers to a context-dependent and pragmatic object (for a detailed defnition, see Johansson 2000:78-81). It is a form of mediated action, a cultural, discursive and linguistic tool that creates a link between mental action, interaction and action situated in context (Johansson 2002:13).

There are several levels of defnition. First, the object is seen as being created by the speaking actor. In the cognitive process the speaker can make a recontex-tualization from other discourses. According to Linell (1998a: 154), recontextu-alization is a dynamic process between discourses and texts in contexts. In this the speaker mediates diferent meanings from these other discourses and texts to the present one s/he is engaged in. Secondly, every instance of RD contains a voice that stages an *other* and thus creates a polyphonic dimension to the utterance (Johansson 2002:12). The voice links the speaker to these other contexts, as it functions as a trace in the consciousness of the speaker (ibid.). Thirdly, it is also textual, as it is used sequentially. In other words, its contextual placement is important, as it allows its functions in discourse to be discovered.

The notion of RD emphasizes the cognitive, linguistic and pragmatic activity of the speaker. In the following, I take up the basic types of RD and the cognitive context of their formation.

Basic types of RD

There are two basic kinds of RD based in the cognitive context that can be explained on the basis of how the speaker constructs them. In Johansson (2000:43-47), I made the first distinction between the types of RD, using Chafe's (1994) cognitive model of displaced and immediate context of speaking. According to this model, there are two main categories of speaking: the *immediate mode* and the *displaced mode.* Here I concentrate on the latter, which is described as follows (Figure 1).

The displaced mode refects the position of the speaker towards other contexts (Chafe 1994:195-201), which s/he relates in her/his speech by the acts of remembering or imagining. The latter has to be understood in a broad sense: it can constitute diferent types of activities, such as evaluation, appreciation and so on (cf. Chafe 1994). By these cognitive activities the speaker relates what s/he has perceived, acted and evaluated in other contexts.

Adapted to RD, the speaking actor recontextualizes for instance utterances from these displaced contexts and thus creates intertextual or interdiscursive links between her/his texts and discourses, as in the following example:

(3) TB: It's been John Prescott who said *let's get private fnance into the railway system*

In this example, the introductory part of RD contains a voice that is a proper noun, referring to another politician in the sociocultural context of British politics in an unspecifed spatio-temporal context. There are no exact indications of time and place in the introductory part; the verbs in the past tense place the utterance in the past. The recontextualizing part presents the opinion of the person mentioned. This type of RD is a recontextualization from the shared sociocultural context of the interlocutors, the IR and the IE; it constructs event-related and existential types of recontextualizations, in that it is based on an act of remembering.

Occurrences of the other basic type of RD, based on imagining, are not rare. They are constructed of several linguistic elements, which characterize the recontextualization as possible, impossible, hypothetical, future-oriented or collective. These may resemble those in the following introductory parts:

(4) You could say to him He didn't say If she says to you He will say Tey say

In other words, a RD of this type presents an interpretation of some kind of speaking actor, with no clear evidence of a speech event that has taken place. This interpretation may be based on the use of a connector *(if)*, a verb form (conditional, future tense), a negative form, or a collective voice. In these types, the RD mediates ideas, issues and points of view to the ongoing interaction. The next theoretical point to be explained is how the RD does this.

RD in the linguistic context

In determining the function of RD, it is necessary to examine the way it is contex-tualized in the sequential organization of the answers. For this purpose, the local and global discursive, textual and interactional organization has to be taken into account. By this I mean, first of all, genre-specifc constraints on turn-taking, on topical episodes and on the type of textuality unfolding in the answers. In other words, the placement of RD in the linguistic context has to be accounted for.

In the interaction it is the interviewer who has the power to organize the turn-taking as well as to propose the topics to be discussed (Charaudeau & Ghi-glione 1997:46-52; Johansson 2000:63). The politician has the obligation to answer. From a textual point of view, the interview contains two types of questions: those that open topical sequences and those that develop the topic. In the topical opening the questions usually have a complex structure (Greatbatch 1988; Heritage & Greatbatch 1991; Léon 1999, 2004; Johansson 2000:151; Heritage 2002). The complex question turn usually contains a presequence that prepares the topic, followed by an interrogative (Johansson 2000:153). The politicians can answer the interrogative or can adopt other strategies in answering, which take up specifc elements of the whole question turn (id.: 107-108). The question turn may be oriented towards agreement or disagreement: in the first case the question has an embedded assertion, in the second a negative orientation in the interrogative (Léon 1999:109, 2004). Here I consider the occurrence in the data of both topic-initial complex questions and those that develop the topic.

In a political interview, topical episodes can be easily distinguished. Here I focus on the types of textual sequences used in topical episodes. In questions which open topical episodes, the IR proposes certain types of cognitive-discursive tasks to be executed by the IE. In this genre, the questions are usually information-or opinion-seeking questions; in the answers, the politician is therefore expected to develop an explanation, a description or an argument. In the analysis, I use the typology proposed by Adam (1992), who posits five prototypical textual sequences: dialogical (interactional), narrative, descriptive, explicative and argumentative. The basic and dominant type of textual sequence in a political interview is naturally interactional; the other types are embedded in it. Here I focus on descriptive, explicative and argumentative sequences (for narrative sequences, see Johansson 2005).

According to Adam (1992:85-95), a *descriptive sequence* consists of four operations. The first is a referential anchoring of the topic. The second operation is that of illustration or aspectualisation, designating the qualities and characteristics of the object of description. Thirdly, there is an operation in which the relations are shown, and, finally, an embedding into another sequence.

In a textual *sequence of explanation* (see Adam 1992:32), the main features are the following: presentation of a problem or an issue to be explained, an internal structure that follows a certain order of dealing with the problem or issue, and finally a conclusion or evaluation.

In an *argumentative sequence,* textual organization is created according to a certain order of argumentation (id.: 104). This order may be progressive, starting from an argument and following its development towards a conclusion, or the other way round, from a result towards a reason for it. To put it simply: this textual sequence is based on a basic pattern of *argument-> conclusion* (the arrow means how the conclusion is reached from an argument). Its objective is to infuence opinions and attitudes. In the following, the analysis starts with this point.

ANALYSIS

Distribution

I first describe the distribution of occurrences according to their emergence in diferent types of textual sequences. Table 2 shows all types of textual sequences, even though narrative sequences are not included in the analysis (see Johansson 2005). As Table 2 indicates, the diferences in the data are not signifcant, only more or less indicative. However, the following observations can be made. In the British data, more than half of all occurrences are found in argumentative sequences, with only a few in descriptive (and narrative) sequences. In the French data the RD was used frequently-in a quarter of all cases-in descriptive sequences, while not quite half of the cases were located in argumentative sequences. The analysis of the linguistic context of the RD will be taken up in 5.2.

The data have also been analyzed to find out whether or not the voices in RD have a clear reference. The references vary in fact from named individuals, or the author of a literary quotation, to plural or otherwise anonymous voices. In the British data the categories of recontextualized voices are the following (Table 3).

The identifed persons are actors in the British political scene. The plural nouns are diferent: there is one firm, parents presented as actors in the public sector of education, and several references to various anonymous authorities *(studies)*. The unidentifed persons and plural voices are also presented as actors in the public sphere. The types of RD indicated by *doctrine, dogma* and *myth* present an argument to be refuted. What is characteristic of the British data is the use of political parties as a voice as well as the unidentifed plural voice. One fourth of voices are proper nouns or personal pronouns referring to an identifed person. There are as many plural nouns that refer to a political party. Nearly half of the voices are the type whose reference is not very clear; in other words, these are cases based on an act of imagining, that is, they do not have a clear reference in any past context (see example (4) in 4.1), bringing out the evaluation of the speaker.

The French data similarly contain a number of references to individuals, named political actors, but also several literary quotations with references to their authors. As for the plural, a large part of the voices refer to groups that can be identifed such as *the Europeans* and *the French.* It has to be noted that more than half of the voices refer to plural voices whose reference is not clear, but designates an unidentifed group of people or the type of RD in question *(argument, fan-tasme).* These cases include the use of the indefnite pronoun *on.* In other words, there are again several cases of the type of imaginative RD.

According to these tables, the type of RD that is clearly anchored to the public sphere is evenemential and factual, and is used similarly in both sociocultural contexts. The main diference lies in references to political parties; this occurs only once in the French data, but is more frequent in the British data. The use of the French indefnite pronoun *on* is used fairly ofen in the combination *on dit que ('it is being said', 'it is said', 'it is to say').* The French data also contain more references to a collective voice, which can be identifed as referring to actors in the private sphere.

Functions of RD in linguistic context

As the previous Section 5.1 suggests, there are some diferences between the British and French politicians in the use of RD in diferent types of textual sequence. In this section I examine the diferent types of textual sequence and the way RD emerges in them, from descriptive (5.2.1) and explanative (5.2.2) to argumentative (5.2.3) sequences.

The politician disagrees with the proposed question, beginning her answer with a negation *(non pas du tout).* The first part of her answer, marked by (a), contains the referential anchoring of the same topic as proposed in the question *(exclusion in the suburbs).* The beginning of part (b) is marked by the connector *mais*

(but). In this part the speaker shifs the topic (from *exclusion in the suburbs* to *unemployed people).* The RD also functions as a description: it shows the situation of one group of people. In the

words of Adam (1992), it is an aspectualisation, illustrating the characteristics of the object of description *(unemployed people).* It contains a plural voice *(tous ces hommes ou ces femmes qui sont en chômage),* and a verb *(se dire);* this is not a reporting verb, but one indicating inner speech, an imaginative or evaluative type of RD. In part c), the speaker further specifes the unemployed people, adding age to the aspectualisation.

Explicative sequence: The second type of textual sequence, explanation, contained occurrences of RD in both sets of data. These sequences emerge when the topic of the talk is a social or political issue focusing on current events. In these sequences the function of RD is to anchor a fact from other contexts in the ongoing discourse. These other contexts are mainly other public-sphere discourses. In the following example, Tony Blair explains how certain issues have been handled, and his own and his party's attitude towards it:

(6) IR: well you're selling of assets

TB: oh for goodness sake David

IR: well what is it

TB: no course it's not asset stripping we're compiling a register

IR: it's selling the silver

TB:

a) No we're compiling a register of those assets that are in the public sector in order to see if there are those that can be better off in the
b) private sector and raise finance (...) we had very strong objections to the way that it was being done and the deal that was being secured for
c) the public sector we didn't object in principle on the railways indeed
d) it's been Tohn Prescott who said *let's get private fnance into the railway*
e) *system* and the reason that we have had to stay in relation to rail as with water we oppose the privatisation for perfectly good reasons (...)

Here, in the middle of a topical sequence in the IR's turns, there is a negatively oriented assertion and an interrogative focused on it *(well what is it)*. The IR's interrogative can be considered as proposing a cognitive-discursive task of explanation. The politician's (Tony Blair) answer is direct and negative, starting with *no*. In other words, it marks a clear disagreement with the orientation proposed by the IR. The RD contains a voice that is identifed by a proper noun, referring to a person who has presented a proposal for handling the issue under discussion.

The answer contains an initial schematisation of the problem in part (a)-here the pronoun *we* refers to the IE's party. Part (b) consists of a reference to a past opinion on the problem. This is followed by a negative utterance *(we didn't object in principle on the railways)* in part (c). Here the politician specifes the domain *(railways)*. The RD emerges in the middle of this turn, in part (d) which develops the topic. This constitutes the point in the explanation supporting the standpoint of the politicians party, expressed previously in part (c). In other words, parts (c) and (d) form a pair, with the latter part supporting the former one. Part (d) also allows the politician to give an evaluation, typical of the end of an explicative sequence, in part (e).

Argumentative sequence: The third kind of textual sequence to be taken up here is the argumentative sequence. Cases where the RD is part of some form of argumentation-whether in agreement or in counter-argumentation by the politician-occur in both sets of data. Here I distinguish two diferent types of use: one where the politician comments on the discourse of the public sphere in some manner, the other where the RD is a point in counter-argumentation.

One frequently occurring topic in political interviews is indicating what other politicians have said and expressing opinions about it. In the following examples the RD is used to bring out the opinions of other politicians, followed by an evaluation and the IE s self-positioning towards the voice. The French data include the following example:

(7) MB: c'est comment adapter un ensei- How to adapt teaching under

gnement alors qu'il y a Fapport pressure from TV and a certain de la télé d'un certain nombrenumber of other means of comtion et c'est oui euh c'est c'est

IR: adapter un enseignement etto adapt teaching and that it

que l'enseignement soit aussi would also be done in conditions fait dans des conditions euh. auuh where there is a minimum of minimum de contort <incom- contort <incomprehensible> préhensible>

MB: c'est le grand de contort mais in the maximum contort but also aussi adapter adapt

IR: et d'efcacité and efectiveness

This occurrence is also from the middle of a topical sequence, in which the IR is not asking questions but ofering comments on the topic *(teaching).* This can also be seen in the amount of overlapping speech in the excerpt. The orientation of the IR's comments is positive, and the IE (Michèle Barzach) does not disagree. The IE's last turn in the excerpt completes the elaboration that has been going on, and the politician moves on to give her own opinion on the topic of part (a). She initiates it in part (b), which is marked by the connector *alors (so).* This is followed by the first-person pronoun *je (I)* and by modality markers by which the IE expresses her (surprised) opinion towards the announcement of the Prime Minister in a certain political situation. Here, in part (c), the RD is an utterance which recontextualizes an example of a new type of political behavior, which is appreciated by the politician being interviewed. The evaluation is given before and afer (b, d)-in other words, it frames the RD with several adjectives and is also underlined by the emphasis of certain words.

In the British data the Prime Minister's comments on the opposition do not receive a positive evaluation:

(8) IR: and er if in fact the single currency was to be accepted as an idea by the by the Labour cabinet not in nineteen-ninety-nine I think Robin Cooks made clear erm but if it was erm in those circumstances would you be tempted to er to do as the Conservatives have said they'll do and in fact allow a free vote of your MPs TB: a) no as we said at the time when this was raised a few weeks ago by the b) Prime Minister who said *it was a*

possibility and then it appeared un- c) clear whether it was or it wasn't and no if a Government decides that d) the Government's got to get its legislation through but there would be a referendum of the British people if there is any question at all of e) a single currency arising in the next parliament then I give you my absolute personal guarantee there would be a referendum of the Brit- f) ish people I would not have a single currency imposed by a Government on Britain

Here, the IE is Tony Blair and the voice is that of John Major, at the time the Prime Minister. In the question turn, and in its presequence, the IR develops the topic *(single currency)* and in its interrogative part, there is a yes-no question *(would you)* proposing a comparison between the possible actions of Tony Blair and those of the Conservatives. In his answer in part (a), the IE first disagrees- the answers begin with a clear negation *(no)*. The RD emerges here at the beginning of this answer in part (a), referring to the words of the Prime Minister. The RD is followed by the politicians opinion in part (b): he states that the Prime Ministers utterance did not give a clear answer on the topic. In part (c), he repeats his disagreement as to the possible actions of the government. This is followed in parts (d), (e) and (f), by a statement of the IE's position. The politician announces his standpoint and possible future actions on the issue, marked by hypothetical markers *(would, if)*. In (e) he produces a speech act of promise *(I give my absolute personal guarantee)*.

Functions of RD in diferent sociocultural contexts

British political discourse: In this part of the analysis I take up the functions of the RD in the British data, to examine its use in the linguistic context of political talk. First of all, Tony Blair uses voices that refer to political actors in the public sphere, as in the following excerpt:

(9) TB:

a) well what is important actually is to make sure that the schools that

b) we have are schools of decent high standards for all our children and

c) I want to say this to you and make it very clear if there are local education authorities that aren't performing well we want to raise their

d) standards too but I don't believe that the Conservatives can turn round afer eighteen years of Government and say *it's all the fault of local authorities*

In example (9) the RD is situated at the end of the turn. In part (a) the politician anchors the topic (good schools); in part (b) he makes a promise, which is emphasized by the use of a metapragmatic utterance focusing on the way of saying *(and I want to say this to you and make it very clear).* In part (c) he continues the topic. In part d), which begins by a connector but indicating an opposing stance, the RD recontextualizes a critique of the IE's political opponent. In the next example he defends his own agenda:

(10)TB: (...) you know we can argue about Labours position in the past but let's argue about what Labour is saying now...

IR: okay now let me ask you TB: what labour is saying now is *that it should be done in consultation*

with business including small businesses since they may be those that

are afected most by it (...)

Here, at the end of his turn, the politician begins to present the agenda of his political party, and the IR gives him permission to do so. The RD refers to a position his party is taking vis-à-vis the social issue in question.

These two cases (9) and (10) present the most obvious cultural characteristics of the functions of RD: the politician uses RD to build up polarized positions. In the first case he presents the real or imagined sayings of his political opponents, in the second he announces his own or his political party's position on a certain matter.

Both are linked to discourse, emphasized with the frequent use of metapragmatic utterances, indicating how the utterances are to be understood (*I want make myself perfectly clear),* and to the speech act of promise. In these instances the RD is embedded in talk in which the politician is either explaining or arguing a social or political issue. The RD functions as a starting or emphasizing point to an agreement, as a supporting argument, or-most ofen-as a disagreement and counter-argument embedded in a negative linguistic context.

French political discourse: What types of RD functions characterize French political talk? First of all, the use of a third person singular voice, as in example (7) above *(Premier Ministre),* is common when accounting for actors and speech events in the French public sphere. Contrary to the British data, however, in the French data the RD is not always used to signal an opposing position; the IE may agree with the other politician, as in example (7) above. As in the British data, the politician may construct instances where he opposes another political person, a party or an idea, but less frequently than in the British context.

Secondly, what characterizes the opposition in these cases is that the RD is directed towards the audience and its function is to show what to think about a certain issue, as in the following excerpt:

(11) IR: vous n'avez pas l'impression queDon't you have the impression rurale et Isabelle Huppert enpression of a cry it's an expres-c'est l'expression d'un espoir.sion of a hope you know if the

In the middle of the topical sequence the IR's question has a negative orientation, which the politician (Jack Lang) rejects at the beginning of his answer (a). Instead, in part (b) he gives his own interpretation of the action he is taking. This is continued in part (c) by a RD that constitutes the first part in an argument *si-alors ('if-then).* This hypothetical utterance is a rejection of the proposal that has been presented in the political sphere (a treaty on GATT)-the politician does not say that he opposes it, but instead prefers to speak in the name of all Frenchmen and Europeans. There is a first person plural pronoun *nous* (*'we'*), referring to them and to the politician, not to his political party. In the *alors ('then)* utterance he announces the consequences if his advice is not followed. In other words, in this type of case the voice is plural or otherwise unidentifed, without a clear reference, as explained (see Table 4). In such cases the politician is sharing her/his thoughts or giving advice.

Thirdly, the RD can also serve to describe or explain a certain political or social state of afairs, as in this last excerpt:

(12) MA: (...) aujourd'hui on est quand(...) today we live in a paradox. a) même dans un paradoxe. les the people who are under 25 do b) moins de 25 ans n'arrivent pas not succeed in entering the labour a entrer sur le marché de travail. market and those who are older c) les plus de 50 ans on leur dit *ça* than 50 are told *that's enough uh suft hein euhuh*

IR: [Incomprehensible] [Incomprehensible]

Here again the politician (Martine Aubry) is not constructing an opposing position, but describing a social situation and how, in her view, it should be understood. In part (a) she states an assertion concerning French society, followed by its aspectualisation in parts (b) and (c). In part (b), the grammatical subject is the people who are under 25 *(les moins de 25 ans).* This part of the description is contrasted with the situation of those who have to leave the labour market, those who are older than 50 *(les plus de 50 ans).* This case and excerpt (5) are examples of several of this type of use of RD in the French data. These are not clearly connected to other types of speech acts, such as promises. Rather, they describe and give an opinion on a certain matter.

CONCLUSION

In this study a cross-cultural perspective was adopted. The starting point was the linguistic element of RD, whose functions were examined in one genre, the political interview, in two diferent political sociocultural contexts: the French and the British. RD is a linguistic device used to recontextualize something from other contexts in the social context of the ongoing speech situation. In other words, it is understood as a pragmatic, context-dependent object. In this study the functions of RD were compared in order to see whether and how they difer in French and British political talk.

First of all, RD is used in diferent types of cognitive-discursive activities that unfold in diferent types of textual sequences in political interviews. Where RD was found to be embedded in French political talk in some cases of description, the British hardly use it this way at all. Instead, in British political talk, RD is used in more than half of cases in argumentative sequences. The cultural diferences are the following: in the British data, RD was first used to create an oppositional stance towards rival politicians and political party; secondly, to inform the audience about the position of the politician her/himself and the political party on a certain political or social issue. Moreover, it was noted that the linguistic context was frequently negatively loaded, and the saying was emphasized with metaprag-matic utterances and speech acts of promises.

The French sometimes did this too, but opposition towards rival politicians appeared less ofen, as did mentions of other political parties. Instead, the French politician might take up her/his agreement with the political opponent. Morever, the French politicians used RD to give an opinion or advice on a political matter. Finally, they described the social situation, giving their opinion about it.

This suggests that the way of responding in these two sociocultural contexts difers even though the discourse topics are the more or less the same. It also suggests that the role played by the politician also afects the realization of represented speech. The politicians interviewed here were ex-ministers in the opposition, whereas Tony Blair was leader of the Labour Party in 1997 and Prime Minister in 1998. The political systems also difered, the French having several political parties and being less polarized. In any case, based on the analysis we are able to say that British political talk is more polarized, clearly signalling the politicians way of thinking about actions, focusing on positions in the public sphere of political decision-making, while the French discussed the issues more widely. The French politicians might state the same type of opinions, but their focus was rather on explaining and describing how to understand the society and political life, without clearly connecting every issue to their role in the decision-making process.

6

Challenges in Political Interviews an Intercultural Analysis

Native and non-native discourse can never be 100% explicit, but rather is characterized by a high degree of implicitness, which is not only true for ordinary talk but also for media discourse. This is of particular relevance for the communicative act of a challenge, which represents a face-threatening act par excellence. This study examines the linguistic realization of challenges in British and German political interviews from the general elections in Britain (1997) and Germany (1998).

It demonstrates language-and culture-specifc preferences for communicating, interpreting and contextualizing challenges. Particular attention is given to diferent sociocultural practices in the context of media communication, in which coparticipants with diferent cultural backgrounds communicate and in which the media interview is watched by an audience with heterogeneous cultural backgrounds.

INTRODUCTION

Culture and context represent extremely complex phenomena, which are dificult to defne since they refer to our knowledge of the world and to our knowledge about the world. Some approaches to culture are carried out in a framework based on the dichotomies nature versus culture and chaos versus order (Sones-son 1989), while other investigations employ a paradigmatic approach based on mental, social and material artefacts (Posner 1989). In linguistic pragmatics, the linguistic realization of particular speech acts has been examined with regard to language-and culture-specifc preferences (Gass and Neu 1996; Blum-Kulka et al. 1989). All of the frameworks presuppose the existence of culture, which is seen as something already given and assigned the status of a product. Thus, there is no need for an explicit discussion of the question of how culture is constructed or reconstructed.

Unlike the rather static frameworks, the sociological field of ethnometholdol-ogy investigates social reality from micro and macro perspectives by focussing on the questions of how the two realms are interactionally organized and how they interact. Social reality entails diferent cultural and intercultural confgurations, which are conceived of as subsets of social reality.

Social actions and communicative actions are embedded in and connected with cultural context which is embedded in and connected with social context. Regarding the conception of an interviewer, for instance, this means that the social role of an interviewer is a more general notion than the sociocultural role of a British or Hebrew interviewer (Blum-Kulka 1987). Ethnomethodologists have introduced a radically different approach to the investigation of society, culture and context by highlighting the individual's role as a social actor, who reconstructs social reality in the micro realm through their social and communicative actions.

The connectedness between social reality, social action and communicative action is based on the premise of indexicality of social action. Thus, the analysis of the social structures of everyday-life activities has become of importance not only for ordinary language philosophers, such as Grice (1975), Austin (1980) or Searle (1969), but also for the social sciences.

According to Garfnkel, the pioneer of ethnomethodology, ethnomethodologists have to undertake "an investigation of the rational properties of indexical expressions and other practical actions as contingent ongoing accomplishments of organized artful practices of everyday life" (Garfnkel 1994:11). Against this background, verbal and nonverbal communication, institutional and non-institutional discourse, private and public discourse, and mediatized discourse are key to the reconstruction of culture and interculture.

CULTURE AND INTERCULTURE

Context and culture have long been conceived of as separate from the communicative act whose environment they represent, and there has neither been a differentiation of context with regard to micro and macro domains, nor has there been a contextualization of culture. Unlike the discrete settings, which look upon context, culture and communicative act as bounded entities, ethnomethodology interprets communicative action as indexical action which interacts with sociocultural context and context, and thus is dynamic.

The premise of indexicality requires a context-dependent investigation of verbal and nonverbal communication, of their constitutive communicative acts and of the linguistic system. As a consequence of the inherent connectedness between context, communicative act and language, meaning can no longer be assigned the status of an independent category. Rather, it is the interpretative result of the interaction between an object, such as a linguistic item or a communicative act, and its immediate and more remote linguistic, sociocultural and social contexts. Because of that, the interpretative result is one of the most important sources of intercultural miscommunication. But how do context, culture and communicative act interact?

In a traditional framework, communication is described as a speaker coding internal messages into external signals, which the hearer decodes. That setting does not accommodate the requirements resulting from the interaction of context, culture and language: it neither accounts for the contextualization of the coding process and the contextualization of the decoding process, nor does it take the contextual constraints and requirements of the sociocultural contexts into consideration. That is to say, the production and interpretation of an utterance require relevant contextual information regarding a possible explicit or implicit linguistic realization. In the framework of speech act theory, explicit utterances are referred to as direct speech acts. Their interpretation does not require the retrieval of a huge amount of contextual information. Unlike a direct speech act, an indirect speech act depends strongly on its immediate contexts. So far, the discussion of the interactive processes between the language system and context has not taken into consideration the contextual constraints of the cultural system. The results of intercultural-communication research (Hall and Hall 1994; Wierzbicka 1991) show that the accommodation of language-external constraints on language production and language interpretation may be a universal phenomenon, but their linguistic realizations in context are defnitely not universal. This is due to the fact that the question of whether a communicative contribution is realized explicitly or implicitly is interdependent on a speech community's preferred and dispreferred modes of realizing communicative intentions. The knowledge about possible linguistic realizations is part of a copar-ticipant's sociocultural competence, which is anchored to a speech community[1] (Gumperz 1977; Hymes 1974).

Diferent speech communities employ diferent contextualization practices, and it is those diferences which lead to intercultural miscommunication. To investigate the diferences more thoroughly, the functional-grammar concept of markedness (Givón 1993) is of relevance: the marked format is structurally more complex, while the unmarked format is structurally less complex; the marked format is less frequent with regard to distribution, while the unmarked format is more frequent with regard to distribution; the marked format is more difcult to process and requires more cognitive work, while the unmarked format is less difcult to process and requires less cognitive work If the concept of markedness is adapted to the investigation of communicative contributions, this means that a contribution which is interpreted as adhering to the cultural modes of verbal performance is attributed to the unmarked format and does not require any extra cognitive work In this setting the "et cetera" strategy applies and the status quo is confrmed (Garfnkel 1994:21). That is to say, the linguistic realization-or interpretation-of a challenge, for instance, is "such as is required" (Grice 1975:45) in a particular context, where it confrms and reinforces the coparticipants background knowledge regarding the sociocultural practice of a prototypical challenge.

If a contribution is interpreted as a deviation from a sociocultural practice, but only a minor one, the strategy "let it pass" is employed and the procedure also follows the "et cetera" pattern (Garfnkel 1994:21). Here, the minor deviation is interpreted as irrelevant as it is looked upon as idiosyncratic and accounted for accordingly.

Should a contribution deviate from the expected cultural mode of behaviour in an unreasonable manner, the coparticipants need to account for the degree of deviation and they may either employ the "unless" strategy or practice "ad hoeing" (Garfnkel 1994:21). The "unless" strategy regulates the acceptance of a particular contribution under specifed conditions, for instance psychological stress. "Adhocing" allows the coparticipant to look upon the contribution as an odd-one-out which is accounted for accordingly, for instance as not being of any immediate relevance.

In general, a contribution is contextualized in the unmarked format. That is to say, a speech community, which may comprise a national culture or one of its subsets, for instance a particular social, ethnic or gendered group, has an unmarked or preferred mode of realizing and interpreting the communicative act of a challenge, for example. Of course, that very general frame of reference needs to be broken down into further constitutive frameworks, that is communicative genres (Luckmann 1995), activity types (Levinson 1979) and communicative projects (Linell 1998).

Those intermediate (meso) frames constrain the linguistic realization of communicative strategies and categorize them into marked and unmarked formats. While a directly realized challenge maybe assigned an unmarked status in a British political interview, for instance, it tends to be assigned a marked status in its German counterpart. Should the interpretation of a contribution and its classifcation as marked or unmarked be inconsistent in a particular context and not hold, its status needs to be reevaluated. Again, clashes between speaker-intended meaning and hearer-intended interpretation are a rich source for a marked interpretation in intercultural communication.

If we accept the ethnomethodological premise that social reality is reconstructed in and through the process of communication and is both process and product-or is both brought to the interaction and brought out in the interaction, to employ interactional-sociolinguistics terminology (Gumperz 1977), we also have to accept the entailment that the social construct of culture as well as its subsets are reconstructed in a similar fashion. Their analyses should, according to Garfmkel, give special reference to "recognizing, using, and producing the orderly ways of cultural settings from "within" those settings" (Garfmkel 1994:31). This means that culture and its subsets are structured constructs, which are in-teractionally organized.

However, we do not generally communicate culture in an explicit mode, but rather presuppose it, or to employ Garfnkel's own words: "much... of what is actually reported is not mentioned" and yet the "unstated understandings" are "required" for the production and interpretation of "recognizable sense" (Garfmkel 1994:10).

That is to say, a contributions presuppositions are part of the sociocultural knowledge of a speech community and therefore do not need to be realized explicitly in everyday life discourse.[2] Again, there is variation with regard to the degree of explicitness in individual cultures, and it is those diferences, which may cause a marked interpretation. But how do coparticipants interpret the unstated understandings, and how do they know what unstated understandings apply in a particular context?

In an ethnomethodology framework, the knowledge about when, where and how to fill in the gaps is part of the coparticipants' sociocultural competence (Gumperz 1977; Hymes 1974). Not only do coparticipants know when, where and how to employ the strategy of gapping, but they also know when, where and how to retrieve the contextual information required in order to make the gaps meaningful. Furthermore, they know how to formulate and interpret messages in a culturally appropriate manner, for instance the speaker-intended meaning of a challenge. Thus, a speech community's conventions regulate the degree of explicitness required for the appropriateness of a contribution. And it is up to the co-participants to act in accordance with the recommended degree of explicitness, or to act in disaccordance with it. Acting in disaccordance, however, is assigned the status of deliberate action for which the coparticipant need to take responsibility.

Conventionalized modes of communication are also referred to as communicative strategies, and are examined in the following.

COMMUNICATIVE STRATEGIES: PREFERRED AND DISPREFERRED MODES

Communicative strategies contain information about how to express a communicative intention, for instance a challenge, in the most efcient and efective manner. From an economy-of-speech perspective, the most efective way of challenging a contribution is realized something along the lines of *I challenge your contribution* or *I do not accept what you have been saying*. In reality, however, the most efcient way of saying something is not necessarily the most efective one. Thus, challenging a contribution does not only need to take into account the level of propositional information, it also has to consider interpersonal aspects anchored to the coparticipants' face needs.

In general, natural-language communication involves a sequence of contributions. For this reason, communicative strategies have to be investigated in a discursive framework (Fetzer 2002) which accommodates the results of preference organization (Levinson 1983; Pomerantz 1984), which have been refned by Lauerbach (1993), who explicitly relates the coparticipants' face needs in the dispreferred format to additional semiotic and language material.[3] Since the additional semiotic and language material indicates an upcoming challenge, it can also be assigned the status of an inference trigger. Since the realization and interpretation of the dispreferred format is not universal, but rather culture-specifc, this may again lead to intercultural miscommunication. Communicative strategies do not only apply to language output and thus to the most efcient and appropriate mode of realizing a communicative intention, but they also apply to language input and the most efcient and efective interpretation and contextualization strategies. Communicative strategies do not only describe the efective and efcient employment of the linguistic code, they also regulate and prescribe a socially accepted mode of verbal and nonverbal performance. They do not necessarily represent the most efcient way of transmitting information by adhering to the Gricean maxims of quantity, quality, relation and manner, but they certainly describe the most habitual, the most appropriate and thus the most accepted mode of communicative performance.

Communicative strategies also have a prescriptive function and thus stabilize a speech community's sociocultural values. Should a coparticipant not adhere to the preferred format, s/he will not generally sufer any sanctions, for communicative strategies do not have a normative, but a conventional status. Yet any deviation from a speech community's preferred format needs to be accounted for since communicative action is looked upon as deliberate action.[4]

Communicative strategies are connected with social and cultural aspects of language use and therefore ofer a very promising field for the investigation of culture and interculture. From a preference-organization viewpoint, there are preferred and dispreferred modes. This entails that there exist less efcient and less appropriate modes of communication. Regarding their connectedness with context, communicative strategies are allocated to the micro-macro interface. Their connectedness with the micro domain is refected on the utterance level, and their connectedness with the macro domain is refected in the micro communicative intentions production and interpretation in accordance with culture-specifc production and interpretation rules. Communicative strategies are not only characterized by internal factors, e.g. cognitive efort and structural complexity, but also by external factors, e.g. the sociocultural aspect of face and the contextual constraints and requirements of institutional communication. This is of particular relevance for the analysis of communicative strategies in the domain of media communication with its dual frame of reference, the first-frame communication on screen and the communication between the first-frame coparticipants and the second-frame audience. Here, the first-frame coparticipants produce and interpret meaning for the direct first-frame communication partner and for the indirect second-frame communication partner, the audience. Because of the multilayered setting, the interpretation of media communication represents a rich source of miscommunication, especially in an intercultural setting.

In the following, those confgurations which count as challenges are examined in detail, and particular attention is given to their connectedness with culture-specifc and media-specifc modes of linguistic realization.

Challenges in context: Challenging a communicative contribution is intrinsically connected with denying its truth and/ or rejecting its appropriateness and sincerity. A communicative contribution can be rejected completely or partially, it can be disagreed with completely or partially, it can be denied, and other contextual references can be non-accepted, such as its degree of politeness or its sequential status. The frame of reference adopted in this contribution is a sociopragmatic approach, which conceives of language as a tool for communicative action. Adopting the theoretical outline and terminology of Habermas (1987), rational coparticipants negotiate the communicative status of validity claims in communication. This means, a speaker postulates a validity claim and directs it towards an addressee, who ratifies the act by accepting it and assigning it the status of a plus-validity claim, or by rejecting it and assigning it the status of a minus-validity claim. A non-acceptance initiates a negotiation-of-validity sequence, in which the non-accepted references of the postulated claim are made explicit and in which their communicative status is negotiated in order to reach some kind of agreement, which is acceptable to the coparticipants.

A negotiation-of-validity sequence is of particular relevance to the analysis of challenges in political interviews because it demonstrates how meaning is negotiated in a dyadic setting, and how meaning is negotiated in a mediated frame of references in front of an audience. In a media-communication setting, such as a political interview, Habermas's conception of communication as an inherently dyadic endeavour is refined with respect to the first-frame interaction between interviewer and interviewee, and with respect to the second-frame interaction comprising the first-frame interaction with the media frame. In order to adapt Habermas's macro approach to a micro setting, the notion of context is made explicit.

Context comprises social context and sociocultural context, linguistic context and cognitive context, which are conceived of as an onion with constitutive layers, metaphorically speaking (Sperber and Wilson 1996). Naturally, the diferent sets of contexts are administered in their own particular ways. Adapting Habermas's frame of reference, a validity claim is anchored to three worlds: the subjective world, the social world and the objective world. Since a validity claim denotes a process-oriented concept which requires ratifcation, it entails both a plus-and a minus-validity claim. In natural-language communication, validity claims are anchored to social and sociocultural contexts represented by the social world, they are anchored to linguistic context represented by the objective world, and they are anchored to cognitive context represented by the subjective world. The tripartite system is schematized in Figure 1.

In the framework of plus/minus-validity claims, challenges can be explicated as follows:

The objective world is defned by the guiding principle of truth, which is based on reference and predication, and on their presuppositions. False validity claims comprise a challenge of reference, predication or of their presuppositions.

The subjective world is defned by the guiding principle of sincerity, which is based on a coparticipant's communicative intention, which is meant as uttered and interpreted as meant. Insincere validity claims comprise the challenge of the speaker's or hearer's sincere intentions.

The social world is defned by the guiding principle of appropriateness, which subcategorizes into another tripartite system of interpersonal, interactional and textual presuppositions, which is defned as follows:

The textual system inherits the overall guiding principle, the Gricean cooperative principle (CP), which is the fundamental premise of the defnition of a plus/minus-validity claim. Here, the maxims of quality, quantity, relation and manner, and the conversational implicature (Grice 1975) are of prime importance. Inappropriate validity claims are defned as challenges which claim that a contribution is in disaccordance with one or more of the maxims, or that its conversational implicature has not been calculated accordingly.

The interpersonal system is based on Brown and Levinson's conception of a model person, their face needs and face wants (Brown and Levinson 1987), and on Gofman's conception of footing (Gofman 1974,1981). Inappropriate validity claims are defned as challenges which claim that a contribution is in disaccordance with the contextual constraints and requirements regarding face and participation.

The interactional system is based on sequentiality and sequential organization. Inappropriate validity claims are defned as challenges which claim that a contribution is in disaccordance with the premise of adjacency and that a contribution is in disaccordance with the contextual constraints and requirements of the turn-taking system (Atkinson and Heritage 1984; Levinson 1983).

Challenges may communicate that a communicative contribution is looked upon as inappropriate, untrue or insincere on the micro domain, and they may communicate that the macro contribution of a communicative genre (Luckmann 1995) is seen as inappropriate or insincere. From a top-down perspective, a communicative genre is conceived of as a macro validity claim, in which the cognitive-context, linguistic-context and social-context references are specifed. No specifcation is required for the objective world anchored to objective context, because the objective context never changes-not even in other possible worlds. Regarding the subjective world, the premise of communicative intention meant as uttered and interpreted as meant is specifed with respect to the macro communicative intention anchored to the macro category of genre. Regarding the social world, which is a context-dependent notion par excellence, specifcation is required for all of its constitutive systems, as is refected in genre-specifc constraints and requirements of a political interview, namely question-answer sequences and neutralism, which is schematized in Figure 2.

Challenging the macro validity claim of a political interview indicates an inappropriate performance with regard to the guiding principle of neutralism (Greatbatch 1992), the constitutive coparticipant-specifc question-answer sequences, the genre-specifc ratifed participation statuses, and the media-specifc constraints and requirements. For instance, an interviewee might choose to ask questions instead of answering them, an interviewer might ask questions about the politicians personal domains, or an interviewer and interviewee might only talk amongst themselves and not to the audience. From the markedness perspective introduced above, inappropriate communicative performance is assigned a marked status, which tends to refect negatively on the coparticipants.

In the following, the linguistic realization of challenges in the British election-night interviews is examined in detail.[5]

CHALLENGES IN THE BRITISH ELECTION-NIGHT INTERVIEWS

The data investigated comprises forty-one short dyadic interviews (2 to 5 minutes) between professional journalists and leading political figures. There are twenty-eight interviews with members of the conservative party ten interviews with members of the labour party two interviews with members of the liberal democrats and one interview with an independent candidate. The focus of the analysis lies on the politicians employment of communicative strategies for performing a challenge and, for this reason, I neither take diferences between public-broadcasting styles (BBC1, BBC2) and commercial-broadcasting styles (ITV), nor particular interviewer styles into consideration. Instead, I concentrate on the communicative strategies employed in the particular context of an election night and account for the diferent strategies used by the winners and losers of the general election.

The interviews with leading members of the conservative party, the losers of the 1997 general election, display numerous negotiation-of-validity-claim sequences. This is due to the fact that the conservatives do not focus on the present moment of the interaction which entails their defeat and loss of power. Instead, they talk about the merits of their former government. The negotiation-of-validity-claim sequences show a higher frequency of markers of the dispreferred format, such as verbs of cognition used with an epistemic function, cohesive links, references to media-specifc constraints and requirements and to the inappropriateness of questions and presuppositions. The verbs of cognition signify subjec-tifcation and reduce the pragmatic force of the argument, and the cohesive links function as textual signposts and indicate some kind of incoherence. While textual-meaning references to ones own argument have the communicative function of boosting the pragmatic force, textual-meaning references to other's argument indicate that the argument has not been fully conclusive. This also holds for references to media-specifc constraints and requirements, which are frequently used as a reason for opting out (Fetzer 2006; Lauerbach 2004). The interviews with the winners display less lengthy negotiation-of-validity sequences, but also a high frequency of verbs of cognition and a high frequency of negative contextualization cues (Fetzer 1997), which are used to attenuate the pragmatic force. While there is a lot of variation in the interviews with the losers, the winners tend to use only one strategy.

In the following, the challenges identifed in the election-night interviews are systematized with regard to their referential domains, namely challenges indexing the inappropriateness of a validity claims content, challenges indexing the inappropriateness of a validity claim's force with a negative evaluation, challenges indexing the inappropriateness of a validity claim by explicitly opting out, chal-lenges indexing the inappropriateness of a validity claim by avoiding the question and challenges indexing the inappropriateness of the macro validity claim.

Challenging the appropriateness of a validity claims content

All of the following examples[6] are responses to interviewer questions, through which s/he intends to elicit a statement about who is to blame for the defeat of the conservatives. All of the conservatives' responses display metapragmatic devices, which intensify the pragmatic force of the argument. In example (1), Stephen Dorell (SD), the Health Secretary, boosts the pragmatic force of his challenge with the adverbial phrase *by any means* and explicitly rejects the interviewers (IR) implicit presupposition that the outcome of the general election has already been decided:

(1)IR Do you agree with Edwina Currie that it was the divisions in your party and particularly the behaviour of the eurosceptics that did it for you? SD I don't accept *by any means* that the results of the election has yet been decided or at least that it is yet known. Erm I do agree with Michael Portillo saying earlier...

In (2), the IR's request for information about who is to blame for the defeat is challenged by SD who again refers to the *unknown result*. Unlike the boosted force in (1), the challenge is attenuated by the negated verb of cognition *don't think:*

(2)IR If a party cannot be forced into unity by one leader isn't it time to change the leader? SD No I don't think that we need to get into speculations about what the lessons are from a result we don't know yet.

William Hague's (WH) challenge in (3) is attenuated by the negated verb of cognition *don't think* and by the discourse marker *well,* which signifes a change in context (Smith and Jucker 2002):

(3)IR Nicolas Winterton you see says that Kenneth Clarke was the fault and that he lost the campaign? WH *Well* I don't think we should I don't think there is any point in apportioning blame around the party....

Challenging the appropriateness of a validity claim's content is frequently anchored to a negotiation-of-validity sequence, in which the challenged presuppositions are made explicit. In (4), the IR requests Malcolm Rifind (MR) to comment on the validity of the claim about him being *confdent* that he will keep his seat:

(4) IR Are you confdent you'll hang on to your seat?

MR I'm extremely hopeful....

IR Being hopeful isn't quite the same as being confdent is it?

MR Well, it's because you're asking me to predict it, I mean are you just wanting me to use the usual optimism that all candidates use or are you trying to find out if I have some privileged access to information? I haven't counted the ballots yet so I don't actually know any more than you do but I'm very happy to sound optimistic.

MR's response indirectly challenges the IR's lexical choice *confdent* and corrects it with the more moderate term *hopeful.* The IR does not accepted that and spells out the inappropriateness of MR's response by saying *being hopeful isn't quite the same as being confdent is it.* In the follow-up move, MR gives reasons for why he prefers the term *hopeful,* and his account is introduced with the discourse marker *well,* the other-reformulation *you're asking me* and the self-reformulation *I mean,* which all signify that he intends to terminate the negotiation-of-validity sequence. The rather elaborate move contains a number of explicit references to the IR, namely *I haven't counted the ballots yet so I don't actually know any more than you do.* This extends the negotiated domain of validity from MR to the IR thus including him and his propositions in the argumentation.

A reference to the not-yet-decided election is also used by other conservatives. In (5), the verbal exchange between Michael Heseltine (MH) and the IR is more confrontational:

(5) IR.... do you accept it hasn't quite worked out?

MH Well the opinion polls haven't worked out

IR Michael Portillo says that it's disunity that was the problem for the Tory party would you agree with that? MH Well I think it's important to have a mature period of refection.... IR Does this imply that the prime minister will resign as leader of the party

MH Well I hope not I've spent

MH challenges the IR's validity claim *it has not worked out* by making the indeterminate reference *it* explicit with the determinate meaning *the opinion polls,* which was not intended by the IR, who intended the pronoun *it* to refer to the conservatives' election campaign. The deliberate mis-retrieval of contextual information is introduced with the discourse marker *well.* The IR does not explicitly comment on the mis-retrieved reference. Instead he takes up the previously introduced discourse topic and specifes it in a subsequent question, in which he explicitly refers to another conservative politician and his reference to the disunity of the conservative party. MH indirectly challenges the IR's claim. This is manifest in the discourse marker *well* and the verb of cognition *I think,* which both attenuate the pragmatic force of the response. The response is rather vague and refers to another indeterminate concept, viz. *a period of mature refection.* Again, the IR takes up MH's vague response and requests him to be more precise and spell out his implications *(does this imply).* MH does not comply but remains vague. This is manifest in the discourse marker *well* and in the marker of subjectivity *I hope.*

The interviews with the winners of the election, the labour party, also contain a number of challenges. Like the conservatives, the majority of the labour politicians refers to the not-yet-decided election. Gisela Stuart (GS) is one of the few who presupposes labours victory. In (6), her challenge of the IR's question is attenuated by the verb of cognition *I think* and the more-fuzzy hedge *kind of:*

(6) IR Yes. Gisela Stuart erm congratulations. Why do you think you won this seat which has been a conservative seat since nineteen twenty-two? Was it just that people were fed up with the Tories? GS No I think it meant much deeper. It was a kind of total disillusionment but also they had lost trust and I see the labour victory....

Alastair Campell (AC) is less explicit in his responses (7), (8) and (9), which challenge the IR's presupposition that labour has won the election. Again, we find the discourse marker *well,* the verbs of cognition *I think* and *I doubt,* and the appreciation device *if you don't mind.* All of the metapragmatic devices attenuate the pragmatic force of the challenge, and all of AC's responses indicate a possible victory which is implicit in the references *a pretty good night* and *we'll get through tonight which seems to be a success:*

(7)IR Well, David, a moment or two ago, about half an hour ago actually, er

Tony Blair came here, he wouldn't say anything, but with us at the moment for any informal chat I'm told is is Alastair Campbell, his press spokesman. Alastair, y/you/you've won, haven't you? AC Well Mr Blair's constituency is not yet declared but erm I think we're having a pretty good night

(8)IR Well, I would doubt that but I think that it's fair to say we've had a very good campaign, we're having a very good night. AC Well I would doubt that but I think it's fair to say...

(9)IR It's gonna be a problem, though, isn't it, all governments with big majorities have problems?

AC Well I think if you don't mind we stick on one night and we'll get through tonight which seems to be a success and then...

In (10), Peter Mandelson (PM) challenges the IR's claim that he is the architect of new labour. In spite of the attenuation device *well,* the challenge is assigned a strong pragmatic force because of the explicit negative operator *not* and the directly negated proposition *I'm not the sole architect of anything:*

(10) IR Now you are of course the architect of this whole campaign and PM Well I'm one of them, I'm not the sole architect

of anything. Another winner of the general election are the liberal democrats. In (11) and (12), their leader Paddy Ashdown (PA) challenges the IRs validity claim in a rather explicit manner. Even though his challenge is attenuated by the discourse marker *well* in (11), the IR's claim is directly denied by the explicit negative operator *not* and the corrected proposition *the liberal democrats are not on the lef.* The pragmatic force is further boosted by a direct reference to the IR with title and last name, viz. Mr. Dimbleby, and a reference to common ground, namely *as you well know.* In (12), the challenge is attenuated by the verb of cognition *I doubt:*

(11) IR So erm Mr. Ashdown, you/you were saying in your speech, when youer when you had the count, er that you looked to the liberal democrats to infuence the changes in the nature of politics and the constitution and all that. There's going to be obviously a hefy labour majority. Do you think that Tony Blair will still stand by that commitment he gave to try and bring other parties in on the left into a sort of new corporative agreement or some such? PA Well the liberal democrats are not on the lef Mr. Dimbleby as you well know we're a radical party but we're an independent and distinctive one...

(12)IR Isn't it a difculty for you that you get this strength, this new strength in the House of Commons, something like two and a half or maybe three times what you had before at the very moment labour roars ahead and gets a vast majority er for itself, thus diminishing any infuence you may have PA I doubt that but let's wait and see how the results play out and in particular...

In (13), the liberal democrat David Steele (DS) challenges the IR's claim in an explicit manner by the denial *I did not say that* while providing the corrected formulation introduced by the reformulation marker *what I said was:*

(13) IR even better had you abandoned the pantomime that you were contesting every seat in Britain and hoping to form a government. DS We had that argument I seem to remember during the campaign IR Yeah, you were maintaining stalwartly DS stalwartly well, we did-IR that you were hoping to form a government. DS But we no it was no no I didn't say that what I said was we had to fight all the seats..

Analogously to the straightforward challenges by the liberal democrats, the independent candidate Martin Bell (MB) employs rather explicit challenges. In (14), he boosts his challenge with the booster *absolutely* and with the straightforward denial *I did not campaign,* and in (15) he uses the direct denials *he can't be vindicated* and *its's just not possible,* which are attenuated by the discourse marker *well:*

(14)IR Now you claim you stood as the Independent candidate for higher stan-dards in public life. Have you smeared and wrecked the reputation of Neil Hamilton? MB No I absolutely have not. I did not campaign at all on er on the charges that are not yet resolved....

(15)IR If he should be vindicated, as he says he will, by Sir Gordon Downey, what will you do by then as elected MP who replaced him. MB Well he can't be vindicated on what is already out there on the record. It's just not possible.

Challenges of the appropriateness of a validity's content are performed by all politicians, whether they have won or lost the election. While both labour and the conservatives tend to attenuate their challenges, the liberal democrats and the independent candidate boost their challenges, which might be due to their particular position in the British election system. In that confguration, smaller parties, such as the liberals, hardly stand a chance of wining the election.

Challenging the appropriateness of a validity claim can be further boosted by attributing a negative evaluation to its force, which is examined in the following.

Challenging the appropriateness of a validity claims force with a negative evaluation

In the data investigated, only the losers of the general election challenge the appropriateness of a validity claim with an explicit negative evaluation. Unlike the challenges of an inappropriate content, challenges with a negative evaluation do not accept the IR's communicative action performed though the claim. The force and the implied sequential status of the validity claim tend to be referred to in a rather general and thus indeterminate manner. The general references are evaluated with strong negative adjectives, such as *ridiculous* by Alan Clark (AC) in (16), *not sensible* by Michael Howard (MH) in (17), Stephen Dorrell (SD) and John Redwood (JR) in (18), respectively (19). Another negative evaluation, *secondary,* is used by SD in (20):

(16) AC Oh that's a ridiculous question

(17) MH I don't think that's a very sensible question

(18) SD... and I don't think it's very sensible to speculate about it when we all know that the result, the true result..

(19) JR... I don't think it's sensible to rush off tonight with all sorts of explanations...

(20) SD Well I think the leadership question is frankly a secondary question

All challenges with a negative evaluation are produced by the conservatives. This maybe due to their particular position of not having anything else left to lose, and it may be due to their frustration.

In the following, challenging the appropriateness of a validity claim by explicitly opting out is examined.

Challenging the appropriateness of a validity claim by explicitly opting out

In the data investigated, only the conservatives use the strategy of *opting out.* The strategy is adopted from the Gricean CP, which is the fundamental premise of the defnition of a plus/minus-validity claim and which is inherited to the social world's constitutive textual system. Against this background, coparticipants can opt out locally if higher-order principles provide good reasons for doing so. The good reasons over-rule the fundamental requirement that coparticipants should make their contribution "such as is required, at the stage at which it occurs, by the accepted purpose of direction of the talk exchange" (Grice 1975:45). In the British data, the strategy is quite frequent and it is ofen based on the claim that one should not speak on behalf of a colleague. Implicit in the strategy is the premise that the moral principle of loyalty overrules ordinary conversational requirements, as is the case with John Redwood (JR) in (21):

(21) IR Do you think John Major can survive this result?

JR. I'm not commenting on anything like that. John Major is the leader of the conservative party and you should allow him time to consider what is best for the conservative party

(22) IR What is your reaction to the defeat of Neal Hamilton in Tatton?

MH Erm well I think that's best up for the history books.

IR Why do you say that?

MH Because I don't see why you think I should comment on something like that which is for Neal a personal tragedy. It's happened, you can have a judgement, I can have a judgement but I'm not going to be drawn on that.

In (22), the IR challenges the legitimate motives of Michael Heseltine (MH) and his reference to the *history books* and requests him to spell them out in more detail. MH complies by making his reasoning explicit in the closing remark *I'm not going to be drawn on that,* which is accepted by the IR, who does not ask any further questions.

Interviewees can also opt out by simply stating that they are not commenting on a validity claim thereby implicating that the claim in question lacks validity, as is the case with JR in (23) and Ian Lang (IL) in (24):

(23) IR Do you think leadership talk during the campaign damaged the cam paigning efort? JR I have no further comments on the campaign. I'm just very pleased that in Wokingham people have backed me again and I will work very hard over the next five years to earn that trust.

(24) IR I mean you you were seen as a possible leadership contender of course afer this election erm obviously not in position to contend for the leadership now, I mean, who who would you like to see succeed John Major?

IL I'm not gonna talk about that now

IR Erm would you would you have run had you still been in Parliament?

IL I'm not gonna talk about that either that's a hype a hype a hypothesis on top of another one. The strategy of opting out is only used by the losers of the general election, and it is used in order terminate the negotiation-of-validity sequence of a particular discourse topic. Opting out can be anchored to a higher-order moral principle or to an individual who voices her or his preferences for closing the encounter.

In the following, a less explicit strategy is examined, the strategy of avoiding the question.

Challenging the appropriateness of a validity claim by avoiding the question

The strategy of challenging the appropriateness of a validity claim by avoiding the question represents a truly dyadic scenario with a lengthy negotiation-of-valid-ity sequence, which becomes more and more confrontational. Because of this, it has a very strong face-threatening potential for both coparticipants who do not intend to give in by accepting the other's evasiveness or by complying with the request for more precise information. In the data examined, only the conservatives use the strategy of avoiding the question in order to challenge the appropriateness of a validity claim. In (25), Edwina Currie (EC) challenges the appropriateness of the IR's validity claim, in which he requests her to confrm a former standpoint by saying *is that still your view.* EC does not comply with the request but talks about her *pro-European colleagues'* positions. The IR challenges the rather general answer by repeating his question *your view* thus indicating that EC has not provided an appropriate answer. But EC does not go along with the IRs request and provides another vague answer. At that point, the IR changes his strategy of challenging her contributions by requesting her to state her own viewpoint. He introduces the anticipated candidate *Mr Michael Portillo* as a discourse topic and requests EC to comment on it. But she does not give in and remains vague, which is refected in the attenuation devices *I think* and *well* and in the rather general references *this area in the Midlands* and *very good and honourable people:*

(25) IR.... is that still your view?

EC Well I know some of my pro-European colleagues feel that that John

Major ought to hang on and perhaps even stay until October or November for the sake of party unity. IR Your view? EC But I think I'm going to su/1 think it would be a tragedy for the man who is an honourable decent man who's uh I think who been very battered .... My preference....

IR Mr Michael Portillo has been mentioned.... Your reaction to him as a potential leader?

EC Well I think in this area in the Midlands

IR And that's Mr Portillo as far as you're concerned. EC Uh, they're all very good and honourable people...

Challenging the appropriateness of a validity claim by avoiding the question seems a very common strategy in political interviews (Bull 2003), and if the interviewer is not very persistent, the interviewee can get away with it. In confrontational settings, there are explicit references to the non-appropriateness of answers and questions, but they only occur in marked interviews (Fetzer 2000). Avoiding the question is necessarily anchored to longer sequences. Here the interviewee blatantly fails to respond thus signifying that s/he does not intend to respond in the interviewer-intended manner, not even if challenged in a follow-up move.

In political interviews, validity claims are not only rejected on the micro, but also on the macro domain of genre with respect to genre-and media-specifc constraints and requirements. This is examined in the following.

Challenging the appropriateness of the macro validity claim

Since political interviews are both public discourse and media event (Fetzer 2000), the appropriateness of a validity claim can be challenged with regard to the two domains. In the election-night interviews, there is not a single instance of challenges referring to the public domain. Media-specifc references and constraints are only challenged by the conservatives. Brian Mawhinney (BW) and Michael Heseltine (MH) challenge the appropriateness of the macro validity claim as follows:

(26)IR Have you spoken to John Major, are you urging him to stay on?

BM I have spoken to the prime minister er on a number of

occasions during the course of the evening and you would erm expect me to give him any advice that he might or might not seek in private not in front of the television

(27)IR And why should the electorate have sleep-walked, in your words, to disaster? MH Well those are the sort of questions we'll have to ask ourselves and, as I said, I don't myself go for the sort of pealing technique within hours of the polls closing I think these will require mature refection.... a way which is very fascinating to the media but it is not the best interest of the conservative party

In both cases, the appropriateness of a communicative act as mediated communicative action, such as giving advice in (26) and analysing an election defeat in (27), is challenged. In general, a reference to the macro validity claim's contextual constraints and requirements does not initiate a negotiation-of-validity sequence. This may be due to the fact that the type of challenge implicates a criticism of the IR, who is portrayed as having performed a request for inappropriate information.

In the short election-night interviews investigated, challenges are classifed with regard to their domains of non-acceptance, namely a validity claim's content and a validity claim's force with a negative evaluation. Furthermore, challenges are performed through the communicative strategy of opting out, which is anchored to the social world's textual system, and they are performed through the strategy of avoiding the question. However, challenges are not restricted to the local domain of discourse. There is also the strategy of challenging the macro validity claim and its contextual constraints and requirements. Here, a challenge of the media-specifc requirements signifes an inappropriate interviewer performance. In the British data, a challenge initiates a negotiation-of-validity sequence, in which the appropriateness of lexical items, pronominal references and presuppositions is negotiated. While challenges anchored to the macro domain and to the micro domain of opting out are brief, challenging the appropriateness of a validity claim's content and avoiding the question tend to initiate rather lengthy negotiation-of-validity sequences in the media event of a political interview.

In the following, communicative strategies for challenges are examined in the German data.

CHALLENGES IN THE GERMAN ELECTION-NIGHT INTERVIEWS

The German data comprise twenty short dyadic interviews (2 to 5 minutes) between professional journalists and leading political figures broadcasted on the ARD, the first public broadcasting channel. There are seven interviews with members of the conservative party, the Christian democrats and their Bavarian sister party, the Christian social union, who lost the general election in 1998. There are seven interviews with members of the social democrats and three interviews with members of the green party, who won the general election in 1998. There are two interviews with members of the socialist party and one interview with a member of the liberals. Unlike the Britain system, the German election system is based on proportional representation and on the first-past-the post system. For this reason, smaller parties stand a good chance of being a coalition partner as neither the conservatives nor the social democrats tend to have overall majorities. Adopting the same procedure as above, the focus lies on the politician's employment of communicative strategies for challenges.

Analogously to the British conservatives, the German conservatives talk about the merits of their former government rather than commenting on their defeat; and like the British labour party, the German social democrats and the greens avoid talking about their victory. In spite of the content-based similarities between the British and German data, the challenged domains of reference and the strategies employed difer signifcantly. In the German sociocultural context, the linguistic realization of challenging the appropriateness of a validity claim's content is diferent; the same is true for the communicative strategies of opting out, avoiding the question and challenging the appropriateness of the macro validity claim. Not only is there variation with regard to the strategies employed, there is also a signifcant diference in the length of contributions and sequences. In the British data, there are numerous rather lengthy negotiation-of-validity-claim sequences, while the German data do not only display less negotiation-of-validity sequences, but also briefer ones. While the British negotiation-of-validity sequences show a high frequency of verbs of cognition and other metapragmatic devices, the German negotiation-of-validity sequences display a high frequency of impersonal constructions, such as passives or the *man-muss Konstruktion* ('one-has-to construction), which attenuate the pragmatic force of a challenge by shifing responsibilities in context.

In the following, challenges of the election-night interviews are systematized with regard to their referential domains, namely challenges indexing the inappro-priateness of a validity claims content, challenges indexing the inappropriateness of a validity claim by implicitly opting out, challenges indexing the inappropriateness of a validity claim by avoiding the question and challenges indexing the inappropriateness of the macro validity claim.

Challenging the appropriateness of the validity claims content

In the following, responses to the interviewers questions about the outcome of the general election and about who is to blame for the conservatives' defeat are examined in the German interviews. In the British data, the pragmatic force of the politicians' challenges is intensifed, and challenging the appropriateness of a validity claim's content is realized quite explicitly and sometimes boosted with an explicit negative evaluation. In the German data, the challenges are realized explicitly and implicitly. The conservative Peter Hinze (PH) challenges the IR's validity claim in an implicit manner by referring to his notion of democracy thus indirectly criticizing the IR's concept. The challenge is further attenuated by the discourse marker *now.*

(28) IR Lassen Sie uns mal spekulieren. Es gibt ja noch 'ne Möglichkeit, dass es doch für Rot-Grim nicht reicht und eine GroEe Koalition ins Haus stiinde. Wären Sie bereit, da mitzumachen? *(Let us speculate for a bit. Tere is still the possibility that there are not going to be enough votes for the SPD and the greens so that there could still be a coalition between the CDU and SPD. Would you be prepared to take part in that?)* PH Also mein Demokratieverständnis ist, dass die erste Frage an den Ge-winner

geht, das sind die Sozialdemokraten, hier sich zu entscheiden, mit wem sie sprechen wollen.... *(Now my conception of democracy is that the frst question ought to be directed at the winner, that is the social democrats. And it is up to them to decide with whom they want to speak...)*

The winners, the green politician Jürgen Trittin (JT) and the social democrats Gerhard Schröder (GS), Oskar Lafontaine (OL) and Franz Müntefering (FM) challenge the IRs' validity claims without any explicit interpersonal devices. They use impersonal constructions, such as *one has to* in (29) and (30), which attenuate the claims force, to some extent:

(29)IR Eine letzte Frage mit der Bitte um 'ne kurze Antwort. Sie werden heute

Abend feiern, haben Sie gesagt,gibt's einen Fahrplan für die nächsten Tage? (One *last question. Would you answer briefy, please. As you said, you will celebrate tonight, is there a timetable for the next few days?)* GS Den gibt's, aber den muss man jetz nicht ausbreiten *(Tal exists, but one docs not have to make it explicit now...)*

(30)IR Sie haben für einen neuen Politikanfang in diesem Land geworben; sie wollten einen Politikwechsel, der sieht im Augenblick noch äufierst knapp aus, denn Rot-Grün ist noch lange nicht ausgemacht.

Oder haben sie bereits en Signal von Gerhard Schröder? *(You have courted for a new beginning in politics in this country. You wanted a change in politics, which still looks rather vulnerable at the moment, because the social democrats and the greens will have a long way to go. Or, have you already had some indication from Gerhard Schröder?)* JT Sehen Sie wir haben noch keine Gewissheit an diesem Abend. Ah man muss das alles mit der nötigen Vorsicht sagen. Wir wissen aber äh.... *(Look, we do not yet have certainty tonight. Erm one has to say all that with the necessary caution. But we know erm...)*

Another strategy of challenging the IRs' validity claims consists of the use of explicit negatives, such as *not going to* in (31) and (32), and *did not* in (31), which are frequently combined with impersonal constructions, such as *that is not going to be discussed:*

(31)IR Marion von Haaren, das ist der voraussichtliche neue Bundeskanzler.

Voraussichtlich muss man sagen, Herr Schröder, weil Sie noch gewählt werden müssen, dazu werden Sie einen Koalitionspartner brauchen. Wer wird das sein? *(Marion von Haaren, this is probably going to be the new chancellor. We have to say probably, Mr. Schröder, because you still need to be elected, and for that you will need a coalition partner. Who is it going to be?)*

GS Das werden wir nich heute Abend entscheiden. Wir kennen ja noch nicht einmal die endgültige Zusammensetzung des Bundestages und deswegen ist darüber heute nicht zu diskutieren... *(We are not going to decide that tonight. We do not yet know the fnal composition of parlia ment und for that reason that is not going to be discussed tonight...)*

IR Haben Sie mit diesem Wahlergebnis, mit diesem Vorsprung vor der Union selbst gerechnet? *(Did you yourself expect that lead over the conservatives?)*

GS Nein das habe ich nicht. Ich habe es deutlich knapper erwartet. Ich habe geahnt und gefühlt, dass wir äh wohl vorne liegen wiirden. Aber in die-ser Deutlichkeit, wie es sich jetzt ankiindigt, habe ich das Wahlergebnis nicht erwartet... *(No, I did not. I expected it to be a lot closer. I have anticipated it somehow and I have had a feeling that we might lead. But I did not expect that clear lead...)*

(32) IR... Ah nach dem derzeitigen Ergebnis geht Rot-Grim, wenn auch knapp.

HeiEt das, dass Sie dann zuerst mit den Griinen verhandeln werden, oder ist dies eine Marge, die Ihnen im Moment noch zu knapp wäre? (*... erm according to the present results a coalition between the SPD and the green party is possible, with a small majority though. Does that mean that you will negotiate with the greens frst, or is that a majority that would be too small for you at the moment?)* GS Ich habe ja schon deutlich gemacht, dass wir darüber nich heute entscheiden, das werden Oskar Lafontaine und i und ich morgen friih besprechen und dann sicher wird das auch in den in der Partei diskutiert werden... *(I have already made it clear that we are not going to decide that tonight, Oskar Lafontaine and I will discuss that tomorrow morning and surely that is going to be discussed in the party...)*

Another strategy of challenging the IRs validity claims consists of the use of inherently negative verbs, such as *wait* in (33) and (34). Since there are no explicit attenuation devices, the contributions are assigned a strong pragmatic force:

(33) IR Ja, Herr Lafontaine, Sie haben die Hochrechnung mitgesehen. Äh es wiirde für Rot-Grün mittlerweile sogar relativ komfortabel reichen. Ah kann sich die SPD da eigentlich noch leisten, was anderes zu machen als Rot-Grün? *(Yes, Mr Lafontaine, you have watched the projections with us. Erm there would be a comfortable majority for the SPD and the greens in the meantime. Erm, can the SPD actually aford to enter into another coalition?)* OL Also wir werden zunächst mal in Ruhe jetzt das wirkliche Ergebnis abwarten. Wir wissen ja auch nicht, ob die PDS im Bundestag ist oder ob sie nicht drin ist.... *(Now we will wait for the real result without any rush. We also do not know whether the PDS is going to be in parliament or not...)*

(34) IR Können Sie jetzt schon sagen, mit welcher Koalition dieses dann pas-sieren wird? Denn für Rot-Grim ist es ja noch verdammt knapp. *(Can you already say with what kind of coalition that is going to happen? Because for the SPD and the greens it is going to be dammed close?)* FM Nein das kann man noch nicht sagen da muss man abwarten... *(No, one cannot yet say that, one has to wait...)*

In the German data, there is no preference for an employment of cognitive verbs when challenging the appropriateness of a validity's content. Instead, there is a preference for explicit negatives and for impersonal constructions, which have the communicative function of boosting the pragmatic force of a challenge. Even the implicitly realized challenge in (28) does not use any markers of subjectivity. Another diference to the British data is the German preference for first-person self-references with verbs of action, through which the politician expresses determinate meaning and spells out what he or she intends to do, and what he or she does not intend to do.

With regard to intercultural communication, the language-specifc preferences are one source of potential miscommunication: the verbs of cognition and the negative contextualization devices in the British data signify that a coparantici-pant is willing to negotiate the communicative status of their validity claim, which does not seem to be the case with the communicative strategy of challenging the appropriateness of a validity claim's content in the German data. In the following, the communicative strategy of opting out is examined, which-unlike the challenges of the appropriateness of a validity's content-is performed implicitly.

Challenging a validity claim's appropriateness by implicitly opting out

In the British data, interviewees frequently opt out in an explicit manner. Or, they simply state that they do not intend to comment on a particular discourse topic any more thus closing it. In the German data, opting out is performed implicitly. In (38), the conservative Norbert Blüm (NB), opts out non-verbally by shaking his head thus signifying that he does not intend to respond in the requested manner. The implicit non-compliance is supplemented by an account, in which NB provides reasons for not responding in the requested manner. At the same time, he agrees with the IR on a very general position, namely that there exists no policy which is flawless:

(38)IR Was haben Sie falsch gemacht? *('What were your mistakes?)*

NB [kopfschütteln] Also ich bin nicht jetzt der äh Besitzer der Gedanken der Wähler. Aber richtigist, esgibtnienefehlerlose Politik.... ([shaking his head] *Now I do not erm own the electorate's thoughts. But it is correct there exists no fawless politics...)*

In (39), the chair of the social democrats, Oskar Lafontaine (OL), opts out implicitly by referring to himself in his role as the party chairman *(der Parteivorsitzende)* and his/her particular responsibilities:

(39)IR Vollkommen klar, dass Sie feiern wollen. Aber ich meine, es gibt doch

Erwartungen in der Partei, in der Bevölkerung, auch bei den Grünen. Sie haben gemeinsam, wenn auch in verschiedenen Rollen, für den Regierungswechsel gekämpf. Wie viel Mandate mehr braucht denn eine Rot-Grime Koalition, damit Sie sagen, das geht auch stabil. *(It is perfectly clear that you want to celebrate. But I mean there are expectations in the party, in the population, also with the greens. You fought together, in diferent roles, for a change in government. How many more seats would a coalition between the SPD and the greens need so that you can say that it's going to be stable?)* OL Der

Parteivorsitzende hat eine besondere Verantwortung in der Partei und er kann nicht leichtfertig herumspekulieren... *(Te chairman has got a particular responsibility within the party and he cannot speculate just like that...)*

In the German data, the communicative strategy of opting out in order to challenge the appropriateness of a validity claim is used by the winners and by the losers, which is not the case in the British data, where it is used by the losers only. In the German data, opting out is performed implicitly. It is not very frequent and therefore not the preferred strategy for performing a challenge.

In the following, the strategy of challenging the appropriateness of a validity claim by avoiding the question is investigated.

Challenging of the appropriateness of a validity claim by avoiding the question

At first sight, the communicative strategy of challenging the appropriateness of a validity claim by avoiding the question does not seem to query the appropriateness of a communicative contribution or of its constitutive validity claims. The postulated validity claim is being ratifed, but the ratifcation move is neither an acceptance nor is it a non-acceptance. With respect to the follow-up move, it becomes apparent, that the ratifcation move does not count as an acceptance because acceptances are not challenged by following-up moves. For this reason, the strategy of avoiding the question counts as a challenge-but as a two-sided challenge. On the one hand, the interviewer takes the interviewees response as a challenge, which requires another challenge. On the other hand, the interviewee takes the interviewer's challenge of their contribution as an inappropriate challenge, which does not have to be complied with. So, a negotiation-of-validity sequence with almost incompatible premises is initiated, which, for this reason, can only be controversial.

In (40) and (41), the conservatives Michael Glos (MG) and Peter Hinze (PH) employ the strategy of avoiding the question. Their responses are challenged by the IR. While MG seems to get away with responding on a rather general level referring to the voters' mentality when being asked to give reasons for the defeat of his party, PH's response in (41), in which he suggests to postpone his answer, is challenged by the IR. PH partially complies with the IR's request by making his previous implication explicit, which the IR accepts:

(40)IR.... warum hat das nicht geklappt? *(Why didn't it work out?)*

MG Es ist natürlich für uns eine Enttäuschung, dass dieser Schwung aus Bayern sich nicht ausgewirkt *(Of course it is a disappointment for us, that the support from Bavaria did not have any efect)*

IR Woran lag das Herr Glos? *(What was the reason for it Mr. Glos?)*

MG Es liegt *(It was)*

IR Am Kanzler? *(Te chancellor?)*

MG Es liegt sicher ein ganzes Stück daran, dass die Mentalität.... *(It is certainly due to some extent that the mentality...)*

(41)IR Ist das heute das Ende des Bundeskanzlers? *(Is this the end of the chancel-lor today?)*

PH Wir wollen jetzt mal den Wahlabend abwarten...*(We want to wait what else will happen on this election night)*

IR Gut also die Antwort verstehen ich... *(Good, well, the answer I understand...)*

PH Das ist n bisschen verfrüht... *(It is a bit too early)*

Compared to the British avoiding-the-question sequences, a politician's evasiveness seems to be more acceptable in the German context, where there is no real controversy and no lengthy negotiation-of-validity sequence. Most of the time, politicians seem to get away with rather general and rather vague answers when requested to provide specifc information. In the German data, the follow-up moves are restricted to two or three turns, which again may lead to intercultur-al miscommunication. For instance, if a British journalist interviews a German politician and if the British journalist employs the strategies identifed for the British context by initiating a controversial negotiation-of-validity sequence, the German politician, who expects two or maximally three follow-up moves, will consider the interviewer to be rude and prejudiced. Should a British politician be interviewed by a German interviewer employing the strategies identifed for the German context, s/he will consider the German interviewer to be rather lenient and not very professional.

In the following, challenging the appropriateness of the macro validity claim is examined.

Challenging the appropriateness of the macro validity claim

In the British data, challenging the macro validity claim's appropriateness is reflected in references to the media domain and its public status. In the German data, there is only one reference to the macro validity claim which refers to the genre-specifc requirement of the turn-taking system. Like the strategy of opting out, the reference to the turn-taking system is realized implicitly. In (42), the conservative Theo Waigel (TW) asks the IR to let him finish his turn thereby implicating that he has been interrupted:

(42) IR Theo Weigel. Herr Weigel, ein herber Verlust für die Union, auch klare Verluste für die CSU, woran hat es gelegen? *(Teo Weigel, Mr Weigel, a dramatic defeat for the christian union, also a clear defeat for the christian social union, what was the cause?)*

TW Das ist ganz klar eine Niederlage der Union. Was die CSU anbelangt, mit achtundvierzig Komma vier Prozent haben wir überproportional gut abgeschnitten. Normalerweise liegt die CSU etwa zehn Prozent iiber dem Bundesdurchschnitt CDU/CSU *(Tis is clearly a defeat of the christian union. What concerns the CSU, with 48.4% we have had a very good result. Normally the CSU is something like 10% above the federal average of the CDU/CSU)*

IR Aber es sind zwei Komma acht, Herr Weigel, *(But it is 2.8 Mr Weigel)*

TW Ja, trotzdem *(Yes, but still)*

IR unter vierundneunzig und vier Komma fiinf, unter dem Landtagswahl-ergebnis *(below 94 and 4.5 below the results of the state election)*

TW Ja kleinen Moment. Lassen Sie mich einen Satz nach dem anderen sagen. Wenn wir nun die absoluten Zahlen nehmen. Und wenn wir nun die absoluten Zahlen nehmen, dann haben wir bei einer höheren Wahlbeteiligung etwa so viel Stimmen erreicht, wiebei der Landtagswahl, aber wir konnten bei der schwierigen

Gesamtstimmung nicht noch Stimmen dazugewinnen...*(A tiny moment. Let me say one sentence afer the other. If we take the absolute fgures. And if we now take the absolute fgures, then we have reached almost as many votes as we had in the state elections, but with a higher turnout, but we could not win more votes in that difcult electoral climate...)*

There is no other instance of challenging the macro validity claim. For this reason, the communicative strategy of challenging the appropriateness of the macro validity claim is assigned a marked status as it is not the preferred mode for challenging the appropriateness of a validity claim in the context of a political interview.

With respect to intercultural communication, the strategy can be another source of in-tercultural miscommunication. Again, British politicians might use the strategy to challenge the interviewer's validity claim and signify that s/he intends to close a negotiation-of-validity sequence, while German interviewers would not interpret and contextualize the reference in the speaker-intended way.

In the German data, the most prominent strategy for performing a challenge in the context of a short dyadic political interview is challenging the appropriateness of a validity's content. While the losers prefer an indirectly realized challenge, the winners tend to challenge the interviewer's contributions in a direct manner. With respect to their linguistic realizations, there is a preference for explicit negatives and impersonal constructions, which boost the force of the challenge. Another preference lies in first-person self-references employed in the context of verbs of action, through which the politician expresses determinate meaning and spells out what action they intend to perform, and what action they do not intend to perform.

The strategy of challenging the appropriateness of a validity claim by opting out implicitly or by challenging the appropriateness of the macro validity claim are not very frequent; they are used by the winners and by the losers. The strategy of challenging the appropriateness of a validity claim by avoiding the question is more frequent but it is only used by the losers in the data examined.

CHALLENGES: AN INTERCULTURAL CONTEXT PERSPECTIVE

Intercultural communication is defned as a communicative encounter, in which participants from diferent cultural backgrounds communicate. A necessary condition for intercultural communication is the premise that the ratifed copar-ticipants do not share identical production, interpretation and contextualization strategies. The application of the functional-grammar conception of markedness introduced above allows for a diferentiation between an unmarked production, interpretation and contextualization, which is performed in accordance with a speech community's conventions, and between a marked production, interpretation and contextualization, which is produced in disaccordance with a speech community's conventions.

In natural-language communication and in social interaction the general premise holds that coparticipants expect unmarked settings and thus similar production, interpretation and contextualization strategies. As a consequence of this, any deviation is considered to be a marked instance of communicative performance and is assigned the status of something that goes beyond ordinariness and therefore is strange. Expecting similar production, interpretation and contextualization strategies in intercultural communication is especially true for those settings, in which the non-native coparticipants have a rather high linguistic competence. Because of that, native coparticipants would expect native-like production, interpretation and contextualization strategies and thus a high sociocultural competence. With a low linguistic competence, deviations in a coparticipants production, interpretation and contextualization of contributions are expected because the coparticipants' prime task lies in the production and the retrieval of factual information. Here, the deviations are accounted for with the practical-reasoning strategies of 'let it pass' or 'unless!

The defnition of intercultural communication also holds for the context of media communication, but needs further refnement with regard to the first-frame setting between direct coparticipants, such as interviewer and interviewee in the context of a political interview, and with regard to the second-frame interaction between the first-frame encounter and the second-frame audience, whose reception process difers signifcantly from the one of the first-frame coparticipants (Fetzer 2000). As a consequence of the multilayered encounter of media communication, interculture can be both a constitutive part of the first-frame encounter with co-participants of diferent cultural backgrounds, and it can be a constitutive part of the second-frame encounter, where the cultural background of the first-frame coparticipants is diferent to the cultural background of the second-frame audience. To make the context even more multilayered, there might also be diverging cultural backgrounds with diverging production, interpretation and contextualization strategies between first-frame coparticipants, second-frame coparticipants and one or more of the second-frame audience's constitutive subsets.

Due to the ongoing process of globalization and internationalization, inter-and multicultural scenarios are becoming more and more common. It has to be pointed out, however, that the complexity of international and global communication is not necessarily a source of miscommunication or of misunderstanding. Should miscommunication occur, possible perlocutionary efects have to be differentiated with respect to efects anchored to the direct first-frame coparticipants and with respect to efects anchored to the indirect second-frame audience.

The multilayered intercultural setting may account for some of the rather negative perlocutionary efects resulting from the performance of challenges in the German-British context. That is to say the German tendency to produce a challenge with a high degree of product orientation and a low degree of interpersonal orientation can, if transferred directly to the production, interpretation and contextualization of challenges in British English, have the perlocutionary efect of being perceived as unfriendly and uncooperative. This is due to the lack of the rather high degree of interpersonal orientation through which the British context communicates the possibility of initiating a process of negotiating the communicative status of a contribution.

Culture-specifc production, interpretation and contextualization strategies are of great importance if culture and interculture are seen as interactionally organized in and through the process of communication. It is at that stage, where national stereotypes are confrmed through culture-specifc production, interpretation and contextualization processes. Against this background, a German speaker talking British English will be allocated to a negative reference group and considered to be bossy, rude and narrow-minded, while a British speaker talking German while adhering to the British strategy of signalling that s/he is open for a process of negotiating the validity of a contribution is also allocated to a negative reference group and considered to be vague, unclear and uncommitting.

CONCLUSIONS

Challenges in political interviews have been investigated in the framework of a plus/minus-validity claim, where they are systematized with regard to their micro and macro contextual references. The tripartite system allows for a systematic investigation of language-and culture-specifc communicative styles for both acceptances and non-acceptances. A challenge is defned as a non acceptance and thus as a minus-validity claim. Depending on the non-accepted domains of validity, communicative strategies are identifed for the German cultural context and for the British cultural context. Culture and interculture are conceived of as interactionally organized phenomena, and communicative strategies are seen as carriers of cultural information. The British and German short election-night interviews of the general elections have almost identical contents: the losers do not want to give reasons for their failure and talk about the merits of former governments instead, and the winners do not want to talk about a victory, which has not yet been assigned an ofcial status. The contents are, however, formulated diferently and German culture and British culture are done diferently by the coparticipants. The culture-specifc ways of expressing a challenge in the political interviews examined confrm the results obtained for unmarked everyday talk: first, the British sociocultural context makes more references to both interpersonal and information domains. Compared to the German sociocultural context, the interpersonal domain is stressed. Second, the British sociocultural context prefers a process-oriented setting, where the institutional identities of interviewer and interviewee are interactionally organized in a more dynamic manner and with more interpersonal needs. The German sociocultural context prefers a product-oriented setting, where the identities are interactionally organized in a less dynamic manner with less interpersonal needs.

The diverging communicative styles have predictable consequences for in-tercultural communication and for intercultural media communication, where British coparticipants speaking German in accordance with the British style for performing a challenge are perceived as diplomatically unclear by a German audience while German coparticipants speaking British English in accordance with the German style for performing a challenge are perceived as stif.

7

Challenge and Support in Al-Jazeera and on Israeli Television

This paper explores patterns of interviewers' challenge and support in TV news interviews conducted by two interviewers-Faysal al-Qasem in Arabic (on Al-Jazeera) and Ben Kaspit in Hebrew (Israel Television, Channel 1), focusing on topic introduction in the openings, explicit comments and elaborative reformulations in triadic interviews with two interviewees.

Based on a micro-analysis and on meta-comments, we argue that Faysal al-Qasem frames the interview from the outset as unbalanced, and the interviewer's identifcation with one of the interviewees at the expense of the other is further reinforced by explicit comments, as well as by elaborative reformulations. In the Hebrew part of the corpus, the opening is mostly informative and neutral, expressions of the interviewer's stance are qualifed as deviations and do not necessarily converge with those of one of the interviewees, and reformulations are symmetrically distributed between the interviewees. These diferences are interpreted in terms of challenge and support.

TE CONCEPTUAL FRAMEWORK

(1) ("Between the Headlines", Israeli Television, Channel 1, December 19th 2002)

162 Lapid You promised me equal time division, and you let him make speeches:

* We wish to thank Dr. Mordechai Kedar and Mr. Richard

Atrakchi for their important input about Al-Jazeera and the socio-political context; the anonymous referees, for their valuable contribution to the analysis; Dr. Miriam Shlesinger, for her enriching stylistic comments; and Dr. Hannah Amit-Kochavi, for her expert advice on transcription conventions in Arabic.

198 Elda Weizman, Irit Levi and Isaac Schneebaum

(2) ("The Opposite Direction", Al-Jazeera, July 2nd 2002)

228Harb: [...] at first, you invent facts and then you believe them and bring guests to confrm

229 Ier: Eh

230Harb: the versi ›n you wish to promote, and you [dare] speak about propaganda through media.

This paper explores patterns of interviewers' challenge and support in news interviews in Arabic and in Hebrew. Specifcally, it focuses on triadic interviews with two interviewees each, and examines whether the examined patterns are distributed symmetrically between interviewees.

In line with previous discussions (e.g. Weizman 1997, 1998, 1999, 2003, 2006a), our notion of challenge is anchored in Labov and Fanshel's (1977) defnition, suggested in the context of therapeutic discourse:

When a person takes an action implying that another person did not perform some of these role obligations, he is necessarily heard as criticizing that other person's competence in that role. This applies to problems of initiating role performance, performing the role correctly, or terminating it appropriately. (ibid.: 95)

This view is very much inspired by Gofman's notion of roles, and mostly by the emphasis on the multiplicity of roles fulflled by each person "in order to be seen as performing his normal role in society with full competence" (ibid: 95). As far as verbal behavior is concerned, Labov and Fanshel (ibid.: 96) go on to say: "If A asserts that B has not performed obligations in role R, then A is heard as challenging B's competence in R". More specifcally,

"If A asserts a proposition that is supported by As status, and B questions the proposition, then B is heard as challenging the competence of A in that status" (ibid.: 97). Hence, "A challenge is a speech act that asserts or implies a state of affairs that, if true, would weaken a person's claim to be competent in filling the role associated with a valued status", (ibid.: 97)

Elaborating on this notion, challenge is conceived of here as *any verbal behavior which might be interpreted as saying or implying that the addressee has not fulflled his or her role appropriately, or has failed to fulfll any component thereof* A basic distinction is made between interactional and social roles.[1] Interviewees' *interactional role* consists, for example, in the obligation to answer properly, to provide information and express opinions, as well as in their right to be given the chance to do as required. Interviewees' *social roles* vary, and their rights and obligations depend on the social roles which are made relevant (Sacks 1995 [1979]; Schegloff 1991, 1992) in the interview, by virtue of which they were invited to the studio (politicians, experts, media figures, ordinary people). If the interviewees are introduced as politicians, their opinions and convictions are important components of their social role.

Interviewees may be challenged either at the interactional level, or at the level of their social role, or at both. Accordingly, interviewees are *interactionally challenged* if the interviewer says or implies that they have not fulflled their interactional obligations properly, and they are *socially challenged* if their opinions are undermined (Weizman 2006a, b).

As has been previously argued, challenge potential may be embedded in the semantic meanings of the utterance, or in such discourse patterns as irony (Weizman 2001), reciprocity (Weizman 2003), terms of address (Weizman 2006b) and others, some of which might be culture-specifc. Thus, for example, when an interviewee responds to an interviewer's question by saying "Dan, as I see it this is an insignifcant question, and in a week from now we won't remember having discussed it" (Erev Xadash [=New Evening], Israeli Television Channel 1, 8.12.91), his response might plausibly be interpreted as challenging the latter's fulfllment of his interactional obligation to restrict the agenda to signifcant issues. This interpretation relies first and foremost on elements of the utterance meaning, such as the criticism in "this is an insignifcant question"; but it is further anchored in the use of an address term (the interviewer's name, "Dan"), which has been shown to carry challenge potential in Hebrew (Weizman 2006b). In this paper, it will be argued that in multiple-interviewee shows, an interviewee may also be challenged by an asymmetrical attitude of the interviewer. Thus, if the interviewees hold conficting views, and if the interviewer identifes with one of them and systematically disagrees with the other, he maybe perceived as challenging the latter, far beyond the expected 'playing the devil's advocate'. We will further analyze the implications to asymmetry to the positioning of the participants in the interview.

In a previous study of two sequential short interviews on Israeli television, conducted by a single interviewer with two interviewees holding opposing views on a highly emotional topic, it was shown that the host challenged each interviewee in turn, and that in each case he used the same challenge strategies. A symmetry between interviewees has been obtained (Weizman 1999). Judging by the two extracts quoted at the opening of the paper, no such symmetry is maintained in the interviews they are taken from: in the first, the interviewee accuses the interviewer of political bias; and in the second, the interviewer is blamed for establishing interactional asymmetry between interviewees. What are the discourse patterns which trigger these protests? Is there a variation in degree and type of asymmetry established by the interviewers examined here? These are the questions this paper proposes to answer, based on a micro-analysis of discourse styles of two interviewers: Faysal al-Qasem on Al-Jazeera, and Ben Kaspit on Israeli Television. A previous analysis of the same corpus explored the interviewers' meta-pragmatics comments on the management of the interview (turn-taking and agenda) and on the violation of Gricean maxims (Levi et al. 2006). In line with the overall purpose of this paper, we will explore other interviewers' patterns: topic introduction in the openings (Section 3), explicit comments (Section 4) and elaborative reformulations (Section 5) in the course of the interviews.[2] We will argue that through the use of these patterns, Faysal al-Qasem consistently favors one of the interviewees. Ben Kaspit, on the other hand, marks expressions of asymmetrical preferences as interactional deviations, makes attempts to compensate for them, and when he does take a stand on a political issue, it difers from that of either interviewee. This diference will be accounted for in terms of positioning. "The act of positioning [...] refers to the assignment of fluid 'parts' or 'roles' to speakers in the discursive construction of personal stories that make a person's actions intelligible and relatively determinate as social acts" (Harré & Langenhove 1999:17). Positioning is dynamic, in that it changes in and through discourse; it afects the meaning and the illocutionary value assigned to a given utterance; it is determined in relation to other participants in the discursive event; and, most important for our purpose, a speaker can self-position him/herself, or be positioned by the other discourse participants (ibid.). Based on the proposed comparison, we will suggest that through his asymmetrical attitude, Faysal al-Qasem positions himself as the author of some of the political convictions he expresses. Ben Kaspit, on the other hand, positions himself as fulflling the traditional interviewer's role of managing the interview.

This interpretation is supported by the interviewees' meta-comments on the interviewers' attitudes, discussed in Section 6. Note that while the analytic approach is of crucial methodological and conceptual importance, it is undoubtedly the overall combination of patterns that determines the nature of interviewers' positioning (Section 7).

CONTEXT AND METHODOLOGY

The analysis draws on a corpus of evening news interviews in Al-Jazeera, broadcast from Qatar, and on Israeli Television, Channel 1. The programs in question are Al-Ittijah al-Mu'aakis (literally "The Opposite Direction"), and "Bein Hako-tarot" (literally "Between the Headlines"), each having one interviewer and two interviewees, representing opposing political views. The two hosts are, respectively, Faysal al-Qasem and Ben Kaspit. The corpus consists of 4 interviews in each language, i.e. 3408 turns in Arabic, and 1157 turns in Hebrew.

The television channel Al-Jazeera is the first Arabic-speaking one to broadcast news and political shows all day long (Usembassy accessed 2003). Broadcasting from Doha, capital of Qatar, with ofces all over the world, it is owned by the royal family of Qatar (Andreus 2003; Fandy 2002), and is financed mostly by the Qatar government (approx. 50 million dollars a year) (Barel 2003) as well as by commercials. However, the Emir of Qatar decided recently to turn the station into a self-sustaining private one (Hammad 2003). The channels slogan is "Ar-Ray war-Ray al-Aaxar", literally: "an opinion and the opposing one". Channel One of the Israel Broadcast Authority (henceforth IBA or Israeli Television) is a public license-fee channel, partly financed by sponsorship ads. In addition to news and current events, it carries entertainment shows, movies, documentaries etc. Its general director is appointed by the Prime Minister and the Minister of Communications (Shalita & Meydan 2003).

The programs discussed here are weekly evening shows. For six consecutive years, Faysal al-Qasem has been awarded the title "the best host in the Arabic world" by the Association of Arab journalists (As-Safeer, January 28, 2003). Ben Kaspit is also a journalist in the Israeli daily Maariv. "The Opposite Direction" always has two interviewees; "Between the Headlines" has either one or two, but the study compares only 2-interviewee shows. The comparability of both programs has been assessed by four experts on Middle East Media. Similarities were pointed out in terms of the combinations between discussion and entertainment, the structure of the program, and the degree of explicitness and aggressiveness of the interviewers. The present discussion is based on the following:

(1)"The Opposite Direction", Al-Jazeera, June 18th 2002. (999 turns)

Topic: The Palestinians in the lands of dispersion.

Interviewees: Dr. Ahmad 'Uwaydi al-Abaadi, a former Jordanian Parliament member, and Dr. 'Ali Badwaan, member of the Central Committee of the Democratic Front for the Liberation of Palestine.

(2)"The Opposite Direction", Al-Jazeera, July 2nd 2002. (724 turns)

Topic: American Media.

Interviewees: Dr. 'Abd al-Hay at-Tameemi, a media specialist from Thames Valley University in London, and Dr. Muwafeq Harb, a specialist on U.S. afairs, and the Director of the American radio station Ash-Sharq al-Awsat, literally: "The Middle East".

(3)"The Opposite Direction", Al-Jazeera, December 31st 2002. (1345 turns) Topic: The vote of Israeli Arab citizens in the general elections in Israel. Interviewees: Saleh Tareef, an Arab parliament member of the Israeli Labor party, and Abd al-Bari Atwan, Editor-in-Chief of the Arabic newspaper Al-Quds al-Arabi.

(4)"The Opposite Direction", Al-Jazeera, June 17th 2003. (340 turns) Topic: Palestinian Resistance Movements.

Interviewees: Muhammad Nazzaal, a member of the political bureau of Hammas movement and Ahmad Subh, the Palestinian Deputy Minister of Information.

(5) "Between the Headlines", Israeli Television, Channel 1, December 19th 2002.

(314 turns)

The subject: Religious and secular parties in Israel.

Interviewees: Eli Yishay, the leader of the religious "Shas" party and Yosef

(Tomi) Lapid, Head of the central anti-religious "Shinuy" party.

(6) "Between the Headlines", Israeli Television, Channel 1, December 26th 2002.

(160 turns)

Topic: The transfer of the Palestinians and political corruption. Interviewees: Yossi Sarid, Head of the extreme lef-wing Merets party and Avigdor Liberman, Head of the extreme right-wing party "Haixud Haleumi-Israel Beitenu".

(7) "Between the Headlines", Israeli Television, Channel 1, February 20th 2003.

(496 turns)

Topic: National Unity Government in Israel.

Interviewees: Minister Tzipi Livni of the right-wing Likud party and Member of Parliament Chaim Ramon from the lef-wing Labor party.

(8)"Between the Headlines", Israeli Television, Channel 1, May 29th 2003. (186 turns)

Topic: The ideology of Israeli Prime Minister Ariel Sharon. Interviewees: Eyal Megged, a writer and Israel Har'el, a journalist.

The micro-analysis is based on the original texts in Arabic and in Hebrew, but the extracts discussed in this paper have been translated into English, for the sake of the presentation, Note that the gloss has been intended to convey the style of the source text, sometimes at the expense of acceptability in English.

3. Topic introduction in interview openings

Openings are usually intended to defne the agenda of the interview, to frame it as newsworthy and to enhance the status of its participants (Blum Kulka 1983; Clayman 1991), and they usually include a statement of topic, background information and a lead-in to the interview (Clayman & Heritage 2002). This, indeed is the case in example (3) from the IBA Hebrew corpus:

(3)[3] ("Between the Headlines", Israeli Television, Channel 1, February 20th 2003)

Ier: Hello and good evening to you, so tomorrow it will probably happen Amram Mitsna will sit again face to face with Ariel Sharon, in Tel Aviv, at noon, a third meeting and probably a decisive one, on the agenda, a unity government-yes or no, hello Member of Parliament Chaim Ramon, good evening minister Tsipi Livni.

Variations may result from editorial considerations or refect the personal preferences of the interviewee. Consider the following opening:

(4) ("Between the Headlines", Israeli Television, Channel 1, December 26th 2002)

Ier: It is time to say good evening to the two of you, Member of Parliament Yossi Sarid eh, head of "Merets" hello, and Member of Parliament Avigdor Liberman aah, the le-leader of "Haixud Haleumi

3. In the transcribed interviews, the punctuation stands for transcription signs, as follows:

, = a brief pause, the number of commas represents the length of the pause

. = falling intonation

? = rising intonation

(.) (?) = mixed intonation, with a tendency towards a falling or a rising intonation, respectively

{} = overlap of two utterances

word = stress

word = increased volume

wo::rd = syllable lengthening

= at turn end and next turn opening-no intervening pause between the two

[laughs] = comments on paralinguistic features

In the transcribed Arabic words,

'= pharyngal vowel

aa, ee = phonemic lengthening

204 Elda Weizman, Irit Levi and Isaac Schneebaum

->-Israel Beitenu", good evening, you were both, eh, prettier when you

were younger, that we've just seen on the short video clip".

Here, the topic is alluded to solely through reference to a previously shown video clip. A humoristic comment ("you were both, eh, prettier when you were younger") probably purports to establish solidarity between the participants (Brown & Levinson 1987) and ease potential tension, and seems to be in line with the use of other solidarity markers later in the interview (note the use of slang in extracts 9,10 below). The concise, essentially informative pattern revealed in ex. (3) has been found to be the norm (in 99.4% of the openings) in a 24-hour corpus of short dyadic news interviews on Israeli television (Weizman 2006b).

The openings in the Al-Jazeera interviews are diferent in three respects: they are relatively long, they follow the formulaic pattern 'A but B', whereby A and B present the pros and cons of the topic in question, and, most important for our purpose, they convey the hosts stance, which converges with that of one of the interviewees, and diverges from that of the other. Example (5) is a case in point. On the agenda-the credibility of the American mass media, mostly when they report on events within the Moslem context:

(5) ("The Opposite Direction", Al-Jazeera, July 2nd 2002. With Dr. Abd al-Hay at-Tameemi, a media specialist from Thames Valley University in London, and Dr. Muwafeq Harb, specialist on U.S. afairs, and the Director of the American radio station Ash-Sharq al-Awsat)

Ier: In the USA there is a liars' club, and each year one American wins the title 'The Most Famous Liar'. Last year, however, and in the current one, no American won it, not because ordinary Americans gave up lying but because this title has become a part of the American propaganda mechanism, as one of the satirists says, and the American media and political circles have proven that they are worthy of the title 'The Most Famous Liar', for the many manipulations and nonsense that they have given the world, starting with Muhammad Ataa's passport inside the ruins of the world trade center through the Anthrax panic and finally blaming a simple person of planning the production of a radioactive bomb.

Until when will the USA underestimate the world's intelligence? Does it really believe the world is that stupid, to believe the panorama of its lies, that wouldn't even fool children? Asked one writer. Why did American media become a means of deception, distortion of facts and fright, in a way that logic would not accept? Why does the USA try to arouse the world through the lie of fear and anxiety of an unknown amorphous enemy, and strive to make the world stupid? Why does Washington keep trying to spread constant panic, and whenever the level of anxiety decreases, it would invent a dramatic story to evoke fear once more? Was it not totally obvious that behind these stories are purposes from hell?

However, what are the proofs of those who doubt American reports? Why are there people who laugh at the American media only because they disagree with its policy? Could it be that the Arabic non-recognition and revolt are nothing but an Arabic-Islamic means to revenge the USA? Why do we not say, that these constant American alertness and fear of terrorism are a proof of their strong sense of responsibility [and commitment] to protect their citizens' life and the worlds security? Is it not of a great injustice to accuse American politics and media of such faults?

This opening has three parts. In the first one, the host tells his audience a short, amusing anecdote about a "liars' club" in the U.S., and in the others he addresses the main issue: the question whether American media are reliable. On the face of it, the second and the third paragraphs may be considered as balanced. Each section is formulated as a series of rhetorical questions, typically characterised by "the addresser's commitment to the answer implied by the question, which is meant to induce the addressee's recognition and acceptance of the message contained in this implicit answer" (Hie 1995:73, and see also Hie 1999). The answers are implied via the background assumptions (Kiefer 1980)[4] which, in turn, support respectively a negative answer to this central question (in the second paragraph) and a positive one (in the third). In the second paragraph, for example, the WH-question "Why did American media become a means of deception, distortion of facts and fright, in a way that logic would not accept?" queries the reasons for the deceptive attitude of American media, while at the same time conveying the background assumption that American media have become a means of deception, distortion of facts and fright'; and the question "Why does Washington keep trying to spread constant panic[...]?" conveys the background assumption

Amongst the vast literature on the presupposition and assumptions embedded in questions, we have chosen to rely on Kiefer's (1980:101) defnition of "background assumptions", as follows:

"Let *p* be a proposition, ? the question operator (which forms yes-no questions out of *p's)* and F that part of *p* that is focused. By *background assumption* of *?p* we shall understand the proposition *p'* which we get by replacing F in *p* by the corresponding Pro-element. By 'corresponding Pro-element' I mean 'somebody' or 'someone' for persons, 'something' for objects, 'some time' for time, 'somewhere' for place, etc." In this account, when asking 'who is leaving?' the speaker normally assumes that the proposition 'somebody is leaving tomorrow' is true. that 'Washington keeps trying to spread constant panic. In addition, the negative question "Was it not totally obvious that behind these stories are purposes from hell?" which closes the same paragraph, is conducive to a positive answer (e.g. Bolinger 1957),[5] i.e. 'It is totally obvious that behind these stories are purposes from hell'. Thus, the answers implied by these questions support the view of the US as deceptive and manipulative. The third paragraph, on the other hand, raises the possibility that this criticism is politically biased. The WH-question "Why are there people who laugh at the American media only because they disagree with its policy?" conveys the background assumption that such bias does exist, and the negative question "Is it not of a great injustice to accuse American politics and media of such faults?" is conducive to a positive answer. Both questions, then, support the view of the U.S. as an innocent victim of prejudice.

This balance, however, is only apparent. First, the background assumptions implied by the questions in the second paragraph seem to be more pronounced than those in the third, due to the use of more emotionally loaded expressions such as "distortion of facts", "the lie of fear and anxiety", "strive to make the world stupid" and "purposes from hell". More important, it is the second paragraph which further elaborates on the claim made in the first: "[...] the American media and political circles have proven that they are worthy of the title 'The Most Famous Liar', for the many manipulations and nonsense that they have given the world". In this statement, the use of "have proven" further suggests that the interviewer's subjective evaluations are in fact widely recognised, indisputable facts. Note that some of the accusations directed at the Americans are formulated as given information, in the form of grammatical subordination (e.g. "because ["the Most famous Liar"] has become a part of the American propaganda mechanism" and "not because ordinary Americans gave up lying"), and are thus less vulnerable to refutation. The jocular tone further drives home the host's criticism, establishing an in-group solidarity (Brown & Levinson 1987) between him and the audience. The close co-textual relations between the two first paragraphs undermine any apparent symmetry in the opening, and gives more weight to the implied accusations directed at the American media.

The opening in (6) has a similar structure.[6] The interview addresses the issue of the elections for the Israel Parliament, and, more precisely, questions the legitimacy of the adherence of the Arabs citizens of Israel to the Labor party. In the background-a coalition of the Labor party with the right-wing Likud party in the last unity government led by Likud Chair, Prime Minister Ariel Sharon, as well as the election of Amram Mitsna, previously a General in the Israel Defense Force and the Mayor of Haifa, as new Chair of the Labor party. As is always the case, the opening is divided into three parts, which detail some of the pros and cons of the Arab vote. As will be shown later, this symmetry is only *prima facie.*

Lhe opening paragraph consists of a series of rhetorical, WH- and negative questions. Consider the following extract from the opening paragraph:

(6)("The Opposite Direction", Al-Jazeera, December 31st 2002. With Saleh

Tareef, an Arab parliament member of the Israeli Labor party, and Abd al-

Bari Atwan, Editor-in-Chief of the Arabic newspaper Al-Quds al-Arabi)

Ier: [...] How are we to bet on the Israeli lef, in the coming elections,

while it turned out, to be, a caricature of the Likud party, or rather its tail? [...] How are we going to bet on Mitsna now, as if his party left Sharon's party, for the sake of peace,, Do those who applaud the Labor party, not know, that it left the coalition only because of the budget? And, doesn't the Israeli left itself, incline to the right, in a shocking way? Has Israel not turned more fascist?

Here, a series of WH-questions convey through subordinate clauses *background assumptions* which favor a complete rejection of the Labor Party. Thus, the question "How are we to bet on the Israeli lef, in the coming elections, while it turned out, to be, a caricature of the Likud party, or rather its tail?" conveys the speaker's criticism of the party's weakness, and the question "How are we going to bet on Mitsna now, as if his party left Sharon's party, for the sake of peace" suggests that Mitsna's Labor Party is not committed to peace. The following negative question further drives this point home, being conducive to a positive answer pointing to the greediness of the party ("Do those who applaud the Labor party, not know, that it left the coalition only because of the budget?"), and the two last negative questions are conducive to the claim that Israel in general, including the political lef, has turned more fascist.

In the second part of the same opening, some of the pros are brought up, mostly through conducive negative questions of the type presented in (7):

(7)("The Opposite Direction", Al-Jazeera, December 31st 2002)

Ier: Didn't Mitsna show an exceptional experience of coexistence of Arabs and Jews while he was Mayor of Haifa? Does the new leader of the Labor party, not use the slogan, that there is no military solution, for the confict with the Palestinians, and emphasize that negotiations should go on, from where they stopped? [...] asks Nawfal. Another Palestinian journalist thinks that the winning of the Labor party should, lead towards a full retreat from the Gaza strip, and the liberation of millions of Palestinians[...]

This apparent symmetry is compromised, however, by the diference in footing (Gofman 1981) between the two first parts: in the first paragraph, the questions are raised by the host himself; in the second, all of them are ascribed to a third party through voicing (Heritage & Greatbatch 2002; Lauerbach 2006). Thus, the two questions in (7) are attributed to 'Arafat's counselor Mamdooh Nawfal, and the last statement is attributed to an unidentifed journalist (no name is mentioned). As a result, in terms of Gofman's (1981) distinction, the interviewer is positioned here as the *author* of the implied cons, and a mere *animator* of the pros. This positioning is further reinforced by the third part of the opening, which consists of a single question:

(8) ("The Opposite Direction", Al-Jazeera, December 31st 2002)

Ier: Why have Palestinians got to the point that they consider Mitsna, as trustworthy, although, he threatened a few days ago, to break their head?

This WH-question, which marks the shift from the opening episode to the interview itself, queries the reason for the background assumption that Palestinians unjustly trust the Chair of the Labor Party, thus supporting the interviewer's objection to Mitsna's candidacy.

In the two interviews discussed so far, an asymmetrical introduction of two conficting stances and the host's subtly marked preference for one of them frame the interview as an unbalanced event whereby the interviewer establishes a kind of "coalition" with one of the interviewees, and positions the other as "less preferred" By so doing, he supports the former and challenges the latter, who is held from the outset accountable for views that are unacceptable to the two other parties.

As we saw, no such framing is manifest in the short, reformulated openings of the IBA interviews. It remains to be seen whether this diference has repercussions for the body of the interview.

EXPLICIT EXPRESSION OF INTERVIEWER'S STANCE

In two of the four interviews in Al-Jazeera, the position conveyed in the opening is further confrmed explicitly in the body of the interview. Let us pursue our analysis of program 3. As demonstrated earlier, the host has conveyed some of his misgivings about the support of the Arabs citizens of Israel for the Labor Party in the first part and in the closing utterance of opening.

Now he addresses an explicit criticism of the Labor candidate for Prime Minister, Amram Mitsna, at the interviewee Saleh Tarif, Member of Parliament of the Israeli Labor party, former Deputy Minister of the Interior and Minister without Portfolio, the first Druze Minister in the Israel government.

(9) ("The Opposite Direction", Al-Jazeera, December 31st 2002)

52Tareef: When he was the commander [...] during the first Intifada in the days of the Lebanon war, he was the only one of the superior commanders in the Israeli army, and he [=who] addressed, and met, with Begin, and refused to go on, and said, I'll resign, and will not agree that such a war will go on, this was his position towards the Intifada, and he resigned from the army, this is Mitsna

53 Ier: Eh

54 Tareef: Eh, {the question is}

55 'Atwan {But he}

56Ier:->-{Just a minute} Mr. Saleh Tareef, what Intifada, the first Intifada,

Mitzna you know, he is responsible for the destruction,, of tens, hundreds of {Palestinian houses}

57 Tareef: he:y brother, e:h

58 Ier:->-And for breaking the bones, of thousands of Palestinians,, I mean he he boasts of it now

59 Tareef: No, {no, he did not-he doesn't boast}

In (52), the interviewee brings to the fore Mitsna's active opposition to the Lebanon war while he served as an ofcer in the army, in an attempt to build a favorable image for him in the eyes of his host. The latter, in turn, is not convinced, and accentuates Mitsna's involvement in the military activities conducted by Israel against Palestinian during the first armed Intifada (56, 58).

The objections to Mitsna's candidacy are further corroborated by the use of highly emotional words such as "destruction of house" (tadmeer al-buyoot), (56) and "breaking bones" (takseer al-'izaam) (58), and through the ironic use of "glorious" (taleed) in the phrase "his glorious, military past and Palestinians' bone breaking" (62). Since this defance is anchored in Mitsna's alleged aggressive activities against Palestinian Arabs, the interviewer thus challenges not only the interviewee's political stance as a member of Mitsna's party, but also the very essence of the latter's solidarity with his Arab brothers, namely-with the audience.

Later on in the same interview, the interviewer criticizes the Israeli Arabs who vote for the Labor party, by qualifying as "facts" (haq'aiq) his controversial evaluations concerning the reasons for their vote (i.e. the infuence of "fundamental

right-wing streams of thought and religion"), and then condemning the voters for ignoring them. He further qualifes their political convictions as "a reproduced cliche" (fkra mubtadhala), thus suggesting that they lack reasoned judgment:

(10)("The Opposite Direction", Al-Jazeera, December 31st 2002)

840 Ier: [33 words omitted] and it seems like the situation of the Labor party, and these groups, has been negatively infuenced in Israel,, by the enormous rise, of fundamentalist right-wing

streams of thought and religion,, also in the USA,, right? The question,, which one of the two is the origin and which is the echo is arguable,,[...] We say that some of the Arabs avoid, or ignore,,

->-these facts,, and this is what explains,, why they reproduce, the

->-cliché, that it is obligatory to help the camp of Israeli Labor party, and the groups close to it,, so that they win,, the coming, elections

Obviously, the interviewer thus challenges Tareef s public role as MP of this very party, whose supporters are so severely criticized. This judgmental attitude is not counterbalanced by a similar approach to the second interviewee. It is therefore not conceived of as "playing the devil's advocate" (Clayman & Heritage 2002:136-138). Rather, it further enhances the interviewer's bias implied in the opening.

Expressions of the interviewer's attitude have also been found in the IBA interviews. They mostly difer from the previous ones in two respects: they are explicitly marked by the host as deviations, and they do not necessarily side with either of the interviewees.

The following extract figures in an interview which addresses the issue of the establishment of a unity government under the leadership of Prime Minister Sharon. In (11) below, the interviewer expresses his enthusiastic support of such a government:

(11)("Between the Headlines", Israeli Television, Channel 1, February 20th 2003.

With Minister Tzipi Livni of the right-wing Likud party and Member of Parliament Chaim Ramon from the lef-wing Labor party)

269 Ier: to go to this government, I call it a historic government, I am not ashamed here to be now in the kind of a situation not only of an interviewer but also of a Zionist patriot, this is a historical government we have never had.

This stance, however, is explicitly marked by the host as a violation of his discursive role ("I am not ashamed here to be now in the kind of a situation not only of an interviewer"). To justify it, he positions himself in a widely accepted national script ("a

Zionist patriot"), and alludes to the legitimacy of its co-existence with his interactional obligations ("not only of an interviewer but also of a Zionist patriot"). Of considerable importance for our discussion is the fact that by expressing his opinion, the host does not compromise the symmetry between the interviewees, since neither of them is in favor of the kind of unity he so enthusiastically opts for: Likud Minister Tsipi Livni supports unity with the religious parties, Labor MP Chaim Ramon refuses to have the Labor join a unity government, and the interviewer envisages an intermediate solution, i.e. a unity government with the Labor party and without the religious parties. The interviewer seems to be well aware of his interviewees' reservations, and enthusiastically proceeds to persuade them:

(12)("Between the Headlines", Israeli Television, Channel 1, February 20th 2003)

74 Ier: If Ariel Sharon proposes a government,,,Labor,,Likud,,Shinuy

,, Mafdal maybe,, you'd agree with me, that this is, a government, unprecedented in the history of Israel, you'd agree with me,,that this is not the government you come from,, this is a difer ent government, you go to,,,could you,, let yourseif,,say,no,,,and leave the country,,with a natural Sharon government, Shas, Agudat Israel, Ixud leumi, Mafdal, whichnlet us say, according to evaluations will not ensure even the American guarantees

Other manifestations of the host's high involvement in the same interview are distributed evenly between interviewees. In (13), for example, when Likud Minister Livni criticizes her fellow-interviewee, MP Ramon of the Labor party, for his unwillingness to join a unity government run by the Likud (177, 179), the interviewer responds by reformulating and justifying Ramon's reservation (180). In (14), on the other hand, the host explicitly rejects Ramon's stance:

(13)("Between the Headlines", Israeli Television, Channel 1, February 20th 2003)

177Livni: [41 words omitted] As a matter of fact what does he say, he says I don't believe you

178 Ier: Correct

179 Livni: In other words, {the thing, just a minute,excuse me,,,in these two and a halt years}

180 Ier:{But he has a case, we have had two and a half or three years, eh, believing}

181 Livni: there were some people of the {Labor}

182 Ier:[to Ramon]:->- {I am working for you}

181 212 Elda Weizman, Irit Levi and Isaac Schneebaum

(14)("Between the Headlines", Israeli Television, Channel 1, February 20th 2003)

408 Ier: This is the government which Chaim Ramon for some reason,,, and I think he is wrong, {does not want to join,, this is a secular Unity government [...]}

Note, that in (13), the host jokingly marks his own involvement as a deviation ("I am working for you", addressed to Ramon, turn 182). By so doing he excludes the possibility of being ascribed the position he adopts, and thus reafrms his discursive position as "playing the devils advocate"

Symmetry seems to be also preserved, to an extent, in an interview confronting Members of Parliament Avigdor Liberman, of the right-wing party Haixud Haleumi, and Yossi Sarid of the left wing party Merets. Here, each of the interviewees is being challenged by personal judgments pertaining to his behavior in the public arena: Liberman is accused of corruption (ex. 15), and Sarid-of excessive centralism (16):

(15)("Between the Headlines", Israeli Television, Channel 1, December 26th 2002)

64 Ier (to Liberman): [6 words omitted] Now to an issue which has both ered he:re for quite some time very many people the corruption in the Likud Avigdor Liberman as a matter of fact...you evaded it at the last minute since it all started with you, the author Of this method, of[...]is our Ivette Liberman, who is now making a bundle

(16)("Between the Headlines", Israeli Television, Channel 1, December 26th 2002)

99Ier (to Sarid): But the alternative of Merets, is a one-person rule, of Yossi Sarid}

100 Sarid: E:h,· corruption,,,corruption,E::h}

101 Ier: Who, everyone says is a dictator, no one challenges his position, getting votes is as easy as pie for you [...]

Indeed, Sarid notices the parallelism: faced with the host's criticism, he ironically echoes[7] the words previously addressed at his fellow interviewee: "E:h, corruption,,, corruption, e:h," 100).

In both cases, the challenge is somewhat attenuated through the establishment of solidarity by the use of slang (Brown & Levinson 1987): "making a bundle", Hebrew "gozer kuponim", in 14, and "as easy as a pie", Hebrew "lokeax bahalixa", in

7. For a discussion of ironic mentions in news interviews following Sperber and Wilson (1981), Wilson and Sperber (1992), see Weizman (2001).

15. Still, this is one more place where symmetry seems to be compromised: the criticism addressed at Liberman is intensifed by the ironic pretense (Clark & Gerrig 1984) conveyed by "our Ivette Liberman", as well as by the estrangement embedded in calling the interviewee by his non-Hebrew name (Ivette), which he had made a point of replacing by a Hebrew one (Avigdor). In addition, the symmetry is broken by the following comment, whereby the host speaks with Sarid about Liberman in the third person, thus establishing a kind of "coalition" between himself and the former, against the latter:

(17) ("Between the Headlines", Israeli Television, Channel 1, December 26th 2002)

138Ier: Liberman the man, what do you think about him, not the politician

139 Sarid: I don't know him so well, but I guess, tha:t his intentions are good, the problem is no:t,

140 Ier: You showed me here some papers, in which it was written that he was a hooligan

141Sarid: you know,, no no, look, what I:s written in here is that [...]

Note, that unlike the manifestations of political bias in the discourse of Faysal al-Qasem, here the interviewee reframes the episode as pertaining to the personal, rather than the political level ("what do you think about him, not the politician", turn 138), a shift willingly taken up by Sarid ("I don't know him so well"). By so doing, the asymmetry is collaboratively keyed (Gofman 1974) as relatively non-serious.

ELABORATIVE REFORMULATIONS

Reformulations are conceived of here as "[the procedure] by which speakers double back on their [...] interlocutor's speech to change or modify their words, thus producing a new (reworded) version that is ofered as a more satisfactory one" (Ciapuscio 2003:211, following Gülich & Kotschi 1995). More precisely, in our corpus it is the interviewer who reformulates the previous interviewee's talk In a conversational-analyst framework, Heritage and Watson (1979, 1980) observe that reformulations manifest the following properties: preservation, deletion and transformation. Any discussion of these attributes is related to such complex notions as 'sameness' and 'similarity' (Sovran 1992; Chesterman 1998:5-15). We have chosen the term *elaborative reformulation* in order to indicate a marked distance between the reproduced interviewee's utterance and its reformulation by the interviewer.[8] A prominent feature of these reformulations is that they elaborate on the original interviewee's words, and further press home the argument embedded in them. Consequently, they seem to position the interviewer as supporting the interviewee whose utterance is reformulated, thereby challenging the other.

In extract (18), the interviewee Badwaan, a member of the central committee of the Democratic Front for the Liberation of Palestine, indirectly accuses his co-interviewee, former Jordanian Member of Parliament Al Abaadi, of identifying with Israel (turn 114):

(18) ("The Opposite Direction", Al Jazeera, July 2nd 2002)

114Badwaan: this is why I mean I request, that we not speak in the name [literally: language] of Israel

115 Ier: =you mean *[ya'ni,* literally: it means]

t-t-you mean Dr. {Ahmad 'Uwaydi al-Abaadi, speaks a Zionist dialect}

116 Al-Abaadi: {if you may, if you may, if you may}

117 Badwaan: {eh,, hm,,, hm,,, yes}

118 Ier: a Zionist language, {if you may [...]}

119 Badwaan: {Te point, a-a Zionist} language

He sofens this accusation by formulating it as a direct request for a change in attitude, and hedges it by the use of we-perspective ("I request, that we not speak in the name [literally: language] of Israel"). The interviewer, in turn, reformulates the accusation, and intensifes it by explicitly naming the target of the accusation ("you mean Dr. {Ahmad 'Uwaydi al-Abaadi, speaks a Zionist dialect"), as well as by replacing the relatively neutral word "Israel" with the more emotionally loaded qualifer "Zionist" (115, 118), which, signifying the ideology underlying the establishment of the state of Israel, carries negative connotations for the Arab speakers and audience. As can be seen in extract (19) below, a few turns later, the interviewer repeats the accusation (133), demands that Al-Abaadi respond (131), and elaborates on it, blaming him for adopting not only Hebrew, but also English. All this time he avoids calling those languages by their accepted names (Hebrew and English), and qualifes them by their emotionally loaded national afliation (the Israeli language, the American language):

(19) ("The Opposite Direction", Al Jazeera, July 2nd 2002)

131 Ier: {I would like}, you to answer him

132 Al Abaadi: =First, {I'll answer, 1}

133 Ier:->- {you speak} the Israeli {and American}

8. In the context of her work on reformulations, see, for example, Blackmore's (1997) discussion of elaboration, including restatement and exemplifcation.

134 Al-'Abaadi: {No, firs-}

135 Ier: language I mean dialect

136 Al-'Abaadi: =First the Israeli

137 Ier: In this part

138 Al-Abaadi: =First {the Israeli}

139 Ier: {aha}

140 Al-Abaadi: Dialect, the Israeli dialect, we don't speak it, neither I nor anybody in Jordan

Thus, the interviewer sides with Badwan in holding Al-Abaadi accountable for what seems to them an ideological misconduct. As suggested earlier, by maintaining this imbalance throughout the interview, the host positions himself as the author of the opinions he defends, and thus supports Badwan, and challenges Al-Abaadi.

The extract in the next example takes place afer al-Tameemi, a media specialist, accuses the American media of deception, and Harb, manager of an American radio station, strongly objects to this criticism. In turn 120, the interviewer claims that Harb failed to answer all his colleague's arguments, and, urging him to provide an answer, reformulates the latter's claims:

(20) ("The Opposite Direction", Al Jazeera, July 2nd 2002)

118 Ier: You said, that you wouldn't {like to answer}

119 Harb: {I've heard some} of it, yes

120 Ier: =aha, you wouldn't like to answer these lies, and it is very easy for a-a person, to sit behind a table and talk about, about such

->-things and fabrications, a-1 mean Mr. Eh, Tameemi a short while

->- ago, hasn't spoken only about lies, but, he said that the American

->- administration and the American media do, political deception,

->- that underestimates, people's intelligence and takes them for

->- fools, as if they were a group of children, and these li-deception

->-doesn't work on anyone anymore I mean, it became visible and

->- there are statistics, I would like you to answer that

121 Harb:I mean I know that there is journalistic deception, and Media deception, and all that is pompous talking that have no no no meaning, [but] there is reality, there are things that happened, and events, there were on September 11th, 19 youngsters, young sters, who bombed, and killed, no less than 3000, innocent people

Here, the host rephrases Al-Tameemi's allegations against the US media at some length. In this reformulation, he uses indices of personal involvement ("these li-deception doesn't work on anyone anymore I mean"), makes additions to al-Tameemfs words ("as if they were a group of children"), and even modifes them, replacing al-Tameemi's afrmation that the US underestimates the *Arab* nations ("us"), by a more general one, i.e. the US "underestimates, *people's* intelligence and takes them for fools".

In support of his disbelief in the American policy and media, al-Tameemi rejects the Americans' claim that they had found the passport of one of the bombers of the twin Towers, Muhammad Ataa. He does so through the use of irony ("I mean, the Americans, nothing, nothing other than Muhammad Ataa's passport came down from the plane and and got to the hands of the FBI?" 200), and by providing what seems to him as scientifc data supporting his refutation (196,198):

(21) ("The Opposite Direction", Al-Jazeera, July 2nd 2002)

190 Al-Tameemi: I'll ask the the

191 Ier: =OK

192 Al-Tameemi: The respected brother in, in, in

193 Ier: =Washington

194 Al-Tameemi: In Washington, afer, what is called the explosions, 9/11, they come out to us of course, eh e-in, the plane which, hit the world, trade center,, they haven't found in this plane anything but the pass, eh {e:h}

195 Ier: port} of Muhammad Ataa [in Arabic-"passport" is 2 words]

196Al-Tameemi: of Muhammad Ataa, Dr., before coming [here] I met a pilot,, I asked him I mean about about about the plane, he told me, and this information, may be scientifc, eh, I mean clear

197 Ier: =aha

198Al-Tameemi: He told me that the plane, weighs around 300 tons when it is in the air, that when it comes down, while it is landing physically it's 3 times heavier,, than its normal weight,, it carries no less than 20 tons of of of of of oil, and if it explodes, its heat level will be, 100 degrees, I mean if you put water, [as they say] in the vernacular, it will melt

199 Ier: =eh

200Al-Tameemi: I mean, the Americans, nothing, nothing other than Muhammad Ataa's passport came down from the plane and and got to the hands of the FBI?

The host then reformulates Al-Tameemi's claims in the form of a question addressed to Harb ("he told you for example, that everything had melted, except for Muhammad Ataa's passport?", 217, 221) and adds another argument, i.e. the claim that the Americans' information about the plane's black boxes is no less misleading (221, 223), unduly attributing it to Al-Tameemi:

(22) ("The Opposite Direction", Al-Jazeera, July 2nd 2002)

217 Ier: For example,, or he told {you for example}

218 Harb: {but, yes}

219 Ier: Does it make sense

220 Harb: =yes

221 Ier: That everything had melted, except for Muhammad Ataa's pass port? OK brother where, are theblackboxes, or two black boxes, in, on the two planes, is it possible, that the passport, didn't melt

222 Harb: Is

223 Ier: And I mean the passports, how to say it, the black boxes, which never, never melt, did melt? He wants you to answer that, I mean he considers it as nonsense

224 Harb: Fir-first, I, I will answer you

225 Ier: Eh

226 Harb: =IT1 give you, I'll give you, I don't know where you got this infor mation, the passport was found

Just as in examples (18) and (19), here too, by consistently reformulating the talk of one of the interviewees and by substantiating the reformulated claims through additions and indices of personal involvement, the host is positioned as asymmetrically supportive of Al-Tameemi, and challenging Harb. This asymmetry excludes a reading of his arguments as "playing the devil's advocate".

In the IBA interviews, there is one apparently comparable case. Discussing the possibility that the Labor Party join a unity government under the leadership of PM Ariel Sharon of the Likud Party, Chaim Ramon, Labor MP, expresses his disbelief in the Prime Minister's promises, and demands that he submit them to the Chair of the Labor Party, Amram Mitsna, in writing. The interviewer asks the co-interviewee, Likud Minister Tsipi Livni, if Sharon might agree to do this, and, since she avoids the question, he declares:

(23) ("Between the Headlines", Israeli Television, Channel 1, February 20th 2003)

363 Ier: {no time tables, I demand, I demand now on Mtsna's behalf,, I demand on-M}itsna's behalf, what he told him on Mon{day, in writing,}

By so doing, the interviewer represents Ramon's earlier demand. However, aware of the challenge embedded in this practice to the co-interviewee, he soon withdraws:

(24) ("Between the Headlines", Israeli Television, Channel 1, February 20th 2003)

380 Ier: Maybe we are making it {to:o hard, it is Chaim and I against you}

By acknowledging the unacceptability of the 'coalition his reformulation has established, the host neutralizes his imbalanced positioning, and re-assumes the interactional obligations underlying interview-management.

META-COMMENTS: INTERVIEWEES BLAME INTERVIEWERS

So far we have seen that Faysal al-Qasem positions himself in and through discourse as being politically biased and consistently supportive of one of the interviewees, while Ben Kaspit is rather particular about marking any manifestations of asymmetrical attitude as deviations, and trying to compensate for them. These observations having been made from the researchers' viewpoint, we turn now to the interviewees themselves: does their discourse provide any evidence for the insights gained from our analysis? The corpus presents us with the following answer: both in Hebrew and in Arabic, interviewees explicitly challenge the interviewers for failing to fulfill the obligations pertaining to their role. For example, in (25) Kaspit is taken to represent the media's hunt for scoops, and in (26) al-Qasem is accused of unreliability and distortion:

(25)("Between the Headlines", Israeli Television, Channel 1, December 26th 2002.

With Yossi Sarid, Head of the extreme lef-wing Merets party and Avigdor Liberman, Head of the extreme right-wing party "Haixud Haleumi-Israel Beitenu)

102 Sarid: { Listen, thds}, I know you [in the plural],, you,, eh, and I do::n't God forbid,,,e:h you are more interested in a merchandise, another merchandise, absolutely, in confrontations, fights, quar rels,, in, in in dirt,,,[...]

(26) ("The Opposite Direction", Al-Jazeera, June 18th 2002. With Dr. Ahmad 'Uwaydi al-Abaadi, a former Jordanian Parliament member, and Dr. Ali Badwaan, member of the Central Committee of the Democratic Front for the Liberation of Palestine)

152 Al-Abaadi {I,, no sir if} you would, {I don't, please}

153 Ier: {aha, yes}

154Al-Abaadi If you please [Literally: May God protect you] Don't put words I haven't said into my mouth Mr. Faysal, {we are on the air and millions of people see me}

However, in Arabic the interviewer is consistently reproached for establishing asymmetry between interviewees, mostly at the political and ideological level, while in Hebrew the interviewer is blamed for asymmetry only once, and it is interactional asymmetry which is at stake.

This diference is well represented by the two examples quoted at the opening of the article. Lapid reproaches the interviewer for violating his interactional rights by establishing *discursive asymmetry:*

(1) ("Between the Headlines", Israeli Television, Channel 1, December 19th 2002.

With Eli Yishay, the leader of the religious "Shas" party and Yosef (Tomi) Lapid, Head of the central anti-religious "Shinuy" party)

162 Lapid you promised me equal time division, and you let him make speeches Harb, on the other hand, is concerned with the interviewers unreliability and *political bias,* which, to his mind, afect the very selection of invited guests:

(2)("The Opposite Direction", Al-Jazeera, July 2nd 2002. With Dr. 'Abd al-Hay at-Tameemi, a media specialist from Thames Valley University in London, and Dr. Muwafeq Harb, specialist on U.S. afairs, and the Director of the American radio station Ash-Sharq al-Awsat)

228 Harb: [...] at first, you invent facts and then you believe them and bring guests to confrm

229 Ier: Eh

230Harb: the version you wish to promote, and you [dare] speak about propaganda through the media.

Later in the interview, he elaborates on his accusations and explicates them (note the words "propaganda" [di'aayaat], and "distortion [of facts]" [tashweeh]):

(27) ("The Opposite Direction", Al-Jazeera, July 2nd 2002)

236 Harb: = Whenever, each time I met with an ofcial of Al-Jazeera I urged them, to translate, into English, the programs of Al-Jazeera, but what I have heard in some cases from Al-Jazeera, and some of the guests it has brought {and some of the propa ganda and the distortion of facts that you [in the plural] do}

More striking are Al-'Abaadfs allegations in (28) and (29), whereby the interviewer is accused of distorting the facts, misleading the audience, depriving the interviewee of his interactional rights and siding with his co-interviewee:

220 Elda Weizman, Irit Levi and Isaac Schneebaum

(28) ("The Opposite Direction", Al-Jazeera, June 18th 2002. With Dr. Ahmad

'Uwaydi al-'Abaadi, a former Jordanian Parliament member, and Dr. Ali Badwaan, member of the Central Committee of the Democratic Front for the Liberation of Palestine)

957 Al-Abaadi: respected brother, all of the entrances [of viewers through Internet]-it seems like they are all prejudiced against my stance, either because I am Jordanian, against Jordan's stance, or they can't understand me because of your interruption, you are a loud mouth, you twisted the picture and tired the viewer.

(29) ("The Opposite Direction", Al-Jazeera, June 18th 2002)

813 Ier:{and these sayings you} a short while ago you blamed the, eh brother Ali of [using] rhetorical phrases, and these say ings of yours are the very essence of {contemptible Arabic rhetoric, I would like to ask you, 55, entrance 55, OK just, a minute

814Al-'Abaadi: {No brother, brother, because you didn't like it, if you may,

no, Mr. Faysal, if you please [literally: may god be satisfed with you]} because you didn't like it when I said about him that he speaks rhetorically, that's true

815 Ier: Aha

816 Al-'Abaadi: =and I tell you

817 Ier: =eh

818Al-'Abaadi: =if you may, let me complete my answer, first

819 Ier: =eh

No comparable accusations are made by the interviewees in the IBA interviews.

CONCLUSION

Interviewers' neutrality, whether genuine or pretended, may be achieved in a number of ways, mostly by asking questions, formulating statements as if they were preliminaries to questions, and attributing statements to a third party via quotations and voicing (Clayman 1988; Clayman & Heritage 2002; Greatbatch 1988; Lauerbach 2006). In the view suggested in this paper, in multiple-interviewee events, (seeming) neutrality may be realized by the establishment of symmetry between the interviewees.

The comparative analysis of two-interviewee discourse events in Arabic and in Hebrew has yielded interesting diferences in this respect. We have shown that in Al Jazeera, al-Qasem's interviews are framed from the outset as unbalanced, and the interviewer's identifcation with one of the interviewees at the expense of the other is compounded by explicit comments, as well as by elaborative reformulations. In Kaspit's interviews on Israeli television, on the other hand, the opening is mostly informative and neutral, expressions of the interviewers stance are qualifed as deviations and do not necessarily converge with those of one of the interviewees, and reformulations are symmetrically distributed between the interviewees. These preliminary findings, we have shown, are supported by the interviewees' own evaluations, manifest in their meta-comments.

In a deeper sense, we suggest that these diferences afect the basic role-design underlying the interviews. Ideological and political asymmetry entail the interviewer's positioning as the author of a viewpoint rather than its animator; the framing of stances as deviations and the preservation of a relative symmetry, on the other hand, reinforce the interviewer's interactional power.

These diferences may suggest that the search for neutrality is not a universal, and that cultures may difer in terms of their perception the interviewer's role. A larger corpus representing a large number of interviewers, a wider range of discourse patterns and topical variation may lead to deeper insights on this issue.

8

Christmas Messages by Heads of State Multimodality and Media Adaptations

This chapter investigates the multimodal quality of Christmas Messages by European heads of state on TV from a functional-pragmatic and semiotic angle. It defnes them as dealing with multiple types of materialities from diferent modes and sub-modes. Section 1 develops the central concept of discourse anchoring as (multimodal) ways through which discourse participants and TV viewers are guided towards and supported in their information processing. Section 2 discusses the discourse facets of Christmas Messages on TV as adaptation of a re-oralised written text to TV features and their media design potentials. Section 3 examines two addresses: the 'multimedia show' by the British Queen in 2003 and the sermon' by the Finnish President in 2004. Section 4 presents a synopsis of message materialities from nine countries giving particular attention to their multimodal grammar'. The Conclusion refects on the growing need of visual representation within the political culture and the complex relationship between what TV viewers see and what they hear.

INTRODUCTION: MATERIALITIES OF TV CHRISTMAS MESSAGES

This chapter addresses the multimodal quality of Christmas Messages by European heads of state from the perspective of TV audiences. On the occasion of Christmas Day, New Year's Eve or

New Year's Day, nations are used to seeing their highest representatives delivering special messages. Not included are speeches on the same occasions by heads of government, since they normally are more (party) political and programmatic in nature. I do neither discuss processes of speech writing and reviewing; their investigation needs access to presidential staff or to a royal institution I do not have (Jochum 1999; Neumann 2004). The paper is based on a corpus of nine televised Christmas Messages (see Table 3.1 below) suppple-mented with the speech texts provided by ofcial websites (including translations into English) or transcribed from the screen. In general, I concentrate on the visual and multimodal aspects of transmission, on what TV audiences *see* while listening to their heads of state.[1]

Heads of state are defned by their *representative* functions. Their duties include state visits, receptions of foreign guests on the same formal level, formal political (constitution-driven) acts and, in general, the representation of their own nation on diferent occasions throughout a year. Ritual communication is rampant at such moments. While their duties are fully absorbed by their main task of being present ceremonially and making the nation audible and visible, on Christmas or New Year s Day their Messages normally bear a *semi-ofcial* character. Personal and individual considerations may amplify topical variation (Sauer 1999, 2000, 2001, 2002). Because Messages cannot only consist of Christmas and New Years wishes, although they are a constitutive part, the question arises *what* is said, and which topics, also visual ones, evoke other types of discourse. For TV viewers also react to the delivery as such and pay attention to *how* heads of state are shown and *how* convincingly they perform. Media features and actualisations of recipient design count.

We therefore regard Christmas Messages, seen as a generic term referring to the corpus, as *communicative events* rather than as pure texts. This implies that communicative practices (of the delivery of public speeches) have to mingle with media practices (of their TV formats). The media practices of our corpus range from the footage of a person sitting at a desk and reading aloud from a manuscript to a person who is shown acting and chatting with other people, moving around while addressing and looking directly into the camera, using teleprompter technology. Besides, as is characteristic of TV settings, Messages are always *framed.* Their most general frame is the announcement by TV announcers, but music, national symbols, Christmas decoration and festivity signs add frames too. How these frames trigger special meanings and what their impact is in terms of the materialities the Messages draw upon is part of this investigation.

A Christmas Message as a communicative event employs two domains: with regard to its content, it embeds *other discourses* including the *personal voice* or *tenor* and, with regard to media potentials, it relies on *other practices.* A mini-mal requirement, as we may assume from earlier investigations (Atkinson 1984; Sauer 2001, 2002,2005; Tiemens 2005), would be an appropriate environment for its content that refects the 'state of the art' concerning its media adequacy. It is these materialities that constitute the Message's impact. TV viewers are expected to fall back on them when processing and constructing their own meanings. Of course, this is not a radically new perspective. In political discourse analysis, however, the recipient-designed materialities are ofen neglected and sometimes not even mentioned. This chapter attempts to work out in detail how the materialities could be taken into consideration as relevant pieces of the meaning potentials that are ofered to the public.

Our corpus and other publications (not in the least publications in the national press covering of the event) reveal what the Messages have in common. The addresses contain accounts (ofen narrations) of last year's events show certain episodes from the head of state's personal perspective accentuate developments of the public opinion during the last year invite the TV viewers to share social values that have been seen as 'problematic' or 'challenging' within the last year re-establish the common ground for public communication by contributing to the social fabric of the community provide a context for individually coloured Christmas or New Year's wishes

Such kinds of verbal actions, visual appearances and other discourse actualisa-tions form the network of every Message. Their combination, however, is vast. Moreover, because heads of state tend to depend on public support, they have to provide visions, opinions or meanings that are both acceptable and plausible.

Consequently, the Messages are 'neutral' rather than 'one-sided'. Yet they are controlled by ideological notions that delineate the national political culture (see also Clyne 1994). In order to avoid political arguments, which might be provoked by the political leaders, Christmas Messages are almost always restricted to those activities which the government as the actual centre of politics does not claim for itself (see Sauer 2001; Neumann 2004). Ideological work is rather done visually and musically than verbally. Considering the use of national symbols and culture-related pictures, and the reference in music and appearance to national customs and Christmas habits, it is very likely that common values are highlighted, or at least welcomed as a bonus.

What is at stake in general is the issue of a *televised* Message. This encompasses heads of state delivering their Messages directly from the screen. No public is visible in their vicinity. A Christmas Message therefore has a sermon-like appearance. Heads of state are shown on the screen reading aloud from teleprompter or manuscripts lying on a desk. So how does what you see contribute to what you hear? Undoubtedly the viewers get more than what they hear, more than an articulated Message text. They also get heads of state in a specifc environment (e.g., standing at a lectern), seen from a specifc camera angle, with or without camera movements, and framed by symbols (like flags, candles, Christmas trees), flowers, props etc. as well as by music (before and/or aferwards). Thus, they get linguistics *and* semiotics. They get meaningful material of diferent kinds, in diferent layers and partaking in diferent practices. This is the reason why we call such Messages 'communicative events' rather than 'texts'. The event is of course text-related, but the text is also event-related, since it aims at communication *and* interaction. No text exists as such, it needs *modes* and *media* to come to life, to become communication. The challenge, then, is to track down these material meaning-making elements of spoken discourse fused with images, music and sounds. It is this *fusion* that calls for scrutiny.

In an early publication, Fiske and Hartley (1978:85-100) suggest that TV, in general, has a "bardic function". Television as a "bard" articulates the established cultural consensus and implicates the members of the culture into its dominant value systems. It celebrates the position of socio-centrality by controlling eccentricity and assures the culture of its practical adequacy in the world. TV exposes potential ideological re-orientation, if needed, and convinces the audience that individual status and identity are guaranteed by the culture as a whole. By these means, TV puts forward a sense of cultural membership. It maybe worth attempting to relate the general "bardic function" of TV to the head of state's representative voice. This entails that the head of state himself or herself is also a kind of "bard" and may be associated with traditional bards who rendered the central concerns of their days into verse. Although the highest representatives do not perform verse (with the exception of some quotes from poetic and literary texts), their performances clearly give room to the central concerns of that year and time. In such a way, a Christmas Message on TV is culturally positioned by specifc discourse practices and sociocultural practices, and may therefore receive acclaim.

One such practice consists of the *doubling of the* bard: ofcially, heads of state possess the highest representative function, but when acting as such, they also act as natural persons. The latter are made explicit when they mention, or react to, personal circumstances like family relationships. Audiences are acquainted with this demeanour. It echoes the "King's two bodies" (Kantorowicz 1957), an (originally medieval) description of the preconditions of every representative public ofce: incumbents have in them the *body natural*, which is mortal, and the *body politic*, which is eternal. This mystifcation is necessary as well as useful, for it allows achieving political acts without provoking resistance against the political power that is executed by the ofce. The public, then, hears ofcial words as belonging to its own repertoire. It responds to both bard and ofce. Against this background, descriptions ofered by heads of state may become prescriptions. This is the price people pay for cultural membership. In Christmas Messages, the magic, to which the common ways of Christmas celebration on TV allude, pertains to this mystic fiction.

In order to gain access to the materialities of Christmas Messages, three lines of investigation are combined in this chapter: Functional Pragmatics, Critical Discourse Analysis and Multimodal Discourse Theory. In Functional Pragmatics, the constellation that is characteristic of Christmas Messages is seen as the *importation* of other discourses into the main discourse. One searches for propositions that bear ambiguous or vague meanings, or one considers other ambivalences and discrepancies throughout the text, in particular concerning discourse anchoring devices (see below) and rhetorical strategies (Ehlich 1994a, 1994b; Sauer 1996, 2002). In Critical Discourse Analysis, this constellation is seen as *intertextual* movement. One looks for what genres, voices and discourses are drawn upon, how they are articulated together and what relationships and identities are constructed (Fairclough 1995). In Multimodal Discourse Theory, the constellation is seen as resulting from the integration of several communicative practices. Its analysis has to refect the diferent *semiotic resources* that establish the meaning-making potentials of the event (Fiske 1987; Fiske & Hartley 1978; Kress & Van Leeuwen 1996, 2001; Van Leeuwen 2005; Lemke 2002; Stöckl 2004; Lim 2004).

In Figure 1 (below), the relationship between the three approaches is shown. My basic assumption is that discourse needs to be distinguished from what I call "discourse shadow" (following Ehlich 1994b): the means of *discourse anchoring* in the ongoing communication, e.g. by deixis (i.e. focussing and re-orientation), morpho-syntax, operative procedures related to information chunking, control of mental actions, articulation and body language. Discourse anchoring operates as harmonisation of the information part of an ongoing discourse with its function and with the very needs of the processing in the reception situation. I link the means of the discourse shadow to semiotic resources that depend on media features.

The origin of this distinction is Bühler's "Language Theory" (1934, English 1990). Bühler developed the so-called "Organon Model" as a unity of every communicative exchange that consists of three general functions: *representation, appeal* and *expression*. Representation is considered to be delimited by the functions of expression (as related to the speaker's signifcative expressive phenomena) and appeal (as related to the hearers perception and attitude). The three functions can be studied if one divides the discourse at hand into language external functions which aim at external goals, e.g. the illocution of speech acts, and language internal functions which aim at discourse anchoring by fostering the participants' processing, e.g. concerning information clustering and focus movement, accentuation and concatenation of content parts. The latter ones form the discourse shadow and provide its recipient design. They depend also on media features and have therefore to be adapted to the semiotic resources used. The discourse shadow anchors the ongoing communication in the situation and combines language means with other semiotic resources. It bridges the gap between the speech text and multimodal practices that are characteristic of TV speeches.

In such a way, the materialities of Christmas Messages may be tackled. In the following section, I discuss the concept of multimodality by combining discourse anchoring, semiotic resources and more general concepts, such as secondary oral-ity and literacy. In Section 3, Christmas Messages from GB (3.1) and Finland (3.2) are examined. They represent two extreme positions: one is very rich in semiotic resources while the other is more like a sermon-like address. In Section 4, a synopsis of the semiotic resources of the corpus will be developed. This is to serve as a first step towards a semiotic grammar of Christmas Messages. In the conclusion (Section 5), I relate my findings to cultural dimensions which are characteristic of Christmas addresses and their materialities.

FROM ORALITY TO SECONDARY LITERACY AND ITS ADAPTATION TO TV

The starting point in analysing a modern Christmas Message on TV is to refect on the change of political *rhetoric* from live oratory to media transmission (Atkinson 1984; Sauer 1996; Tiemens 2005). This change afects the speaker's role con-cerning their screen appearances; it is ofen referred to as a "decline" of rhetoric.[2] In classical antiquity, speaking meant personifcation, performance and content management at the same time by *live oratory:* organised spontaneity, catching applause and spellbinding eloquence. The semiotic resources classical orators had at their disposal consisted of place and time, body movements, dress, gaze, verbal craft and actors' skills. Nowadays, medium conditions determine the semiotic resources to a great extent. What was adequate in live oratory no longer functions appropriately when transmitted by television.

Because the primary orality of oral culture has been infuenced by the emergence of written communication and the development of other technical media (in particular TV), we now live in the age of secondary orality. To use Ong's own words: "It is essentially a more deliberate and self-conscious orality, based permanently on the use of writing and print, which are essential for the manufacture and operation of the equipment and for its use as well" (Ong 1982:136).

This secondary orality governs the reality of modern political discourse. When politicians appear on TV, we may discern a range of realisations of this orality. As for some politicians, it is obvious that they act spontaneously, although their spontaneity is "cultivated and domesticated" (Ong 1982:137). Others routinely formulate sentences that sound like written passages even if a manuscript is neither used nor memorised. Their routine is a result of education and instruction, which normally means learning from books and written examples. A third group produces well formulated oral texts which were indeed written in advance and therefore re-oralised for such an occasion. TV audiences mostly can see that the speakers rely on manuscripts. These three realisation forms of secondary orality, although there are of course more of them (Holly 1995), demonstrate that the concept of secondary orality is plausible, but needs to be further refned.

The routine and the text-dependent groups both echo an inclination towards old speech attitudes. Politicians on the screen ofen execute *declamations,* a term borrowed from rhetoric. They 'declaim' rather than 'do' speech acts. Moreover, it was declamations that formed the basis of Western education. People have had to learn written texts in order to be able to equip their ongoing or future oral communication. Without texts their oral skills would not increase. The speech habit of declamations still infuences the way representative politicians act in public. When they represent the nation, they act as *declamators*-of texts written by others. The declamations are clearly script-bound since the ritual nature of a representative speech and the representation situation accentuate the need for a reliable text basis. If we compare a Christmas Message with, say, a spontaneous appearance, such as a reception or the like that shows heads of state acting and chatting with people, then their overtly script-bound character comes to the fore. In general, spontaneity shown by representatives and transmitted by mass media is normally carefully planned and ofen rehearsed. At least, it is a result of refections and professionally supplied preparations (Holly 1995; Neumann 2004).

In the light of these considerations, a Christmas Message bears an 'overculti-vated' air. The consequence of this practice (or, more precisely, "discourse practice", as Fairclough (1995) calls it) is that a Christmas Message uses a kind of *secondary literacy,* an overtly re-oralisation of a written text. This occurs in combination with a TV script or a planned footage. Its literacy is based on the fact that the written text provides the relevant content. Additionally, the availability of the Message text on ofcial web sites or, as is the case, for instance, in the Netherlands, its publication by the national press, contributes to this air of literacy. Its second-ariness shows in the sermon-like presentation style: speakers *enact* the text as if performing by memory, although they use the teleprompter technology or read from a manuscript. Seen this way, secondary literacy equals the oral re-articulation of a written text by a speaker reading aloud.[3] Accordingly, secondary literacy is re-oralised written text-whereas secondary orality is textualised (writing-oriented and medium-related) orality.

Christmas Messages are embedded in the nations Christmas celebration. This embeddedness asks for more than declamations as it is unthinkable that heads of state 'declaim' the wish "Happy Christmas to you all". They must be more convincing-more 'live'. In such a decisive moment, they must be less script-bound, e.g. by smiling, putting their reading glasses down, looking into the camera, making an inviting gesture, articulating enthusiastically etc. The communicative practices applied in a Christmas Message, thus, borrow (and must borrow) from other practices that are less script-bound. The secondary literacy has to be mitigated by other ways of addressing and other semiotic resources used.

In general, TV viewers gather more than the re-oralised text alone. They *see* a speaker speaking and acting at the same time. TV audiences respond to meanings which are related to "televisuality" (Atkinson 1984). The medium features and their semiotic resources are predominant. It depends on the chosen realisation whether the Message is seen and heard along the lines, to take extreme cases, of a 'sermon or a 'multimedia show'. On the one hand, a 'sermon' is characterised by the fact that speakers are alone on the screen and create a relationship with their recipients that depends more on the speech content than on the few other semiotic elements. When heads of state speak directly from the screen then only the variation of camera shot sizes (from medium via medium close-up to close-up) and camera movements may lower their intenseness. According to Atkinson (1984), this is a situation not convenient as far as TV features are concerned. The Finnish example (see below) belongs to the sermon-like Messages that are customary in most of the European countries. It urges the recipients to concentrate on the Message content, although the way of performing (concerning gaze, body language, articulation, dressing code, the use of props etc.) may cause a range of responses, from fascination to disappointment, from sympathy to compassion.

On the other hand, a Christmas Message as a 'multimedia show' presents not only an orator, but also video sequences of him or her in diferent environments, sometimes even other people who themselves contribute to the Message content by delivering statements. This last example refers to the style of the British Queens Christmas Message from 1997 on. The British example (see below) demonstrates a strong inclination towards mass media expertise and expectations, at least preparedness for innovative media exposure and willingness for experiments. It is a long way from live oratory to the 'multimedia' approach.

Seen from this perspective, the challenge is to bring about more correspondence between words and pictures, what people hear *and* see. The semiotic resources have to be richer, with respect to either the performance itself or its frames. As for the frames, the audiences' expectations may depend on Christmas customs and thus be *culturally* determined. In Figure 2, the factors that infuence the representation style and the use of medium features are summarised.

The written text of the Message is predominant in that it provides the very content. The first step is to re-oralise this text, i.e. to find a balanced way of its realisation in accordance with the speaker's oral style and body language. This is also what the rehearsal entails. The second step is the adaptation to the TV features in order to achieve an apt performance. That means that the 'Christmas culture' has to be refected, not only in the choice of topics, but also in the choice of music, room decoration, props, symbols and the like. The third step is the choice of media design and how the televisuality is realised. Camera movements, sequence of shots, montage, size, angle, dynamics and other means are called for. The fourth step is to consider both the cultural elements expected and the discourse anchoring means, for they have to be visually and verbally adequate in order to support the processing of the Message. Because Christmas Messages contribute to the head of state's representative function they use the sociocultural practice of public representation. And they allude to some other culture-related practices, such as evoking national traditions or appealing for (ideological) values. The "multi-lay-eredness" (Clark 1996) refects the medium adaptation of the discourse anchoring as well as its semiotic resources. The question mark (in Figure 2) indicates that the anchoring might be questionable insofar as comprehension support in words *and* pictures *and* sounds is a risky business.

The point of view adopted in this paper is that the transcript of a Christmas Message, as provided on ofcial websites, does not sufce as the only source of investigation. Access to its *multimodal* nature is indispensable. Accordingly, a description of the visual and acoustic quality of the performance is a minimum requirement. A Christmas Message has to be treated as a TV programme in the first instance. Its materialities are seen as providing the information design the recipients are facing when they listen *and* view.

It depends, however, on the concept of multimodality whether the fusion of spoken discourse, sounds and pictures may be approached. Multimodality ofen tends to 'add' another communication mode to an existing mode. Considering the complexity of modern mass communication, this is undesirable (Lemke 2002). It was the idea of "design" (Stöckl 2004), and more in particular "media design" as related to "semiotic resources" (Lim 2004), that was able to combine communicative and discourse practices, on the one hand, with multi-layered discourse, on the other hand. Both domains merge into a multimodal theory of communication (Kress & Van Leeuwen 2001:111): A multimodal theory of communication... concentrates on two things: the *semiotic resources,* the modes and the media used, and the *communication practices* in which these resources are used. These communicative practices are seen as multi-layered and include, at the very least, discursive practices, production practices and interpretive practices, while they may also include design practices and/or distribution practices.... The key point here is that meaning is made not only with a multiplicity of semiotic resources, in a multiplicity of modes and media, but also at diferent 'places' within each of these.... In any one mode *all* realisational elements are available for the making of signs, and are used for that. From the moment that a culture has made the decision to draw a particular material into its communicative processes, that material has become part of the cultural and semi-otic resources of that culture and is available for use in the making of signs.

In such a way, the prospect of adaptation of a text to media features and the combination of diferent semiotic resources comes into focus (Lemke 2002). This is what multimodal discourse analysis is meant for. However, whereas Kress and Van Leeuwen (2001) treat multimodality, in general, as a range of semiotic resources related to communicative practices and discuss examples of diferent kinds and in a variety of designs (as does Lim 2004), a representative address transmitted by television is exactly the other way round. Its purpose is-more or less-fixed, although its realisation is flexible. Its text stands, but the other elements need to be constructed in an appropriate manner. The Message has to reckon with the complexity of TV meaning-making potentials. In this paper, multimodality is therefore seen as the *result* of the adaptation of a Message to TV features. The medium is TV, its modes depend on the meanings it is able to carry.

According to Stöckl (2004), language, image, sound and music are considered *core modes.* They are either realised in visual or auditory *sensory channels,* which have certain *medial variants,* like static vs. dynamic, or animated writing vs. text on screen, and speech. Furthermore, we distinguish *peripheral modes,* such as nonverbal means and para-verbal means, and *sub-modes,* such as size, angle (camera), lighting, colour, 2-dimensionality, rhythm and volume. TV as multimodal communication, then, applies the four core modes and their sub-types in full.

As for *communicative practices,* the way TV programmes are usually made determines what audiences may expect, already know or respond to when viewing and listening. Here, the live performance of a Christmas Message, although it is faked, is predominant. This entails specifc *presentation practices {discourse practices),* such as live vs. recorded, but in particular spontaneous speech vs. written to be spoken, and their sub-types, like directly to camera/audience, to other participants, and voice-over during diferent images. Also the *distribution practices* have to be taken into consideration: the frames of the Message, its musical context as well as the Christmas-related props, that contribute to what viewers may manage to grasp. In general, the performance is furnished with *sociocultural practices* if the speakers succeed in relating its content to their "body politic" as well as "body natural" (Kantorowicz 1957) and if they confrm their very role by performing as a "bard".

The written text of TV Christmas Messages as prepared by the head of state's staff matters in that it is the basis of the address. Yet it is written with the aim of adequate re-oralisation. It is therefore the main facet of the speech delivery that all kinds of anticipations, which are characteristic of the "apparatus of literacy", have to be "translated" (Lodge 1997:214-215) into re-oralised instances-and pictures. Thus, the anchoring of the Message in the reception situation (Ehlich 1994a, 1994b) has to be performed in conformity with medium features, in general, and (socio)cultural determinations, in particular.[4] Accordingly, the discourse shadow is not only actualised by words, body language, gaze, but also by pictures (Chandler 1994) and by sounds people may pick up on the way (Van Leeuwen 1999, 2005). Consequently, the signifcance of anchoring refers to the need to anticipate what the audience may encounter-and to the fact that a TV Message is "immediate" and even "vivid" (Lodge 1997). Its evanescence challenges the nature of the written text basis. Given this contradiction between secondary literacy and film dynamics, it is likely that the adaptation to television features, while, at the same time, referring to cultural expectations, will depend on fortuitousness. The multi-modal nature of a Christmas Message carries too many indeterminate factors to deal with easily.

In Figure 3 (below), a network of decision-sensitive points is developed which infuences the wording and structure of a Christmas Message as well as its adaptation to the medium features and its anchoring in the reception situation. Anchoring and TV adaptation are related to the discourse practices of the Message. Furthermore, its sociocultural practices are acknowledged. We regard them as related to the general cultural-political purpose of the construction of *social cohesion*. This is one of the most essential tasks a head of state has to fulfl (Ensink & Sauer 2003). It is linked to his or her role as a bard in giving the community a proper voice. It does not only concern the way the text is written, but also the way its content is realised in accordance with the medium, cultural traditions of the country and performance skills of the representative. Even certain "design practices" (Kress & Van Leeuwen 2001, 5: "design stands midway between content and expression") need to be taken into consideration, namely dressing, hairdo, room decoration, lighting and colours, Christmas symbols, national symbols and the like. It is likely that these practices underlie all decisions concerning *what* is depicted *in what way*.

In the following section, a Christmas Message from GB and one from Finland are investigated. The GB example (3.1) belongs to a multimedia show style, whereas the Finnish example (3.2) is sermon-like, as it would be in most other European countries. Both realisations refect the use of semiotic resources, as related to TV medium potentials on the one hand, and to the speech content on the other hand. However, the solutions chosen vary. In Figure 3,1 pay attention to the media design character of TV adaptation and anchoring, and to the sociocultural practices involved. To a certain extent, I also deal with the Message content in order to detect verbally conveyed sociocultural practices, such as certain topics. Due to lack of space, however, I cannot give a full analysis. Yet I try to combine the three methods of analysis as referred to in Figure 1 above. Moreover, because a Queens representative role difers from the one of an elected President, the Messages may represent two ways of dealing with the highest public ofce and its eternal and temporal nature. This enables us to outline two cultural political settings ("cultural values", according to Clyne 1994) and to relate them to the actualisa-tions of the recipient design means.

As announced by the British press, the Queens Christmas Message 2003 was broadcast for the first time from outside a royal residence.[5] At the usual time, at 3 p.m. on Christmas Day, the Queen appeared on BBC 1.[6] A transcript of the Message-of which the texts (and some photographs) are available from the ofcial website-including descriptions of pictures and inserted footage is used in order to give an impression of its multimodal character.[7]

- [Beginning sequence: National Anthem, played by the military band of the Household Cavalry, Windsor, in traditional uniforms, Queen's car arriving, Q stepping out, shaking hands with commander, anew the band, then text *Te Queen,* Windsor flag]
- [Queen, in Combermere Barracks, Windsor, (afer having come forward from behind) is now standing between two tanks, one of them decorated with red crosses, in blue dress; the camera zooms from M to MCU so that at least one tank could be seen. Talking directly into the camera] (A) I am sure that most of you will be celebrating Christmas at home in the company of your families and friends, but I know that some of you will not be so lucky. This year I am speaking to you from the Household Cavalry Barracks in Windsor because I want to draw attention to the many Servicemen and women who are stationed far from home this Christmas. I am thinking about their wives and children, and about their parents and friends. Separation at this time is especially hard to bear.
- [voice-over Q (video footage from Iraq with original sounds underlying Q's words): soldier in battle dress, camoufage style, patrolling in the streets of an Iraqi city, friendly with children and other people)]

  (B) It is not just a matter of separation. The men and women of the Services continue to face serious risks and dangers as they carry out their duties. They have done this brilliantly.

- [v-o Q (video sequence: control post in a desert landscape, soldiers controlling cars, searching through a house, giving food to children)]

  I think we all have very good reasons for feeling proud of their achievements-both in war, and as they help to build a lasting peace in troublespots across the globe.
- [talking directly from the screen, MCU, standing in front of a tank]

  (C) None of this can be achieved without paying a price. I know that all our thoughts at this time are with the families who are sufering the pain of bereavement. All those who have recently lost a close relative or friend will know how difcult Christmas can be.
- [Interruption: video footage from an aircraft carrier, meeting of soldiers with commander, then servicemen and women in diferent shots] Commander: In less than an hour's time this ship will be brought on four hours notice to execute operations in Iraq
- [v-o Q (video sequence: soldiers climbing up helicopter, climbing up jet fighter, preparing aircrafs)]

(D) These individual Servicemen and women are our neighbours and come from our own towns and villages; from every part of the country and from every background. The process of training within the Navy, the Army and the Air Force has moulded them together into disciplined teams.

- [v-o Q (video footage: soldiers marching, tanks riding, control post controlling people, observation post from a tank)]

They have learnt to take responsibility and to exercise judgement and restraint in situations of acute stress and danger. They have brought great credit to themselves and to our country as a whole.

[Interruption: inserted video report of a reception of the Queen in Combermere Barracks, with several soldiers]

Q: So how long have you been with them/with the regiment/ have you been away and back again?

[v-o Q (video footage: reception in the Barracks, Q chatting with diferent groups of ser vicemen and servicewomen, original voices can be heard sofly)]

(E)I had an opportunity recently at the Barracks to meet some of those who played their part with such distinction in the Iraq operations. I was left with a deep sense of respect and admiration for their steadfast loyalty to each other and to our nation.

[Interruption: continuation of video report of a reception of the Queen in Combermere Barracks, with several soldiers]

Soldier: I was in Iraq, yeah, where I made my service/my job was to fix the-uh tanks.

Queen: [...]

Other soldiers: [...] [Length is nearly two minutes]

Queen chats with 5 diferent men and women, focussing on the theme of "team building" and "teamwork", also on "regiment as family".

[talking directly from the screen, MCU, standing, from a royal residence (Sandringham House, Norfolk)]

(F) I believe there is a lesson for us all here. It is that each of us can achieve much more if we work together as members of a team. The Founder of the Christian Faith himself chose twelve disciples to help *him* in his ministry.

(G) I was reminded of the importance of teamwork as I presented, for the first time last sum mer, the Queen's Awards for Voluntary Service by groups within the community.

[v-o Q (video footage: reception in Buckingham Palace, Q presents the Awards to diferent groups of people, original noises can be heard sofly)]

I have been struck by how ofen people say to me that they are receiving their award on behalf of a team and that they do not deserve to be singled out. This annual award recognises the team rather than the individual.

[Interruption: inserted video reports showing social activities by the Award-winning groups, accompanied by a short introduction of the kind of activity, interrupted by an direct talk into the camera by a representative of the Award-winners]

Text: *Swansea Old Peoples Welfare* Voice by *Iris Aubrey,* later on for a short while also directly: In total we have 20 volunteers and they are worth their weight in gold. They work hard, they are good tempered, they are pleasant and without them we would have to close. Most of the people we deal with, about 90% of them live alone, have got some sort of infiction and they need to get out and to know that people really care about them. Winning the Queens Jubilee Award was a great achievement for the volunteers to be recognised for what they do. Text: *Asian Blind Association, Coventry* Voice by *Bhanamuti Dabhi,* also directly: Being a visually impaired person in the Asian community it was hard for me to get help and support. We have got people from all religions and cultural backgrounds, they speak in diferent languages, we do social activities, we do counselling, fill beneft forms whatever. Without the help of the volunteers we won't be able to run the group.

Text: *Ferryhill Town Youth, County Durham*

Voice by *David Foster,* also directly:

We first started 10 years ago in 1994, we started with one team. For us, in a deprived area, if the football wasn't here for the children, they would just be on the streets anyway getting into trouble and we felt that something needed to be done. We've very proud of it, I mean, 5 teams of boys and girls is a lot of children off the streets every weekend.

Text: *Epsom and Ewell PHAB, Surrey*

Voice by *Julia Giles,* also directly:

We have disabled youngsters, we have able-bodied children we bring them together to have fun and they don't even know that they're integrating they are just having fun doing diferent activities. I think it would be quite difcult to describe a stereotypical volunteer because we have such a variety of people. We have people that come in from the city and take off their suit and change into their jeans, we have people that come and help from local hospitals, all walks of life help out here, which is fantastic. The feeling you get from helping other people is a great sense of achievement.

[v-o Q (video footage from [text] *Gatehouse Oxford,* where obviously homeless people get food]

(H) In this country and throughout the Commonwealth there are groups of people who are giving their time generously to make a diference to the lives of others.

[talking directly, M to MCU to M, Queen is standing in room in Sandringham House, Christmas tree on the right, visible are also diferent family photographs on mantelpiece and Christmas cards, see photograph]

As we think of them, and of our Servicemen and women far from home at this Christmas time, I hope we all, whatever our faith, can draw inspiration from the words of the familiar prayer [pretending to read from the book but not doing so]:

Teach us good Lord

To serve thee as thou deservest;

To give, and not to count the cost;

To fight, and not to heed the wounds;

To toil, and not to seek for rest;

To labour, and not to ask for any reward;

Save that of knowing that we do thy will.

[Closing the book]

It is this knowledge which will help us all to enjoy the Festival of Christmas.

[With a shy smiling] A happy Christmas to you all.

[Closing sequence: the same traditionally uniformed military band of the Household Cavalry playing the Christmas carol "Hark The Herald Angels Sing"]

For full comprehension, it is necessary to see the pictures, to pick up acoustic and visual signals, to listen to the speech and the diferent texts by other people, and to assimilate the diferent semiotic resources used. Thus processing its multimodal content and integrating diferent communicative practices seem to be an issue that is really at stake here.

At face value, the Christmas Message 2003 is organised symmetrically with respect to music, pictures and words. It comprises three parts. The first part establishes the topic of the *state* or *nation state* (A-F), the second one the topic of social activity by *voluntary work* (G) and the last part the *Christmas wishes* (H). All parts are linked by the Queen as the main actor in them and by the topic of "teamwork" that applies to the military and social side of the community. The three parts are ratifed by the underlying Christian morality, since the Queen refers to Christ and his twelve disciples "as members of a team" (F) and uses this reference later on too (G, H).

The beginning is ofcial: National Anthem, played by a traditionally uniformed brass band (beginning sequence), visit at the Barracks and starting the address standing in front of tanks (A, see also the first photograph), then meeting with servicemen and servicewomen (E), and of course the reference to the war in Iraq, also with inserted footage from Iraq (A-D), including the Queens reference to the dead (C). In this section of the Message we also find a certain "dramatising strategy" (MacArthur 1999) insofar as the information the viewers are provided with has been turned into dialogue (E: Queen chatting with soldiers). In such a way, the practice of small talk and the discourse practice (by TV viewers) of overhearing such talkunderpin the practice of representing the nation. The "body politic" merges into the "body natural" (Kantorowicz 1957), visually as well as acoustically[8]

The second passage starts with the topic of Christianity ("I was reminded of the importance of teamwork" G, referring to F). It consists of video sequences of the presentation of the Queens Awards for Voluntary Service and includes special transmissions in words and pictures by four award-winners. These sequences enact a *documentary* practice. They function as a *eulogy* of volunteers in Great Britain and of the community itself (G). The length of that part is nearly half of the whole Message. Even the fact that the long footage of volunteers' work might take the viewers' minds off things contributes to what maybe called the Queen's serving role in society i.e. having an open eye for social relationships. In this passage, it is the Queen's ofce that is foregrounded so that her "body politic" connected with social questions is acclaimed.

Afer this chain of volunteers' footage the Queen suddenly stands in San-dringham House (already for a short moment in F, but mainly in H). From a room, very well known from earlier Messages (see also the second photograph), she first *declaims* a prayer referring to the teamwork topic, then closes the prayer book and wishes her viewers a happy Christmas with a shy smile. The Christmas carol "Hark The Herald Angels Sing" in sound and pictures is the last sequence, played by the same military band as in the beginning and closing the frame.

Although the Message takes no more then nine and a half minutes, and although the speed with which the change of addressing from the screen, voice-over, film sequences and other people in words and pictures shown is very high, thus obeying the general requirements of modern TV, the main line is presented quite clearly: war in Iraq and ofcial politics, social work and royal duties concerning the welfare sector, political morality and social achievements. Yet the se-miotic resources used and the diferent frames applied (music, military, the topic of teamwork, volunteers, Christmas symbols, religious references) may cause a problem of integration. This comes especially to the fore, if one listens only once to the Message, as an ordinary audience would.[9]

The meaning making depends on the *anchoring* devices. Visually, there seems to be no problem, since it is the Queen who symbolises the nation in words and deeds. Even the bright blue of her dress contributes to the impression of the unity of discourse. As she wears the same dress in all the sequences, this signals to the viewers that the diferent activities happen within the same context. This is also refected in pictures which illustrate several formulations other speech (see also Sauer 2001, 2005), thus supporting the meaning visually. Acoustically, however, the words of the address, the words to be picked up from the Queens chatting with people and the words by several social welfare representatives do not match to that extent. It is even a bit cacophonous.

In sum, the documentary style of the Christmas Message, which results in its multimedia show style, relies on the written text, but is deliberately adapted to the needs of televisuality *(sensu* Atkinson 1984). The Queen interrupts her orator role and is shown chatting with people, which, together with report-like footage from Iraq, resembles a year's review rather than a Christmas Message (Sauer 2001). This functions as a form of intertextual discourse (Fairclough 1995) and makes the Message more political. From time to time, the TV features are predominant in that they may distract the viewers from the Message content. Its multimodal realisation goes much further than what the discourse shadow requires with respect to the anchoring concerning text cohesion, focus control and (speech) acts which are well supported. However, interruptions by video footage and other people may disengage the viewers' attention. Consequently, it is the Message's "media event" character (Wardle & West 2004) that has to be taken into consideration. The makers of the Message, who had already in advance taken care of press releases of the 'new' way of addressing, were obviously more interested in its innovative design than in its content. For them, the Queen appearing between tanks in the Barracks turned out to be more relevant since these pictures might stay longer on the viewers' retinas. Accordingly, the visual quality of the Message was their very concern notwithstanding the fact that the Message text did not go that far.

This becomes especially clear if we look at the closing part of the Message recorded from Sandringham House. It reminds us of the sermon style of a Christmas Message that prevailed before 1997 in the United Kingdom and is still widespread in the other European countries. However, because the room where the Queen delivers her last words-a conclusion, a prayer declamation and a Christmas wish (H)-is not a study and not related to work, the viewers are, so to speak, made welcome to her *home.* One sees a living room in Christmas time: a Christmas tree, Christmas cards on the mantelpiece and hanging on tape from it, a three-piece suite (style 'Chesterfeld') with a cofee-table decorated with cards, and more cards on the dining table in front of the Christmas tree. This arrangement maybe considered a 'material' expression of the *domesticity* which, according to Ong (1982), is characteristic of the era of secondary literacy: speech under TV infuence that is dominated by pseudo-spontaneity It induces a *pseudo-home.* This sense of domesticity has the advantage of mitigating the scandalous footage of armoured servicemen in Iraq and the Queen standing between tanks, although they are curiously decorated with Red Cross flags. A certain degree of preposter-ousness thus might be perceived in these arrangements.

On this Christmas Day the Queen functions indeed as a bard. Her voice states the concerns of the year 2003 that are reinforced and proved by relevant footage. Moreover, the alternations between direct speech from the screen, voice-over passages and footage of her chatting with soldiers bear a rhythmic character, a bardic manner too. They contribute to a vivid style and evoke national pride in the British Army, the welfare institutions and the volunteers. It is all the people who fulfl their duties, as the Queen does. Viewers are invited to respond to these proud people, who are not only named, but also shown. Even the "Herald Angels" sound proud. Pride, then, is part of the social fabric of the community and suggests satisfaction in whatever way it may be achieved. It is at that stage where the Message turns into the emotional side of the sociocultural practice of social cohesion. The public may also become aware of traditional meanings of the English culture (uniforms, flag, National Anthem) matched with intercultural relationships represented by the award-winners by voice and look. The Christmas Message is explicitly modern in form and media practices, but at the same time traditional in content. The traditional impact naturalises the eternal ofce of the Queen, who observes the hurly-burly of daily politics from a distance. It is her role of being there which is demonstrated incessantly. These pictures are powerful in that they celebrate the Queens divine omnipresence and bestow the "mystic fiction" (Kantorowicz 1957) on her.

THE FINNISH PRESIDENT: NEW YEAR MESSAGE 2004

The Finnish President, Mrs. Tarja Halonen, delivers her New Year's Message 2004 on New Year's Day at 12 noon on TV first in Finnish, then in Swedish, the second language of the country.[10] She sits at a desk in front of a movable wall to which a great oil painting is attached which depicts several sailing boats and vessels approaching a coast, presumably Finland's. The mahogany desk is decorated with four props: a small Finnish flag with Presidential coat of arms, a table bell belonging to her role as chairwoman, a bouquet of white flowers and a table lamp. A speech manuscript lies on the desk, but she almost always looks directly into the camera, obviously using the teleprompter. The room is separated from a much larger hall since on the right-hand side of the screen (only for the few moments when the shot size is M, see Figure 4, below) three windows and a few chairs can be seen that belong to the original hall furniture. The presentation style is calm; the shot sizes are, with the exception of the establishing long shot of the very beginning and the medium shot at the beginning and the end of the speech, only MCU and CU; the average length of the shots is nearly 1 min., but it can also be considerably longer. There is a certain tension between what is said and how it is pictured since the text content units (say: sections) do not clearly correspond to the sequence of shot transitions.

normal text = directly addressing from the screen (which is always the case)

[text in brackets] = [descriptions and explanations, also transitions via searching for the next camera or looking at manuscript, despite the use of the tele-prompter]

M, MCU, CU = medium shot, medium close-up shot, close-up shot

S-4 (46s) = shot num^^^ ^

[S-l (20s) Beginning sequence: establishing long shot of the Presidential Palace in Helsinki, music of the National Anthem (partly), then zooming in on the Finnish flag on the top of the Palace tower.]

[S-2 (33s) Superimposition: President in M sitting at a desk in a study-like part of a greater hall, in front of a wall with an oil painting attached to it. Then a short smile.]

(A) Citizens, elections are an important part of democracy. Following last spring's parliamen tary elections, our country received a new coalition Government. Afer Prime Minister Jaatteenmäki's brief Government, the same parties formed a new Government. This Government headed by Prime Minister Vanhanen has now established its position.

This year is also an election year. Elections for the European Parliament will be held in June and local elections in October.

[S-3 (29s) Looking at desk where the manuscript lies, which is obviously meant for search ing the next camera, cut to MCU]

The signifcance of the European Union has increased in our daily lives. Co-operation is needed in more and more areas. The position of the European Parliament has been strengthened and its signifcance will continue to increase in the future. Local authorities have a key task in arranging services in our welfare society, such as social services, health care and education. It is thus important for our daily lives whom we elect to make these decisions.

Let's exercise our right to vote!

[S-4 (46s) Cut to CU (other camera)]

(B)International uncertainty and armed confICts continued last year in diferent parts of the world. The situation in Europe and Finland's position have remained safe and stable, however, and our relations with all our neighbours are excellent.

During the past year security policy has been actively discussed in our country. Discussion has particularly concerned the development of co-operation in the European Union and the preparation of the Government's security policy report. The question is how we can best take care of Finland's and Finns' security in the future.

Co-operation between the Government and the President of the Republic in preparing the security policy report has gone well. Parliament will receive the report sometime this year.

[S-5 (38s) Searching for other camera, cut to MCU]

I myself have emphasised the following points concerning our security policy: (a) Finland does not face any security threat which in itself would require us to change the basic structure of our security policy. (b) Finland's defence has always been primarily up to us, regardless of whether we belong to an alliance or not.

(C)The European Union's Intergovernmental Conference last year did not reach a consensus on a new Constitution. The Union still has its present treaty and there is plenty of time to negotiate a new one. Negotiations should continue without delay, however.

Finland wants to develop the European Union as an equal community of member states so that it corresponds to citizens' needs and wishes as well as possible. The Union's justifcation and acceptability depend on these things as well as the division of power, which is also important.

[S-6 (79s) Cut to CU]

Membership of the European Union and active participation

in every sector of it have promoted Finns' well-being and have also strengthened our security policy position.

Finland considers it important to develop the Union's civilian and military crisis management capability. The Union should promote peace and stability in Europe and other continents. The Union's ability to prevent and manage crises is above all political and economic, but military capability is also needed in crisis management.

Our point of departure has been that we are prepared to help other member states if they need help. On the other hand we assume that others will help us if we need help. The consensus achieved in the Intergovernmental Conference regarding this matter is a good compromise.

[S-7 (Ills) Looking at manuscript, cut to MCU]

Ten new members will join the Union at the beginning of May. This is a good thing for all Europeans, although enlargement still involves many challenges.

Finland is dependent on international trade. The efciency of the Union's internal market is a precondition for our welfare. An efcient internal market will help us succeed in global competition.

(D) Finland has been regarded as a winner and success in globalisation-and even an example to others. With the reduction of barriers to international trade we have been able to export our products and services around the world. Of course we also have experience of the dark side of globalisation.

Important matters are of common interest around the world. Peace, stability and prosperity in our neighbourhood and farther away promote and strengthen Finns' prosperity and security.

[S-8 (50s) Searching for other camera, cut to CU]

Finland works in the UN, the World Trade Organisation and other international forums to create rules and develop co-operation to govern globalisation. In its present form globalisation is not fair and does not ensure sustainable development. Everyone must return to the negotiating table to revise the rules of international trade and investment.

[Looking at manuscript, without transition]

The nation-state must be strong to meet the challenge of globalisation. We know that our own success has been based above all on people-on expertise, innovation and co-operation.

Our social welfare net helps people but also supports participation in tightening international competition. Globalisation is about participating and adapting to changing circumstances.

[S-9 (48s) Looking at manuscript, cut to MCU]

(E) We have done well, but we cannot become complacent. Our challenge is also to succeed in tomorrow's globalisation.

Our key success factors will remain education, research, expertise and entrepreneurship. We need active measures to spur innovations and to develop and market them. Smooth co-operation between the public sector, education and business is extremely important.

In my international tasks I have become even more certain that we must take care of ourselves. Finland must create a national globalisation strategy for the future. This requires co-operation between the Government and labour market organisations. On the basis of discussions I am convinced that this work is being approached with the necessary determination.

[S-10 (56s) Looking at manuscript, cut to CU]

Unemployment is still our most serious social problem. In many workplaces people are worried about their jobs. Yet at the same time Finland faces a shortage of workers. We must continue to invest in properly educating our children and young people and helping adults develop new skills. Work is the foundation for our national wealth and well-being. Success in tightening international competition requires continuity in working life and possibilities for lifelong learning. The modern working world requires flexibility. The basic point of departure, however, should still be people and their need to balance work and family life.

Children's welfare has been a common concern in recent years. Most children are better off than before. Still, all too many children need help. Parents' care is the primary way to ensure children's welfare and prevent mental health problems. We all have a shared responsibility for children and families as well.

[S-ll (99s) Looking at manuscript, cut to MCU]

Defciencies in mental health services have been repaired. A great deal has been achieved particularly in children's and young people's psychiatry. New prevention and treatment models have been created along with new co-operation networks.

I believe it is important to devote serious attention to preventing and treating mental health problems. Particularly resources should be available in children's psychiatric research and care and in diferent forms of social support.

(F) I have ofen talked about culture being people's spiritual home in our rapidly changing world. Culture also has a growing economic signifcance. Successfully combining artistic ereativity and economic production has resulted in nationally signifcant products. We could even say that industrial design is part of our national identity.

Finnish architecture, design, music and other culture also have international appeal. In diferent fields of culture and the arts we have strong international successes.

Our challenge is to improve diferent dimensions of cultural expertise. This requires respect for our cultural heritage, attention to creativity and the development of cultural production. Finland has opportunities to make cultural production a signifcant national industry.

Our own culture is developing and receiving infuences from outside. It would be good if our country could attract immigrants to start businesses and hold jobs. Immigration should not be viewed only on the basis of our own needs, however. Immigrants should be treated as neighbours who have equal rights and obligations.

[S-12 (27s) Looking at manuscript, cut to M]

One of the most important values of a multicultural society is tolerance. Tolerance does not mean that we would approve, under the guise of cultural traditions or customs, violations of the principles of democracy, human rights and the rule of law. We must strengthen these together.

(G) Finally, I would like to thank you on behalf of my husband and myself for your co-operation and numerous contacts.

Thank you also for the greetings I received on my birthday. Your support and interest in the management of common afairs has been important.

I wish all of you a good year in 2004.

- [S-13 (3s) Fading out, dark screen]
- [S-14 (88s) Fading in, M, beginning of Swedish address]
- [S-15-S-23 (645s=10min45s) Delivery of the Message in Swedish, with less speed than in Finnish, cuts to MCU en CU, more or less same transition pattern as during Finnish speech]
- [S-24 (35s) Looking at manuscript, cut to M]
- [S-25 (4s) Final sequence: picture fades out, coat of arms of the Finnish President on blue background, silence]
- [TV announcer]

The Message takes 11 min. in Finnish and 14 min. in Swedish, together 25 min., including beginning and final sequences. The text is organised in seven main topics. Each topic begins with a description in general terms and is then followed by a focus on Finnish contributions, refections or problems, and finally a statement is made concerning what has already been done or still needs to be done in the future. There are only two exceptions. The first topic (A) begins with a direct address and the statement that "elections are an important part of democracy". It ends in a request formulated as an invitation: "Lets exercise our right to vote!" The last topic (G) is coloured personally. The President thanks for co-operation and birthday greetings, mentions her husband, smiles and finishes her speech with a New Year's wish.

The thematic organisation is a typical example of a representative speech in 'sermon' style, addressing the audience directly from the screen. Its overall rhetorical strategy is that of a *laudatory speech* (Sauer 2001, 2005). This entails that there is also some criticism in order to prepare the audience for measures that will be taken by the government in the future. Because the President's role is representative and not party political, the political dimension concerns general developments and expectations rather than government businesses. Consequently, she relates descriptions and advice giving to her task and experiences which she herself had gained during the last year in her ofce. In such a way, the problems which the Finnish have to deal with are formulated in such a manner which may involve the viewers in their solutions. This is, among other things, done by the change of I-clauses and we-clauses (see Ensink 1996). The I-clauses accentuate that she knows what she is formulating, and knows that the audience knows too. Moreover, by using I-clauses she brings to the fore her personal engagement in the issues she is dealing with. In such a way, the I-clauses link the actual speech content to previous discourse-her own or other. The we-clauses, however, have no such clear status. She uses them in order to speak about "we = the Finnish people" including herself (like in A, D, E) or to refer to the government's decisions (like in B, C). In other cases she simply treats Finland as a "person": "Finland wants... Finland considers it important..." (C).

The topics, the perspective of the descriptions and the form of advice are shown in Table 1. The Message is quite general in content and moderate in tone. As far as she is inclined to give advice, she formulates mainly approvingly rather than admonishingly, positively rather than negatively. She seems to be more interested in the future than in the past and obviously avoids the genre of a year's review, which could have been expected on such an occasion. The fact that there was a crisis in government and a change of the Prime Minister (A) is imparted but not assessed. Yet she mentions several earlier developments in diferent social and political fields that have to be picked up and improved in the new year.

There are, however, some peculiarities. The first point is the topic of security policy (B). It belongs obviously to the President's duties insofar as she plays a role in contributing to the national security report. Regarding this report, she pleads for continuation of the Finnish policy of neutrality concerning Finland's defence, although she avoids the word neutrality herself. The formulation of two essentials ("points") indicates that she desires to participate in the continuing discussion. Because there has been an ongoing debate on whether Finland should join NATO or not, this functions as a clear intertextual and interdiscursive tie to previous political discourse. It stimulates the TV viewers to mobilise their (political) memory. The second point is related to culture (F). It begins with an I-clause: "I have ofen talked about culture being peoples spiritual home in our rapidly changing world". This is again an intertextual link and concatenates the actual speech with her earlier discourses. It underlines her trust in the importance of cultural afairs. She favours the Finnish successes in industrial design abroad and emphasises them as part of the "national identity". Her appeal to make "cultural production a signifcant national industry" links infuences from outside-which she considers necessary ("It would be good if our country could attract immigrants")-with the Finnish way to deal with ("Immigrants should be treated as neighbours"). In this context, however, the concept of tolerance is used in order to show that Finland does not tolerate violations of democratic principles. The idea of a multicultural society therefore is strongly focussed on Finnish values as parts of more general occidental values. In such a way, she claims and reassures at the same time; she claims that there is a need for immigrant workers and she reassures the audience that there exists no real threat to the Finnish culture.

The last point is connected with the President's personal situation. In her closing statements (G), she becomes a wife who has a husband, and a woman who had received birthday greetings. Furthermore, she considers her own work "the management of common afairs" and encourages the audience, also by smiling at last, to show interest in it and support her in her job. Finally the wishes for a good New Year 2004 follow. This is one of the rare moments that the "two bodies" (Kantorowicz 1957) appear explicitly.

Considerably little attention is paid to the anchoring of the Message and to the adaptation of the overtly script-bound text to TV features. The text topics are in principle realised in short sentences in the form of statements, but their coherence is not much supported by language means. The Message structure that may help to generate an outline of its complexity is neither made explicit nor clarifed otherwise. The most characteristic feature of the text is that of a list. If recipients are distracted for a short moment, they cannot easily continue from where they were lost. Thus, the Message has the lulling efect of a litany. Maybe this is not inconvenient since she indeed acts like a preacher giving a sermon. Moreover, the discourse anchoring during the Finnish Message focuses the TV viewers repeatedly on the political role of the President in diferent discourses. In such a way, the Message content presupposes a certain political knowledge and experience.

This communicative practice, however, hardly takes into consideration that the screen presentation requires more than verbal content alone. Hence a poor practice, albeit well-known in representative speeches. As a matter of routine, the re-oralisation of the written text that can be seen as a manuscript lying at the desk dominates the style of the speech. What people see when they listen to the verbal content is a 'talking head'. The desk at which she speaks and its environment, in particular the background that is used (the painting, see the photograph), establish the impression of a study. Because the audience might be aware of the fact that this study is constructed by artifcial props and clearly separated from a greater hall, it is a *pseudo-study* that frames the Message. What is depicted is a fictitious room in which the real President enacts her speech. Consequently, the public is invited to participate in this semi-real business. The transmission itself is oscillating between the serious content and its theatrical framing. This functions as an overt appeal to the audiences imagination. It may create a certain feeling of involvement, a mutual job done between public and President. Accordingly, the sociocultural practice of social cohesion is not so much related to the role of the bard, although the years review style contributes to this a bit, but to a strong, even *authoritarian* voice that confronts the viewers with their need of being advised and coached. This treatment is quite rough. "We have done well, but we cannot become complacent" (E), is an appeal to political morality that might be associated with Protestant ideology, albeit mitigated by the claim of Finnish normality.

There is only one moment when pictures and words coincide. The emphasis on Finnish design (F) is linked with "respect for our cultural heritage". Apart from the fact that this passage equals the rhetorical strategy o*ffshing for compliments,* it also draws the audience's eyes to the things that are pictured at this very moment. The mahogany furniture (the desk and the chair) harmonise on the one hand with the red colour of her hair and on the other hand with the colour of the vessels in the painting. Accordingly, the arrangement of the pseudo-study as well as her dress and hairdo signal interest in and attention to design. We do not know whether this impression is intended or not, what we do know, however, is how the TV viewers are treated. The colour harmony, the lighting, the things shown and the topic of Finnish design work together appetisingly It is this multimodal quality that, albeit for a few moments, transcends the overall sobriety of the Message and produces the sense of hope and optimism that is inherent in a New Years Message.

Whereas, in the British Queens Christmas Message, the viewer is confronted with many vantage points by diferent cameras and video footage inserted, the Finnish New Year's Message works only, with the exception of the cover shot of the Presidential Palace, with one single vantage point. As Figure 4 (below) shows, this is done by two cameras that frame the Finnish President by turns in medium close-up shots and close-up shots. Only the beginning and the concluding shot of the address (in Finnish as well as in Swedish) is realised as a medium shot. But this means no change of the vantage point. Without any exception, the Finnish President remains in the centre of attention.

The medium close-up and close-up shots, in general, have a very slow cutting rate. The duration of the shots ranges between 29s and even 141s, which is exceptional slow in the context of modern television (Tiemens 2005). This increases the viewers' concentration on the speaker. There is nearly no possibility to see other picture content than the talking head. Even if the viewers are familiar with the speaker and her addressing style, the visual content they are provided with implies special attention for the *movements* the speaker is doing during her address. What we see is that the Finnish President performs generally two movements: she looks at her manuscript for a short moment, on the one hand, and she searches for the other camera (one of the two cameras that are present), on the other hand. Both movements obviously function as signals to the camerapersons to change the frame. What is more, as the transcript (above) shows, the change of camera frames does not correspond with the speech text. So speaker movements and change of camera frame tend to disengage the viewers, at least to contribute to a certain irritation.

There is another factor that contributes to the impression that the "televisu-ality" (Atkinson 1984) in the Finnish Message seems to be underestimated. The medium features neglect the potential semantic connections between picture content and speech text: "semantic connections refer to those instances in which the visual images are linked to the verbal text of the speech" (Tiemens 2005:400). How could one choose visual images that would match or reinforce verbal references in the text? Above, I mentioned already the short coincidence between Finnish design props and the topic of design in the speech. But this lasted just for a few moments, the following topic change then caused a mismatch. This is, however, a very strong view of the situation. Concerning the structure of the address, its culmination point maybe considered the good wishes at the end. An adequate match would be the speaker in close-up and smiling, as is the case in most of the speeches of our corpus. But this does not seem to be the case in Finland. Here the end of the New Years Message is framed in medium shot! We do not know why, but it seems that the director has chosen a kind of formal *parallelism:* both the beginning and the end of the address in Finnish as well as in Swedish are framed in medium shots. Concerning the TV features and their meaning-making potentials, this is a surprising choice.

Figure. Shot content, camera framing, shot length of the Finnish President's New Year's Message 2004

S-1 (20s) Establishing LS [long shot]: Presidential Palace in Helsinki, music of the Na tional Anthem (partly, only two "lines"), zooming in on the Finnish flag on the top of the Palace tower

S-2 (33s) Superimposition: President in M sitting at a desk in a study-like context, in a greater hall, in front of a wall with an oil painting attached to it, at the right side of the hall chairs are standing in front of windows. Short smile

S-3 (29s) P looking at manuscript, searching the other camera, cut to MCU

S-4 (46s) P cut to CU (other camera)

S-5	(38s)	P searching for other camera, cut to MCU
S-6	(79s)	P cut to CU
S-7	(Ills)	P looking at manuscript, cut to MCU
S-8	(50s)	P searching for other camera, cut to CU
S-9	(48s)	P looking at manuscript, cut to MCU
S-10	(56s)	P looking at manuscript, cut to CU
S-11	(99s)	P looking at manuscript, cut to MCU
S-12	(27s)	P looking at manuscript, cut to M
S-13	(3s)	Fading out, dark screen
S-14	(88s)	Fading in, M, beginning of Swedish address
S-15	(77s)	P searching for other camera, cut to MCU
S-16	(56s)	P looking at manuscript, cut to CU
S-17	(50s)	P looking at manuscript, putting page aside, cut to MCU
S-18	(50s)	P looking at manuscript, cut to CU
S-19	(97s)	P searching for other camera, looking at manuscript, cut to MCU
S-20	(74s)	P looking at manuscript, cut to CU
S-21	(69s)	P looking at manuscript, cut to MCU
S-22	(81s)	P looking at manuscript, cut to CU
S-23	(141s)	P searching for other camera, looking at manuscript, cut to MCU
S-24	(35s)	P looking at manuscript, cut to M
S-25	(4s)	Coat of arms of the Finnish President, silence

In this section, the semiotic resources with which Christmas Messages and New Year's Messages are assembled will be documented.[11] No attention is paid to the speech content so that no interpretations will be given on how content and TV features may infuence each other. According to the concept of multimodality as multimodal materialities developed in this chapter, the figures show how European heads of state are exposed when presenting their Christmas or New Year's Messages. Considering that the speakers (or their staff or government) might incline to enhance their means of recipient design, they have to select a certain presentation style and to link them to the semiotic resources available. In order to diferentiate these resources and the corresponding communicative practices, we concentrate on the *core modes* of language, image, sound and music, the *sensory channels*, their *medial variants*, their *peripheral modes* and *sub-modes* (Kress & Van Leeuwen 2001; Stöckl 2004) as well as on the *discourse practices* (the frames that are used and the anchoring signals), *production practices* (the design of media features) and *sociocultural practices* (which also depend on the content that is not included here; Sauer 2005). First, the semiotic resources of the corpus identifed on the occasion of Christmas 2003 or New Year 2004 (Table 2) are compiled. Secondly, a synopsis (Table 3.1-3.3) is given of specifc elements based on a rough categorisation rather than a systematic empirical examination, which contribute to the 'syntactic' meanings that might be established by the corpus (Figure 5). The semiotic resources used and their combinations are seen as contributing to what in future maybe termed a 'semiotic grammar of Christmas Messages'.

Genre-specifc elements

In Table 2 (below), the opening and closing frames are treated separately as they represent a traditional media practice. The *images* and the *music* and *sound* before and afer the speech proper form a bracket which signals to the audience that the Message is an exceptional TV programme. The other appearances of the semiotic resources belong to what I want to call the message style of a speech, since they are based on choices by the speakers themselves, their staf, and their political and media advisers. Another domain of choices concerns the room from which the transmission takes place; traditions and traditional interiors maybe of infuence and personal considerations concerning how a head of state wants to be exposed as well.

The message style elements are divided into *visual* and *auditory* ones. *Speaker-related and visual elements* are posture, body and hand movements, the dynamics of face, looking behaviour (in particular the use of teleprompter technology), tools, dress and desk All these categories appear in diferent configurations. *Te speakers context* is also *visually* represented (context-related means): useful are distinctions, such as room, lighting, manuscript, props and background. *Audience-related visual elements* consist of looking into the camera and recipient-directed gestures. Also subtitles and a sign interpreter are regarded as visual supports of the audience's interpretation of the speech and therefore categorised here, although they add a layer to the transmission, a technical one. As for *speaker-related and auditory elements,* the quality of the speaker's voice and the use of one or more national languages matter. *Audience-related and auditory means* are forms of direct address, greeting formulas, the use of you-clauses, some speech acts, repetitions and of course the wishes at the end of a Message. *Recipient-directed* material articulation means, such as warmth or intenseness, also need attention. The so-called interruptions by footage in documentary style play a specifc role. They happen, as far as I can see, only in the GB Christmas Messages from 1997 onwards. They have to be treated as particular sequences: sometimes with the Queen's voice in voice-over format, sometimes as a short report of receptions or visits, sometimes in other combinations.[12] But they always add a meaning dimension, which hardly could have been articulated otherwise. Therefore they create innovative *discourse practices* and may evoke specifc *sociocultural practices,* like the one of modernism in monarchy.

Table 2 displays the recent repertoire of sign making in Christmas Messages under the conditions of mass communication. It presents an exemplary inventory of potential realisation forms, a vocabulary. The chart does not show all possible categories of the collection, since this depends on what one wants to categorise. Nor does it refect all possible combinations, other than the ones I myself propose by distinguishing the frames before and afer the speeches and interruptions.

The following step therefore is the "concatenation" (Sauer 2002) of semiotic resources. In order to arrive at a syntax of these resources, we have to get grasp at their combinative potentials. The only way of doing so is to *compare* the speeches of the corpus with one another, and to pay specifc attention to the resources used.[13] As the heads of state's choices verify *their* syntax, we might be able to find some patterns, which are characteristic of the genre. These syntactic means show which solutions are opted for in the European countries in order to expose the head of state to the public in Christmas time (for sermon-like transmissions, see Figure 5, below).

In Table 3.1 (below), the corpus is introduced. What is interesting from the point of view of multimodal discourse is the attention paid to the framing of the Message: structure, length and complexity of the *opening sequences.* The announcements by television presenters were left out since they are clearly separated from the Message itself. Most countries use the Presidential or Royal Palace as an *icon* in order to clarify what may be termed the centre of the nation. This is very ofen accompanied by the National Anthem (or, as is the case in N, a Royal Anthem) played or sung (sometimes with subtitles) and followed by flags or coats of arms. However, some countries have no real opening (A, DK) or a very short one (D). That means that Austria and Denmark start *in medias res,* i.e. both heads of state can be seen immediately on the screen. It is perhaps because of this sudden appearance that the Danish Queen begins with a smile which is connected with her putting on the reading glasses. In NL, the religious setting refers already to the content of the Message. It is realised by sacred music during which shots of the palace are shown. Only in GB the opening sequence is not only a salute to the Queen but also a kind of report, which functions as a communicative practice borrowed from journalistic genres. It marks the fact that the Queen delivers her Message outside her residence: she is shown arriving at an unusual place, the Combermere Barracks, so that recipients can see she is really outside and therefore in the midst of society. The report dimension of this footage documents, as it were, that the Queen is 'moving'.

All opening sequences, as far as they had been produced, also refect the time of the transmission. If it is at noon or later, daylight is shown; if it is in the evening, then the lighting is clearly artifcial. The latter adds some magic to the delivery, in particular when a palace is illuminated in the snow (D, N). The opening sequences focus the audiences globally on the meaning of the speech: only in NL and GB where a certain tradition of variational realisations of the format exists, the relationship between the pictures (GB), the music (NL) and the speech content is developed in such a way that viewers may infer a general meaning. However, their potential assumptions concern rather feelings and sentiment than a clear indication of the content that will follow. In Table 3.2, the semiotic resources of the place, the Message delivery style, the props on the head of states desk or in his or her environment, and the closing sequences are compiled. Whereas the question whether or not to make use of the teleprompter technology and thus to dispense with the showing of the manuscript may depend on the experiences and preferences of the diferent heads of state, the room from which the Message is delivered and its decoration are clearly in the centre of decisions and arrangements.

The speakers and their appearances form the core activities. Everywhere we see festive clothes, albeit with some diferences. The most remarkable examples are the Danish Queen, who obviously prefers *très chic* fashion and exclusive jewellery, and the Norwegian Crown Prince, who seems to be on his way to a New Years Eve party immediately afer the broadcast. The speakers usually sit at a desk so that only the upper part of the body is exposed. The Spanish King sits on a chair with no desk which turns out to cause a bit of discomfort, whereas the British Queen stands and moves around. The movements, in general, are restricted: hardly any hand motions (ofen combined with holding a manuscript), some hand motions in order to accentuate the tenor of a passage and a lot of hand motions (A, E) which obviously aim at encouraging the publics involvement. In such a way, *speaker-related resources* may comprise some clearly *audience-related* units produced by hand motions, gaze and looking into the camera.

Heads of state obviously prefer the atmosphere of a study in order to display their working context even on a festive occasion. The occasion itself is referred to by Christmas symbols, bouquets, candles or more general means that indicate a festive moment. The rooms are mainly arranged and decorated as though they were studies. We call them *pseudo-studies* since the audience may see that these rooms are not real ofces (as workplaces). Sometimes however, the rooms have the air of a home and are therefore termed *pseudo-homes.* A pseudo-home looks like the head of state's home and gets the viewers to suppose that the speaker lives there (E, GB). Even family photographs contribute to this purpose. However, viewers cannot be sure that their impression is realistic. It is this oscillation between feeling invited and being part of the fabrication that is profted from.

Apart from Christmas-related props, national symbols, like flags and coats of arms, are used in general. Only Austria combines the national flag and the flag of the European Union. The Dutch and the British Messages use the flags of their royal families: the flag of the House of Orange flutters on top of the Palace in The Hague, whereas the kettledrums of the military band are decorated with the flag of the House of Windsor.

The 'natural' context in which these national symbols are shown thus provides an air of self-evidence which avoids carefully the danger of bombastic nationalism, as is also the case with the Finnish President's mini flag. In sum, the props demonstrate an aloof style of the Message so that few distractions from its solemn content can take place. The compositions of the props unveil a certain relationship between the *production practices* and the *sociocultural practices.* They gently inform the audiences that the royal representatives are exposed to the mass public with reference to eternal traditions (ofen shown in paintings of predecessors), whereas the elected representatives incline to more specifc discourses: education (indicated by books, D), technology (shown by computers, A) and business (demonstrated by the desk design, FIN). Regarding E and GB, the pseudo-homes are predominant. They demonstrate normality, at least in Christmas customs and family photographs that contribute to the "body natural" (Kantorowicz 1957). In NL, the room presents a fictitious environment; it is no-ones place, neither study nor home, and therefore evidently the result of a temporal arrangement.

The last category of this chart is devoted to the closing sequences. Do these sequences mirror the opening ones or do they add special meanings? Four closing sequences are symmetrical (A, B, D, E). The others represent either a variation (same pictures with another piece of music, NL; a short picture of the coat of arms, FIN; a Christmas carol, GB) or something completely diferent. The Danish Message comes to an end by a military ceremony: the guard of honour rises flags, salutes the National Anthem and marches through the Gate of the Royal Palace. This refers unmistakably to the ofcial character of the Queens role as head of state. Yet in Norway, the singing of the National Anthem with text in subtitles is accompanied by film pictures in helicopter view of the Norwegian landscape and its seasons all over the country, thus glorifying its beauty[14] and stimulating the audience to respond to this promotion of Norway.

Semiotic grammar

In Table 3.3, the camera work and the sub-mode of colour are taken into consideration as these constituents of TV media practices concern domains of meaning making which are both unavoidable and essential, such as number of cameras, their placement and their operations. They may even respond to the verbal content, e.g. a close-up shot at a crucial moment or the zooming in on the speaker in order to concentrate on the ongoing passage. The fact that audiences are not accustomed

14. In Norway, the National Anthem on TV, for instance on National Day, is always pictured this way. The role of the "bard" the Crown Prince personifes is taken over by "nature" that sings the praise of Norway as a cultural entity.

As for the sub-mode of colour, the colour scheme of a Message also needs to be accounted for. I see colour as a "sub-mode" (Stöckl 2004) or a "combinational not in itself existing mode" (Kress & Van Leeuwen 2002) that belongs to the *lighting* of an address. Apart from national colours in flags, which play a restricted role here, the combination of composition elements 'colours' a speech at hand. I distinguish daylight and no daylight Messages and seek for patterns which organise both transmission types. In the case of daylight transmissions, mostly diferent shades of white are used, in combination with beige, light yellow and the like. But there are also some clear contrasts, produced by red, brown, gold and the mahogany of furniture. The floral green of flowers and bouquets belong to both transmission types. It depends on the intensity of spotlights whether the floral green is contributing to a natural or artifcial appearance. The night transmissions prefer a darker set of colours, which make contrasts appear more conspicuous and constructed. What is shown behind the speakers counts in particular. If a zooming out camera or a medium shot is used then one sees some open doors which allow insight into diferently lighted rooms (B, N), thus giving an impression of depth. Globally speaking, the colour schemes applied in Christmas Messages tend to *harmonise* the exposure of the head of state with his or her representative function. They play down the strangeness of a speaker addressing her or his audience from the screen and *naturalise* the artifciality of the 'faked' live transmission.

The materialities of sermon-like Christmas Messages

Afer the examination of, first, the vocabulary of semiotic resources and, second, their potential syntactic relationships in the genre of TV Christmas Messages, I want to summarize the sermon-like transmissions. Their construction is simple: frame X, delivery of the speech, frame X or frame Y. Most of the frames are combinations of music (played, sung or both) and national symbols like palaces and flags. In these cases, the frames mark the representative function of the head of state so that there is no doubt that it is him or her who delivers the Message. As for the picturing of the Message itself, syntactic relations are only discerned if the camera work is related to the content of the speech or to other semiotic resources. There are only some moments, where a camera, mostly in medium close-up or close-up, depicts the speaker directly addressing the audience with a gesture or smile. Apart from these rare moments in which language, body language and camera operation coincide, no other syntactic relations have been established. Variations concern the decoration of the rooms and dressing style.

Figure 5 shows the materialities of the sermon-like Christmas Messages. As is characteristic of the secondary literacy of representative addresses, the performance of a *talking head*-or more precisely: a *talking upper part of the body*-sitting at a desk relies heavily on both the content of the speech and the re-oralisation by means of body language and articulated voice. The camera movements and the sizes of the pictures, which are presented in Figure 5 by the left part, oscillate between focussing (the speaker as centre) and contextualising (the speaker within a visible context, the decorated room). The discourse anchoring therefore depends in part on the speech content. What is shown and how it is shown, which are presented in Figure 5 by the right part, may support these discourse practices. I distinguish between a naturalistic way, which accentuates the speaker's individuality, and a traditional way, which underlines the ofce (and its burden). The former denotes the way politicians act in public, and the latter contributes to the eternal quality of a monarch. The discourse anchoring then draws upon the ability of the audience to relate the ongoing performance to earlier speeches and appearances or to respond to the royal ofce and to produce loyalty anew. I consider these picturing modes linked with the "body natural" vs. "body politic" (Kantorowicz 1957) distinction. It makes political representation flexible in that it invites the viewers to take into account that a Christmas Message however heartily worded is a semi-ofcial discourse. The speakers body language as caught by the camera contributes to such an interpretation. Normally, the authority of a head of state is beyond doubt. But if he or she performs a Christmas Message then their hand motions, gaze and the articulation-in conformity with the content-may contribute to the sociocultural practice of'coaching' rather than reiterating the status quo (Sauer 2001). The point is that such sort of considerations needs to be supported by the multimodality of the semiotic resources which are combined only to a certain extent syntactically. The material realisations of Christmas Messages as presented in this section yet open up the possibility of thinking and analysing them in terms of grammar.

CONCLUSION

The multimodal character of televised Christmas Messages-as demonstrated in this paper-ofen leads to a certain mismatch between what is shown and what is heard. In some cases, the clash of manner and meaning is undisguised. What you see is completely diferent from what you hear. The adaptation of the Message script to the medium television is predominantly restricted to the embodiment of the speaker as a person who is exposed to the viewers. Some speakers are more suitable for their role than others. Moreover, if representatives acknowledge the necessity of multimodal communicative practice and its relatedness to expectations that are, among other things, determined by media habits, then they are able to respect the visual layers that contribute decisively to the business of performing. Yet this is not only a question of personal inclination. It depends also on the willingness to pay more attention to the way public discourses are realised in general. This demonstrates that the cultural common ground, the anchoring and the adaptation to the medium features allow a considerable range of realisations. It is the domain of the semiotic resources that should be treated with more creativity and inventiveness, both from the perspective of analysis and from that of speech making. A lot of systematic work has to be done in order to discover how far one can go multimo daliy.

Although the speeches of our corpus may be regarded as tokens of a type, that is the genre of Christmas Messages, there are considerable diferences concerning their use of multimodality Because the semiotic resources of a culture, according to Kress and Van Leeuwen (2001: 111), depend on the moment a "culture has made the decision to draw a particular material into its communicative processes" and therefore consider specifc resources as part of this culture, the diferences found in the corpus may also be seen as culture-related. However, how culture infuences the multimodal discourses of Christmas Messages has not yet been worked out in full.

We distinguished two diferent groups of Messages: those by royal heads of state and those by elected ones. As far as multimodality is concerned, we made another distinction between a documentary and multimedia style transmission (GB and in Norway's closing sequence) and a sermon-like speech (by the majority of European representatives). We found that the sermon-like Messages used semiotic resources within a rather restricted framework. We also found that neither their royal nor their elected representativeness was able to explain the difer-ences between them. The documentary or multimedia style of the British Queen, however, seemed to be afected by a strong inclination towards modernity, which is refected in experimental, innovative TV performances. This turned out to be specifc for the role of the monarchy in GB, which had been challenged by various attacks and problems (Wardle & West 2004). In the case of GB we thus detected a *cultural* element, an element specifc of that culture of royal representation. It made the representation a media event. In the Norway Message, the closing sequence was culturally loaded too. It refected the subtle ways of dealing with nature and the nations landscape, which the verbal content of the Message just touched upon by shortly mentioning environmental problems. The association of Norwegian landscape and environment thus functioned as a cue of culture-related considerations and ideological claims.

Bibliography

Ajay Dash: *Basic Concept of Journalism*, Discovery, Delhi, 2007.

Appleby, Paul H.: *Policy and Administration*, Birmingham, AL: University of Alabama Press, 1949.

Arun Bhatia: *Theory and Research in Interpersonal and Mass Communication*, Akansha, Delhi, 2005.

Basu, Prahlad K.: *Governance and Public Administration for Poverty Reduction*, Salvador, Brazil, 1997.

Brecher, Michael: *The Politics of Succession in India*, Connecticut, Greenwood, 1976.

Carl J. Friedrich: *Constitutional Government and Democracy*, Boston, Ginn, 1950.

Charles H. Kennedy: *Ethnic Preference and Public Policy in Developing States*, Boulder, Lynne Rienner Publishers, 1986.

Charles Howard McIlwain: *Constitutionalism: Ancient and Modern*, N.Y., Cornell University Press, 1958.

Conway, Margaret : *Political Analysis: An Introduction*, Boston, Allyn and Bacon, 1972.

Dunner, Joseph: *Dictionary of Political Science*, New York, Philosophical Library, 1964.

Durgadas Roy: *Financial Intermediation in Economic Development : The Indian Perspective*, Rajat Pub, Meerut, 2009.

Eldridge, P.J.: *The Politics of Foreign Aid in India*, New York, Schocken, 1970.

Ezra, N.: *Bureaucrats and Policy Making*, New York, Holmes & Meier, 1984.

Gargan, J.: *Handbook of Local Government Administration*, New York, Marcel Dekker, 1997.

Heimanson, Rudolph: *Dictionary of Political Science and Law*, N.Y.: Oceana Publications, 1967.

Jagannath Pati: *Media and Tribal Development*, Concept, Delhi, 2004.

Jalal, A.: *Nationalism, Democracy, and Development: State and Politics in India*, Delhi; New York: Oxford University Press, 1997.

Joshi, Vijay: *India: Macroeconomics and Political Economy, 1964-1991*, Washington, World Bank, 1994.

Karan Sareen: *Encyclopaedic Dictionary of Multimedia*, Ivy Pub, Delhi, 2004.

Krishna Menon: *Media Communication and Photo Journalism*, Manglam Pub, Delhi, 2008.

Max, Beloff: *Foreign Policy and the Democratic Process*, Baltimore, Johns Hopkins University Press, 1955.

Nilesh Kumar Singh: *Religion, Media and Public Sphere*, MD Pub, Delhi, 2009.

Pradip Ninan Thomas: *Strong Religion, Zealous Media : Christian Fundamentalism and Communication in India*, Sage, Delhi, 2008.

Prakash Gandhi: *Principles and Practices of Mass Communication: A Theoretical Perspective*, Kanishka, Delhi, 2007.

Ramesh Chandra: *Analysis of Media and Communication Trends*, Isha Books, Delhi, 2004.

Ranjan Parhi: *Indian English Through Newspapers*, Concept Pub, Delhi, 2008.

Sachin Bharti: *Mass Communication and Society*, Aavishkar Pub, Delhi, 2008.

Schmidhauser, R.: *Supreme Court: Its Politics, Personalities and Procedures*, New York, Holt, 1960.

Subbarayappa, B.V.: *Science in India: A Changing Profile*, New Delhi, Indian National Science Academy, 1984.

Suketu Ohri: *Industrial Toxicology and Bioremediation*, Dominant Publishers and Distributors, Delhi, 2010.

Uday Sahay: *Making News : Handbook of the Media in Contemporary India*, Oxford University Press, Newyork, 2006.

Index

□□□